John Davison
first started investigating the Yardies while
working at The Sunday Times of London where he was
one of the longest-serving staff writers. He spent more
than ten years at the newspaper covering news, investigations and features.
While a foreign reporter and defence correspondent
for the newspaper, he worked on assignment in Kenya,
Europe and Bosnia during the civil war. He also worked
at The Gleaner newspaper in Jamaica on a prestigious
Commonwealth Press Union Scholarship.
John Davison was nominated for the 'Reporter of the
Year' prize in the 1995 British Press Awards, and was
commended in 1991 and 1990.
Before joining The Sunday Times, he spent two years at
the Birmingham Post and Mail, covering news, features,
theatre and jazz.

He now works as a freelance writer and television
journalist, and lives in London.

First published in Great Britain in March 1997 by VISION
Paperbacks, a division of Satin Publications Limited.

VISION Paperbacks,
a division of
Satin Publications Limited
3 Neal Street
Covent Garden
London WC2H 9PU
Email: 100525.3062@compuserve.com

Cover design and layout: Justine Hounam.
Typesetting and design: Pixel Press.
Back Cover Image: Rex Features
Printed and bound in Great Britain: The Bath Press, Bath.

©1997 John Davison/VISION Paperbacks
ISBN: 1-901250-02-4

VISION Paperbacks

So as sure as the sun will shine,
I'm going to get my share, now,
what's mine,
And then,
The harder they come,
The harder they fall,
One and all.

Jimmy Cliff

John Davison

GANGSTA

The Sinister Spread of Yardie Gun Culture

ACKNOWLEDGMENTS

In the preparation of this book, there are many people to whom I owe a great deal. Particularly, my thanks go to all those who ran considerable risks in talking to me. Not all can be named, but you know who you are.

From the Metropolitan Police, I must thank John Brennan and Steve Barker. It was through them and the indefatigable Brian Fotheringham from the Immigration Service that I became involved in this subject in the first place. I am also indebted to John Jones for his openness and support during my research, and also to 'Bellyman' from the 'Hotel' for his good humour and hospitality.

For his insights into the situation in Birmingham, my special thanks go to 'Gringo'. For looking out for me there, I am grateful to 'Toad' and all at the 'Front'.

In Kingston, I must thank Sheila Watson for her interest and willingness to show me around. I also appreciate the help and frankness shown to me by Colonel Trevor McMillan.

In New York, my thanks go to Joe Green and the boys at the 67.

Finally I must remember those who have put up with me during the writing of this book. It wasn't easy, for any of us.

Contents

INTRODUCTION

O N the morning of Wednesday March 13, 1996, a local eccentric and gun enthusiast called Thomas Hamilton walked into a primary school in central Scotland and started to shoot. A few minutes later 16 children and a teacher were dead, as well as the killer himself. The whole of Britain was shocked into mourning of a depth not seen for 30 years, while an astonished world asked how could this happen in the small, civilised country they had heard so much about? 'The Slaughter of the Innocents' was the common theme of newspaper headlines that week, accurately reflecting the sense of horror in editions which dedicated up to 20 pages to the story. Breast-beating opinion columns, meanwhile, demanded to know how the Dunblane Massacre had been allowed to take place and, in particular, did this mean that Britain was now living in the shadow of the gun? The issue of guns and gun culture was thrust to the top of the political agenda and debates about the ownership of legally held weapons, such as those used by Hamilton, and the influence of the 'gun lobby' have continued ever since.

Three days after the Dunblane murders another shooting took place, but this one went unrecorded even in the local media. The contrasts are instructive. The scene of the second incident was not an idyllic small town with an ancient cathedral and a genuinely 'close-knit' community, but the main shopping centre in Wembley, an unlovely suburb in north-west London. No one was killed, or even hit, but 35 rounds were fired from an assortment of hand guns. Those involved were not psychologically disturbed loners with a grudge against society, as was the case with Hamilton, but rival factions of black drugs dealers engaged in a turf war for control of the highly lucrative local trade in 'crack' cocaine. A member of one gang had been shot in the leg the week before, and this was a retaliatory ambush against his assailants. No one there, it is safe to assume, was the holder of a gun licence.

Of course the image of five-year-olds being mercilessly gunned down at the start of a gym lesson was singularly frightening, in particular for anyone with children of a similar age. I covered the Dunblane story for The Sunday Times, and saw other hardened 'hacks' there break down in tears as details emerged and the journalists' thoughts turned to their own loved-ones. Nothing had delivered the same shocking impact to the nation as a whole for 30 years - not even, arguably, the massacre of 16 people at Hungerford, Berkshire, in 1987, or the carnage caused by the explosion of

Above: Earl Broach, a feared Yardie gunman, poses for the camera kissing the barrel of his beloved automatic

PanAm Flight 107 over Lockerbie, Scotland in 1988. The Dunblane victims were, after all, almost entirely children - the 'innocents' of the subsequent headlines and the painfully reproduced school photographs. No one, especially myself who saw it at first hand, would suggest this reaction was in any way inappropriate.

In terms of a general indicator of the way British society has moved, however, I would suggest that the unnoticed events in Wembley three days later were far more significant.

During hours of Parliamentary debate and sound-bites after Dunblane, little more than a nod was made towards this other problem of illegally held firearms. The political parties fell over themselves to advocate more and more stringent controls on gun licences, in response to highly effective lobbying by the families of Dunblane victims. The Conservative Government out-bid its own official Cullen Report before it was even published, while the Labour opposition pushed for a total ban on all handguns. In the end legislation was rushed through to limit ownership to .22 target guns, which would have to have the firing mechanism removed before being kept at home. Campaigners and opposition politicians said this still was not enough, while on the other side a protest march was organised for something called 'Shooter's Rights'.

Sadly, in the context of the real threat to the public from guns, all this is irrelevant - some would say even laughable. Five years ago, when I began the research that has eventually yielded this book, there was no real gun culture in Britain. People had thrilled to, or been appalled by, the antics of Rambo and other gun-toting American imports on the big screen, and serious concern had been voiced about the effects of these on the popular consciousness. Indeed Michael Ryan, responsible for the slaughter at Hungerford, had been dubbed as a Rambo-type fantasist. The culture and the mentality behind that attack, however, was completely alien.

A large part of the shock to the British system following Hungerford was the discovery that people in this country actually had guns at all. There had been plenty of violence over the preceding decade - from the weekly running battles of football hooligans to the full-scale riots in predominantly black inner-city areas such as Toxteth in Liverpool, Brixton in south London and Handsworth in Birmingham. On the Broadwater Farm estate in Tottenham, north London, Police Constable Colin Blakelock was savagely hacked to death by a mob during one such disturbance in 1985. But guns, even in these 'front line' areas, were still virtually unknown. Police officers who spent years patrolling there say they simply never came across them.

The situation now is very different. In certain parts of inner-city Britain guns are a daily reality, as they have long been in many American cities, and even the previously taboo idea of a routinely armed police force is seen as being inevitable. That such a change should come about so quickly and so completely is a social phenomenon of huge significance, and yet it has happened while most people were looking the other way. It has reached the stage, in fact, where a dozen armed men can have a shoot-out on a Saturday afternoon in a London shopping centre and no one, publicly, even notices - even while the nation is engaged in an orgy of self-examination about the rights and wrongs of gun club membership.

THE PURPOSE of this book is to chart and examine one central thread in this development, the rise of 'Gangsta' gun culture and those who have brought it to the street corners of this country. It is about the Jamaican criminals who have become known as 'Yardies' and the enormous impact they have had on the British crime scene. Originally the term 'Yardie' meant nothing more than someone from Jamaica - or 'Yard' as it is known. However, it now describes one of the most feared groups of violent drug dealers and robbers ever seen in Europe.

The Yardies are not the only reason for the growing influence of guns. Others include the collapse of the Berlin Wall, with the resultant open market in weapons from the former Eastern Bloc, the increased ease of importing guns from Europe following the relaxation of European Community border controls, and even the sale of Gulf War trophies by returning British soldiers. One point of view is that it all would have happened anyway, and that the relative immunity of Britain to guns in the past was just an historical peculiarity that must sooner or later have been reversed.

Even if that were accepted, however, it is indisputable that a vital catalyst which in the event helped to bring about these changes was provided by the Yardies. The view of this book, in fact, is that their role has been the pivotal one. Quite simply, the criminal use of guns has increased parallel with the domestic drugs trade and in particular with the emergence of 'crack' cocaine. From the outset that section of the market has been dominated by Jamaican criminals and their British-born associates, and remains so today. The use of guns, and the culture that goes with it, has been a central feature of Jamaican 'badness' for 20 years, and it spilled over into America and Canada before it ever came to Britain.

The pattern of crime and firepower has remained consistent throughout, as have the links between Jamaican criminals in the principal centres of Kingston, the Jamaican capital, New York and London. Recent evidence suggests that this informal network is now extending its operations to continental Europe. In Britain the new gun culture has brought with it an image of glamour and easy money which has proved seductive to certain

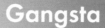

elements within the young, indigenous black community and so has further deepened its influence. Gangs of 'home boy' criminals now also see the gun as a vital business and style accessory.

If this is a controversial view, it is not an isolated one. A series of confidential police reports over the years have identified the emerging problem and called for action. One of the more recent of these, produced by the strategic research unit of the National Criminal Intelligence Service (NCIS), looked at the whole issue of drug-related violence. In assessing its effects, one section states: "The damage that drug-related violence by ethnic Jamaican and other black British criminals is doing to the law-abiding black majority gives cause for concern, particularly as many young blacks now see 'Yardie' style criminals as role models and accept extreme violence as a way of life." But this is not the only problem it highlights. "There is a danger that media reporting of violent crime depicting the 'gun-carrying Yardie figure' will result in a significant section of the black community being stigmatised," the report says.

Nevertheless, its pages paint a gloomy picture of the situation and are full of references to the peculiarly Jamaican element of the drugs-and-violence scene. Referring to a 1991 report by the National Drugs Intelligence Unit, it says: "This research showed that in London, some of the groups (predominantly of Jamaican origin) who traded in drugs did not hesitate to use firearms. Their principal objective was to take control of the importation and distribution of illegal drugs and thereby accrue the financial rewards. The unstable and perfidious nature of group members made them particularly dangerous." Using this earlier research as a bench mark, the NCIS report goes on: "It is clear that although drug violence in the UK has not matched levels in the United States, the situation is worsening."

Its overall conclusion is stark and unequivocal: "Ethnic Jamaican and other black criminals engaged in trafficking pose the most overt current threat in terms of drug related violence in the UK."

THE OTHER main theme of this book is to document and assess the response by British police and other law enforcement agencies to the problem. As the few quotations above show, there has been no shortage of intelligence information about the nature of the challenge faced. The question is whether that information has always been properly acted on, or whether more could have been done to prevent the development of the current situation.

In the course of my research I have been given unprecedented access to police operations and strategic thinking in this area, and I have seen a great amount of dedicated work carried out by the relatively few police officers, along with those from the customs and immigration services, who have specialised in combating Yardie crime. Whether those efforts have always been properly directed, however, and whether there has ever been the political will at the highest levels to take the necessary action is a different story. Frequent changes in emphasis and focus on the problem, on occasion amounting to a refusal to publicly acknowledge its existence, have severely hampered the effectiveness of the response. As a result people have been shot and killed, including police officers, who might otherwise have escaped harm, and gun culture, of the illegal variety, has been able to further exert its insidious influence.

The reasons for this official vacillation are numerous and complex. Some can be seen to stem from simple mistakes of perception, others from perhaps inevitable tensions which take place within large organisations faced with huge demands on limited resources. First and foremost, however, has been a shying away from the highly sensitive issues of race which the problem has generated. Dogged by past and continuing accusations of racism, police forces have been unwilling to take consistent and robust action against those elements within the black community who constitute that problem. Because this dilemma is understandable does not detract from my view that the way it has been addressed has, overall, amounted to a serious abdication of responsibility.

FINALLY, and in relation to the previous point, it is important to state what this book is not about. It is no part of my purpose to score racist points or to encourage others to do so. I have no wish, in the terms used by the NCIS report, to 'stigmatise' the black community.

In one sense the Yardie phenomenon is not essentially a black issue. The historical origins of the problem, which are examined in great detail in the following pages, lie in Jamaica and nowhere else. Not in Trinidad and Tobago, not in Barbados, not in Nigeria or Ghana. I am not, then, propounding a theory of a generalised 'black menace' stalking the land. Neither am I suggesting that all Jamaicans are Yardies. It should go without saying, but of course it is true that the vast majority of the population who have their origins in Jamaica are as decent, honest and hard-working as anyone else. Indeed, given the enormous influence that churches continue to have in the life and culture of the island, it could be argued that many of the moral standards imported from there are higher than those found in our own increasingly secularised society. A trip through the countryside on any Sunday, when families on the road rigged out in their best clothes seem to spend all day going to and from church, is perhaps the best time to see this other Jamaica. But none of this can change the fact that there is and has been a particular problem with Jamaican 'bad bwoys', both in that country and abroad. To say so, while stressing that this is not an appeal for stereotyping, is not a racist statement.

It is interesting to note that the same levels of sensitivity do not seem to apply when discussing other crime problems amongst ethnic minorities in this country. When fear of a cocaine explosion was at its highest, no one shrank from terms like 'Colombian Drug Barons' on the grounds of incitement to racial hatred in describing the fabulously rich men who controlled much of the trade (and were, actually, Colombian). Few seemed to get upset when it was revealed that highly organised gangs of Nigerian fraudsters were taking millions of pounds out of state benefit systems. Most recently, endless articles have been written about the coming of the Russian Mafia without any vocal complaints from that country's embassy. Clearly there are different factors at work when you are talking about elements within a long-established black community that has a history of discrimination against it, and to not see that would be naive. In turn, however, it is hard to see how a reluctance to even acknowledge this problem, with the black community as with the police, can be in anyone's best interests. To suggest, as has been written, that Yardies in Britain are some kind of myth conjured from a fetid joint imagination of the media and London's Metropolitan police is, simply and dangerously, wrong.

For there is another sense in which this is very much a black issue. It is

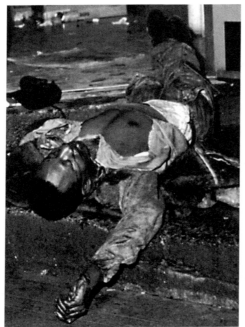

The life and death of a gangsta: Earl Broach (above) is killed in a doorway (right)

the black community which is literally staring down the barrel of the new gun culture. Parents in 'black', and already underprivileged, inner city areas are the ones who most have to fear their children being taken by a bullet, crack, or the 'gangstas'. If 'black-on-black' shootings such as the one in Wembley are no longer worthy of comment, either because the information is suppressed or because no one is interested, then we really are living in a racist society.

Chapter One

HANDSWORTH REVOLUTION

" IT'S the youth, man, it's the youth. All they're interested in is money, trainers, cars and pussy. Education is too slow for them, even a job is too slow. They want it now."

The speaker is Gilly, a huge 'dred' (Rastafarian) DJ, who has just finished his early hours set at the Frontline 'blues', an illegal music and drinking club. Reggae sounds continue to pound out through wreaths of ganja smoke and exclusively black heads nod sagely to the beat, as we cram into a relatively quiet corner of the kitchen to eat goat curry and put the world to rights. Gilly is talking about the state of affairs in his own community of Handsworth, a run-down area of Birmingham. But just as the 'blues' scene could easily be taking place in parts of London, Bristol or Nottingham, his bleak view could equally be a description of life in many areas of inner-city Britain.

Standing at about six-foot-five, at least half as wide across the shoulders and with a resplendent mane of rasta 'locks', Gilly is not a man you would wish to argue with anyway. His opinion, however, has a personal, tragic context to add to its weight. Days before our conversation he had seen his eldest son, 19, sentenced to 12 years imprisonment on robbery and drugs charges.

"He's been locked up before, and I told him he would have to settle down. But he wouldn't listen," says Gilly, who is 36, with a dismissive shrug. Another one bites the dust.

From elsewhere in the kitchen come other contributions about the delinquent tendencies of the local 'yout'. "We got all kinds of gangs, all kind of crews," says Shelley, the man on the pans. "There's the Burger Bar crew, now. They're into drugs and stealing cars. Then there's that bunch of girls who stuck up a bus."

A bus? Girls? "Yeah, man. They stick up a bus with knives and rob everybody on it," says another grey-hair, laughing in spite of himself. "Like a fucking stagecoach robbery."

Indeed, later that very day, a youth – said to be a leading light of the Burger Bar crew – was arrested after police raided his house in Handsworth and found two firearms with ammunition, £30,000 worth of 'crack' cocaine and large bundles of cash. On Sunday of the same weekend the local Post Office was robbed and left boarded up. Locals would now have to travel further afield in order to 'check their books' for benefit money. "Soon we'll have nothing left in Handsworth," said a Frontline regular, staring down the Soho Road the day after.

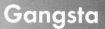

Back in the kitchen, at about 4am on Saturday morning, and Gilly offers to take me 'on the road' to visit some other kicking (and illegal) night-spots.

One, which at first sight appears to be normal semi-detached house, opens up like the Tardis to reveal a very organised operation. Two large, ram-full rooms accommodate music and dancing with the kitchen and bar serving from the middle. Gilly taps a blind wall to another room. "That's where the gambling goes on," he says.

He has to shout above the gut-shaking bass thump of Jamaican music. One growling rapper is singing the praises of gun power, along the lines of: "If you hafna' got a gun, you got nuttin' to say roun' here." Another, although backed by an equally aggressive rhythm, is appealing for 'Respec' to be shown to women.

Outside, as we leave, a group of predominantly white prostitutes shivers on the pavement under the watchful eye of their black minder.

Another blues, or 'shabeen', is accommodated in a single terraced house. It is alarmingly full, including the precipitous staircase, and the only man with room to move is the DJ who operates in the corner of the main room behind metal grills.

A third is in an innocent looking bungalow on a residential street. A group of youths are huddled round the entrance. "You see them guys?" says Gilly as we approach. "They're bound to be dealing something."

Inside, elegantly word-processed notices on the wall say: "BEWARE MUGGERS. People leaving this club have been mugged. Be careful." Welcome to the ghetto.

THIS IS a strange, alien world which most people in Britain never see. To my personal shame, I worked as a journalist in Birmingham for two years in the 1980's and never came close. It is not without its attractions. But Handsworth, and places like it, have been the crucible of frightening changes over the past few years which are of profound importance to society as a whole.

The gun, and 'gun-play', is now the hard currency on these streets. It was brought by the Yardies, say locals, and their own youth has adopted it with enthusiasm. Things are predicted to get a lot worse before they get any better. Since the summer of 1995, Handsworth and nearby areas have seen five murders, at least six attempted murders and numerous other shootings by gunmen. Guns are openly worn in public, and policemen have been threatened at gun-point. Local officers fear that it is only a matter of time before one of them is shot dead in the course of their duty.

If it all sounds a bit like Northern Ireland, then this is no accident. The rise of gangsterism from roots in a sectarian/political conflict runs on surprisingly parallel tracks in both situations, as will be examined in more detail in later sections of this book. The atmosphere in the black ghettos is also similar in many respects to that found in areas of Belfast or Londonderry, which are also known locally as 'ghettos'. Alongside the violence, both areas share the characteristics of closed, exclusive communities where everyone knows everyone's business. Once inside, along with the fear is a similar easy warmth, a raucous, dark humour and a determination to have a good time despite all.

The startling difference is that while the streets of Ulster are patrolled by a heavily armed police force and several thousand specially trained troops, the lines in Britain's black ghettos are held by small groups of dedicated local officers, for the most part unarmed and often fighting against a lack of resources and political will as well as violent criminality.

Another difference is that while death or punishment shooting among drug dealers in Belfast prompts acres of front-page news coverage and hours of television reports, identical violence in other British inner-cities is often ignored by the media or purposefully kept quiet by the police. Again, some of the gun-related incidents in Birmingham that I have already mentioned were not even reported in the local press.

This is not to ignore the wider historical and political aspects of Northern Ireland. Nor would I advocate martial law in British cities. But as with Dunblane and the Wembley shoot-out already mentioned, the contrasts reveal an interesting, I would say damning, picture of perceived priorities and public sensibility. Put bluntly, it is fair to assume that if more white people were being shot and terrorised then the response would be very different.

Police on patrol in Handsworth, Birmingham.

'CHERIE' loves the ghetto. Handsworth is her 'manor', she says, and she couldn't live anywhere else because the ghetto is open and honest and there is 'no bullshit'.

Certainly this sparkling, diminutive mother-of-four, whose name I have changed, shows a refreshing candour when discussing her own past and present. A long career as an 'exotic dancer' began when she was 16 - "OK, a stripper, and a damn fine one I might add," she offers within minutes of meeting her in the Frontline - and it was a career that took her "to more countries than most people could mention in five minutes." As if to prove the point, her accent veers from muted Brummie (Birmingham dialect), to black-British street, to Jamaican patois, to west-coast American and back again in the course of a single conversation.

She is 38 or 42, depending on what day you catch her, and cheerfully affirms that her children, ranging from age four to 18, are all from different fathers. Her latter years, she says, have been spent in prostitution, shoplifting, 'general hustling', a short spell in prison - and crack addiction. Although still lithe, she doesn't dance any more. Instead she walks with a pronounced limp. It is the legacy of being thrown from a third-floor window by a Yardie crack dealer in a dispute over £20.

"It was in 1992, when I was working in the red light district of Balsall Heath (part of Birmingham). This friend of mine had borrowed £50 from a dealer, re-paid him £30 and said I would give him the other £20. So he comes to me for the £20, but the trouble was I didn't know about it, so I said to him, 'I don't owe you no £20'. I hadn't known him previous, you see, and anyway I don't take shit from nobody," rattles off the irrepressible Cherie.

"Next thing, now - I don't know if it was a gun or a piece of lead piping or what - but I feel this hard thing poked into my side. I am marched into this house, up to the third storey, I'm knocked out with a plank, or whatever, and subsequently thrown through the window. I got away with a broken left hip and left elbow," she says. "I landed on concrete."

Despite spending three weeks in intensive care and a total of 12 weeks in hospital, Cherie thinks she had a lucky escape. "It nearly killed me psychologically. But at the same time, if my system had not been numb with cocaine I would have died from fright. It's what saved me," she says. Then, with a rather naughty smile, she adds: "That's my excuse for keeping on using it." Joking apart, and in spite of having taken and occasionally sold the stuff over a number of years, Cherie is in no doubt that crack is what lies at the heart of her community's current problems. She saw it arrive, watched it flourish from her vantage point on the street and then saw the violence and the gunmen follow.

The ferociously addictive nature of crack has been well documented since public fears were first raised about it in the late 1980's, but it is worth recording again, from one who knows, just what we are talking about. Cherie says simply that it is an 'evil' drug that derives its strength from operating psychologically rather than just giving a physical high - making people think they are capable of anything. It is an escape that is so powerful because it is so complete, and the need to get back there becomes irresistible. When she was earning big money on the street and by 'escort work', she could spend £1,000 a night if she wanted to. "And I have done," she says.

You might be on the way to the shops to buy a pint of milk, but before you ever get there you will find that you have 'raised' £15 or £100 through theft, hustling, conning or 'blagging' in order to buy another hit. Then the day just disappears.

"All you are interested in is getting another stone. You will sell God off the cross in order to get that one pipe," she says. "It's Satan himself that crack stuff. It's Satan himself."

The links between crack, prostitutes, and the Yardies are important on a number of levels. Firstly, keeping girls on the street is a standard way for a dealer to raise finance in order to buy and import cocaine, which is then turned into crack. Equally, a lot of prostitutes are only doing what they do in order to pay for a crack habit, and so they also become an important market. Finally, the girls might also be used as couriers to go to Jamaica or America in order to bring the cocaine back.

This is how Cherie remembers the whole situation beginning, in around 1986. "That's when I first saw it, how the crack-heads used it and what they would do to obtain it," she says.

At the time there were a few dealers, then mostly in 'weed' or marijuana, who were running street girls and who decided to move into this new drugs market. "They got a few good looking white girls who were prepared to go across the water and bring the stuff back. A few black girls followed them, and while they were over there they meet some nice-looking guy, they meet a Yardie, who wants to come over here." That, she says, was the start of the latest influx of Jamaican criminals. The pattern of girls sponsoring Yardies to come to Britain, and then giving them a base when they get here, has persisted ever since.

By 1988 Cherie was working at a strip club called the Revue Bar and was given a chance to go to Amsterdam to do some work. While there she met two Jamaican girls who also wanted to come to Britain, not to work as strippers but to sell crack. "When I came back in '89 I brought them with me. Maybe I was a bit naive or green to do that, but . . ," she shrugs.

Already the scene was changing. "Two main Yardies came over [she will not divulge their names] and they started an epidemic over here. It got way out of control and became a way of life for people round here." They had

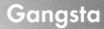

set up shop in a club called the Nightspot and were making a big impact with ostentatious shows of easy wealth. "Their heaven is England. They had so much money to spend it was almost pathetic," says Cherie.

The local youth, keen to get in on the act, were by then offering their services. "We're talking up-and-coming youths, maybe age 15 or 16, and they show the big guys that they have the know-how to pull in the money. They also got started into crack," she says. And so the downward spiral began. "You've got to be a really strong person to control it. It's destroyed so many lives."

And the Yardies now? "They have got one aim and one aim only. To sell crack cocaine for money. They don't care how they do it, who they use or how they get here. Once they get here they have got it made." They are still the most powerful influence on the scene, she says, because they have the most money. But like growing numbers of people in the indigenous community, she is no longer impressed. "I don't like them and I don't like what they stand for - which is violence and exploitation." One example of this she has seen is street girls being beaten up by Yardie dealers just for buying 'gear' from other people.

The Yardies' main mistake, however, was to get too big and to provoke a power struggle with gangs of the local 'home boys'. It is this struggle that forms the backdrop to many of the recent shootings.

The picture, as ever, is not a simple one, but the common factors are crack and money. Some of the locals, as mentioned, became and remain willing lieutenants of the Yardies. Others bought the cocaine or crack wholesale from them and sold it on the street for their own profit. As time went by, some of these then set up independent operations and started to kick against Yardie dominance of the lucrative market.

The attractions of being a big player were just too great. "The local boys, now, are saying 'We've got it'. They've got the means, they've got the know-how and they've got the whole community behind them," says Cherie. "They've got the girls, they've got the shit and they've got the money. And money is power. From them having crack in their pocket they can have anything they want."

And so they started to say something else. "They're saying: 'We were born here. This is our community. We have a right to it here. You've come here thinking you can run it over us. But it can't work'." Reprisals, says Cherie, were inevitable. "The Yardies can't lose face, so they blow a few heads off, using crack as the excuse. Now they are just shooting people for the sake of shooting people."

Ironically, the commodity that started it all - crack - is now in decline in the area, according to Cherie. Over the past three or four years it has been gradually going out of fashion, and a lot of the formally big users have been sent to prison for robberies they carried out to pay for the drug. As the violence has escalated over the same period, people are also less inclined to come into the area to 'score'. Where a dealer might once have made £10,000 a day, he is now lucky to make £2,000. As things have come full circle, even the street girls are selling crack for themselves and keeping the money. "The Yardies are having it tough now," she says. "They've been forced underground."

This shrinking market and the increased competition within it has only served to fuel the incidence of gun-play. The influence of the drug may be on the wane, but the gun culture which it spawned is here to stay. In local minds there is no doubt where it came from. "The violence and the guns were brought by the Yardies. Before you wouldn't see a home boy resorting to violence to get his crack sold. But the Yardies, that's what they stand for."

It's a style that has become highly infectious. "The home boys are following the Yardie style, they're coming the Yardie style, like big bad men," says Cherie. The process seems to be part self preservation, part deadly image. "Gun warfare is a novelty for the home boys, they're not used to it. Before they were knife men, but you can't fight a gun with a knife. To look big, act big, talk big you have to follow the Yardie way, and that is gun warfare. It's the only way you can get heard," she says. "They're making records about guns, they're not making records about knives."

As a result, she adds, it is now easy to get shot at, 'knifed up' or run over in Handsworth. So is she still in love with the place? I get another flash of the naughty smile: "The concept of life down here is totally different," she says. "It's nice, but it's deadly."

THE KILLING began in earnest on the night of June 21, 1995, on a terraced street in the Lozells area near Birmingham's 'front-line' (centre of activity) at the house of a small-time weed dealer called Timothy Thomas. He was known locally as 'Ganja Lips'.

The house was a popular spot in the area. 'Lips' was a renowned cook of Jamaican food, and his friends, with equally exotic street names like 'Dreddy', 'Cry-Cry' and 'Country Boy', would gather there most evenings to eat, drink and smoke weed. During the day he would sell 'draws' of ganja from his back door to people that he knew, but he was a vocal opponent of crack.

"Ganja Lips was a nice fella, always smiling always laughing. If you're sad he can make you happy, no matter, in a minute in seconds," said one local. "He was just a nice guy."

Just before midnight on the fatal night, three armed men came to call who were looking for more than food or a bit of fun. They had come to rob,

and before they left Lips had been shot dead and two of his friends wounded.

Lips was in the house with one friend called Keith Charles, or 'Principal', and their assailants bundled both men upstairs at gun-point and demanded money. Charles was waiting for his girlfriend, Pat West, to come and pick him up. When she arrived and tooted her car horn in the street one of the robbers went out to her, produced his gun again and forced her inside to join the other two in the front bedroom. All had their wrists bound with tape and were made to lie on the bed. She had some jewellery taken and the demands for money were repeated. Lips left the room at one stage, but it is not known whether any cash was handed over.

On his return he made a dash to escape out of the window, and the gunmen opened fire. Lips was hit in the chest, but still managed to get away and ran 50 yards down the road before collapsing. In the escape attempt he was also shot in the leg. He died in hospital later that night.

The gunmen had all left the bedroom to chase Lips, but afterwards two of them returned and opened fire on the remaining terrified figures on the bed. Charles wriggled about to try and avoid the shots, but was hit in the right groin. Pat West later discovered that two coins in her cardigan pocket, a £1 coin and a penny piece, had been dented by a bullet, deflecting it and possibly saving her life. After the gunmen had left again, both victims also made their escape through the window and Pat West broke her ankle in the fall.

One theory is that a local Yardie gangsta had brought in out-of-town gunmen for the robbery. It is thought to have been planned to coincide with the summer solstice when the maximum amount of money would have been in the house after locals had been stocking up with weed before leaving for the huge Glastonbury rock festival in the English West Country. Another idea is that it was just a case of mistaken identity, and there was no money in the house anyway. Two men stood trial for the shootings in December 1996. One was acquitted and the other, at the time of writing, is facing a retrial. No third man has yet been identified.

The brutal logic of the incident, as seen locally, was explained by one source, we'll call him Wayne. "That was just a direct set-up," he said. "But a man comes to rob you, you've got all different type of people. I mean a man pulls a gun on you, you might empty your pockets or you might say 'Fuck that. You're going to have to kill me'. Well Ganja Lips was that kind of person. If it was a knife he'd say, 'You're going to have to stab me. You ain't going to take my little money in my house, or whatever, what I have worked for.'"

The rules, it seems, are ones that both sides understand in such a confrontation. "The geezers that have gone there to do that now, it's on top, so they are going to have to play their cards out, innit? Which they did," said Wayne. In other words, having shown their hand the gunmen couldn't let Lips live because then he would be looking for them. "They played their cards out, Ganja Lips took the bluff and ended up dead." It's that frighteningly simple.

The next victim in this story is an altogether less popular character than Lips, a home boy gunman and crack dealer we will call Gilbert. He cannot be identified for legal reasons. "He upset the whole community all on his own," was the view of another local commentator.

His problems stem from the fact that he broke the basic rule of the drug dealing world - to stay on top you must "never get high on your own supply" - and became a dedicated user as well as a distributor. A common symptom among heavy users is a creeping paranoia that leads to unpredictable, violent behaviour. Gilbert, in the local parlance, had gone seriously 'para-cat'.

By the time that he was shot, on December 24, 1995, Gilbert had also already acquired a considerable reputation for 'badness'. In Handsworth it is widely believed that he was responsible for the murder of a man in a local blues club, after being told that he could not smoke his crack there. He was charged with the murder but walked free from the trial, and locals say this gave him the air and the arrogance of someone who thinks they are untouchable.

Again there are various theories as to why he was targeted, perhaps not altogether surprising for a man who was known to have a lot of enemies. Some say he was involved in a drugs rip-off from a Yardie gangsta and was shot in reprisal, others that it was over an attempted robbery of a local sound system, which was also backed by one of the Yardies. The most straightforward explanation was that he had been beating up on his girlfriend, some concerned friends had brought in heavies to 'sort him out' and things had got out of hand.

What is supposed to have actually happened was that he went to see his girlfriend at the house of a relative on Christmas Eve, and had started smoking his crack pipe and causing an argument. A group of four Jamaicans who were also in the house suddenly appeared and the row intensified. In the end a handgun and a sawn-off shotgun were produced, Gilbert was handcuffed, gagged, forced into a car outside and driven away. He was taken to the Hilltop golf course, some three miles away, taken out of the car and told to run. As he did he was blasted in the back by both barrels of the shotgun.

Miraculously he survived. Rather like the experience of Cherie, it is assumed that only the fact that he was 'cracked out of his head' at the time saved him from dying of trauma.

Two men appeared at the Old Bailey in October 1996, charged with the attempted murder. But the trial collapsed when the principal witness - Gilbert himself - failed to show up. He had disappeared once before in the trial process and was only found then after being arrested for pulling the emergency stop cord on a train. This time, however, the police had no such luck.

He was arrested a few weeks later, however, and was in custody at the time of writing, charged with robbery. The word on the street is that far from learning from his near-miss with death, he was still up to his old tricks of terrorising the neighbourhood before his latest arrest.

After Gilbert's shooting, the bullets started to fly thick and fast around Handsworth. Just three days later Trevor Lee Hamilton, or 'Shines' was shot dead at his home in Handsworth Wood. He was a known associate, or 'spar' of Gilbert's so there may have been a connection. But no one has yet been arrested for his murder.

On January 14, 1996, a crack dealer from nearby Wolverhampton was killed in London. He had been down there to pick up a consignment of the drug, but before closing the deal discovered that he had been sold £4,500 worth of candle-wax in what is becoming an increasingly popular type of drugs trade 'sting'. When he tried to object and fight back, he was shot.

By mid February, the home boys in Birmingham were starting to show their teeth. Members of a notorious local gang burst into a wedding at the Winson Green community centre, forced a Jamaican to the floor and shot him in the legs. He was then dragged outside and a gun placed to his head. As the trigger was pulled, however, the gun apparently jumped. The shot went into the pavement and the man, known as 'President Sass', escaped with his life.

Far from being regarded as lucky, however, Sass is said to have been another victim of mistaken identity. He had come up from London just for the wedding, and happened to be sitting next to the man that the boys were really after. One version of why the raid took place is particularly chilling. It is that a member of the home boys' gang had previously robbed a local Yardie and that he in turn had sent for reinforcements from London. The 'soldier' in question, so the story goes, was planning to hand-grenade the local boy's house, and the wedding attack was an attempted pre-emptive strike. "The home boys decided it was time to make a name for themselves," was the view of one local.

Two weeks after that, the home boys were at it again, at another blues in nearby Newtown where a 'sound system' believed to have Yardie links was playing. Sound systems are now the staple diet on the Jamaican music scene, and, as they often form the rhythmic backdrop to violence, they deserve a short explanation here.

Essentially starting as groups of DJs playing records like any other, the systems have developed a whole new form of performance over recent years through the DJs 'rapping' between and over the songs to stamp their own personalities on them. To the untutored ear the effect is chaotic, as songs are switched, mixed and interjected with rapid-fire patois 'lyrics' from the teams of DJs. Pre-recorded sound effects are also liberally thrown into the mix, with variations on the theme of gunfire being particularly popular.

The systems have become hugely successful, packing out dance halls with hundreds of people at a time and playing for big money, with each having their own dedicated followers. 'Clashes' between two or more different systems are also a feature of this scene, where each plays for a few minutes in response to their rivals, and success is measured by the reaction of the crowd. One extreme form of appreciation, imported direct from Jamaica, involves real gun-fire - when gangstas pull out their weapons and fire into the air in a 'gun salute'. Police have long suspected links between some of the systems and the bad men, to the point where sound equipment travelling between Jamaica, the USA, Britain and the European Continent has been used for smuggling drugs.

On this February night in Newtown, the system in question was at least closely followed by local Yardies, and the home boys are said to have gone along to see what they could take. First they tried to rob the girlfriend of one of the DJ's, called 'Bubbler', and then they decided to rip-off the man himself by laying in wait in the car park. When Bubbler came out of the club and got into his car he found himself surrounded by youths brandishing two hand-guns and a sawn-off shotgun.

As Wayne has already explained, not everybody in this world is intimidated by such things. Bubbler was another. He refused to even get out of the car and was shot at point-blank range in the head with the shotgun, through the car window.

The first signs that the home boys were prepared to shoot back had actually come a few days before the Sass attack. Then, at a club in Small Heath, a notorious Yardie known as 'Run Eye' (his name comes from the fact that one of his eyes waters a lot thanks to a bullet that creased his temple in a previous shoot-out) had got into an argument with a group of locals, pulled his gun and fired on them. But he came off worse from that encounter with shot-gun pellets in his leg, and he went back to his base in London to re-group and return for revenge. The escalation of warfare was only prevented by the fact that he was arrested for immigration offences and deported before he had the chance.

The biggest name Yardie to be shot in Birmingham, however, is said to have died at the hands of his own. He was 'Junior' Chaplin, who for more

than a decade ran a drugs and prostitution operation in Handsworth and Balsall Heath. He was killed with four shots from a 9mm handgun on March 1, 1996, while sitting in his car outside a Caribbean take-away shop.

He is an even less popular character than Gilbert in the community, known to have a penchant for drug rip-offs, set-ups and swindles as well as gun play. One judge, in a recent trial during which Junior's name figured prominently, summarised him as a man, "with a reputation for carrying a gun, who hits people round the head and takes their jewellery". Perhaps because he is dead, he has also taken the posthumous blame for some more serious crimes. Some believe that he was the man who set up Ganja Lips for the hit, others say he was responsible for both the attack on Gilbert and the death of Shines in retaliation for an attempt by them to rip him off. He is not widely mourned.

Some, however, were impressed by his larger than life attitude. A standard night out would involve him going into a club and immediately ordering two or three bottles of champagne which he would distribute among a gaggle of attentive girls. He always had plenty of money to spend, and would cruise around the neighbourhood in hire cars, paid for each week in cash by other devoted females. It was in one such car that he was shot dead. On a number of occasions that he was arrested by police, it was his girls who gave him an alibi.

The first attempt on his life happened in early 1995, outside a club then called the Rialto, which sits just across the Soho Road from the Frontline blues. The story there was that he was shot by a home boy who had just been recruited to a rival Yardie gang and was given the job as an initiation to serious badness. He was then paid in crack to get himself started in business. Junior did not lose his life that night, but did have his dignity seriously dented - he was shot in the buttocks.

Clearly rattled, he shifted his whole operation to Balsall Heath for a while, running crack and girls out of three houses on the same road. But a number of police raids on the addresses all but put him out of business and he was forced to return to Handsworth and to expand into other areas like Wolverhampton. Eager to re-establish himself and his 'face', he went about with a worse 'attitude' than before, threatening people with guns and setting up robberies of drugs from other dealers. "He was saying, 'you can't touch me because I'm bad'. But other people didn't see it like that," said Wayne. "He got too big for his boots and a rival gang wiped him out, just wasted him. Simple as that."

His final offence reflected the changing balance of power on the Handsworth scene. Realising that he would have to stay sweet with the rising influence of the home boy gangs, it is said that he was taking gear from Yardies and giving it to the new kids on the block. It's not something that you can get away with for long. The killing itself is not thought to have been a planned affair, just an opportunistic 'hit' by someone who was in the right place at the right time.

"Who ever did it is very brave," said one local police source. "Junior's boys are after him. He's living on borrowed time."

HEIGHTENED police activity in the area following all these shootings quietened things down for a while. But then in May a gangsta known as 'Yardie John' was found dead at a house in Ladywood, with a single bullet wound to the head. The house had been raided earlier in the year by customs officers, when cocaine and two firearms were found, and Yardie John's demise had all the signs of another drugs rip-off gone wrong.

That, for 1996, was the end of the killing, but the guns had not gone away. During the summer two cars were seen speeding down the Handsworth 'frontline' of Villa Road, with gangsta's shooting at each other through the windows. Again: "Just like a stage-coach shooting", said one observer. In October, a man escaped from Walsall Crown Court after producing a knife and stabbing a prison officer. Later the same day police in Handsworth heard that he was in the area in a car, and three detectives confronted him as he was parked by the side of the road. The man brought out a sawn-off shot gun, pointed it at the policemen and said: "You want some of this?" Unarmed, the officers had to beat a hasty retreat, pursued down the road by the man waving his gun.

The early hours of Sunday November 3, saw more open gun play on the street following another stand-off between Yardies and home boys. The scene was So'premes night club in West Bromwich, where a disagreement on the dance floor between the two factions had led to a Yardie pulling a gun and the home boys being unceremoniously kicked out of the club. At about 3am, when the triumphant Jamaicans were emerging onto the street, they found that the home boys were waiting for them - with guns.

"I saw this one guy with a gun run across the road, take up a position on the corner and start to fire shots down the side street. Other guys were

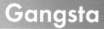

smashing up a car parked on the corner, just kicking it in," said one witness. "It was like a scene on the telly, man. People were running about all over the place and girls were screaming. It was chaos."

Other witnesses said they saw a group of men with handguns and a pump-action shot gun lined up across the road and shooting into the crowd as it came out of the club. If anyone was hit, it was not reported. Next day, however, police found the wadding from several shot gun cartridges. None of this incident appeared in the local papers.

The next night more shots were fired as the inevitable retaliation for the retaliation took place, near the Handsworth club where Junior was originally shot, now called Thasha's. Yardie gunmen lay in wait for, and then confronted a group of the home boys who were on their way to the club. Word on the street was that one youth took four shots to the chest as his friends ran away, but he survived. He was wearing a bullet-proof vest.

Chapter Two

TOAD

TOAD is a man who knows a lot about the gun-play epidemic in Handsworth. He had to face down Junior when that gangsta pulled a gun on him in a club, he was in the same house when Gilbert was taken away and shot, and he counted the murdered Shines as a good friend. Toad has also picked up his own bullets - he was shot four times after intervening in an argument at another local blues club - but he lives to tell the tale.

His story of that night and its aftermath warrants telling at length, both as an account of an incredibly lucky escape and as an illustration of just how thin the line between life and death has become in the ghetto.

"It was a Thursday night in July 1995, and I was in this pub for a game of pool when I saw him. I had never seen him there before, so I'm thinking, 'what's he doing here?'." says Toad, starting at the beginning. The name of this man has also been changed, we will call him 'Tiger'. With him were two other Yardie characters who were outside their normal stomping ground. One we'll call 'Albert', and the other is known as 'Soldjy' after a spell

Toad, real name Rudolph, pictured in Birmingham

he spent in the army. "That man knows his guns," says Toad. Both had recently been released from prison for firearms offences.

Toad greeted them but soon left to go on to Thasha's. At the club the three turned up again. Toad saw one dodging between pillars on the dance floor and another brandishing his gun. Concerned now that he might be a target, Toad started making inquiries, but a friend told him that if he stayed out of the way he would be OK. It was said that the previous night the three had been involved in a shoot-out with a group of home boys. Tiger had a dispute with one of their main men, and had 'gathered his crew' to 'sort it out'. The clash had been inconclusive, and so they were out again to try and find the man. "They'd come out with blood in their eyes," says Toad, "I heard that Tiger had been smoking crack and drinking white rum, saying that he'd kick down every door in Handsworth to find that guy."

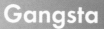

Nothing else happened at the club. When it closed, Toad caught a taxi with two other friends and went on to a blues club (by coincidence, one of those I was to visit with Gilly).

"Well I was just going into the back room, and as the door closed behind me I walked into a man with a gun saying, 'I'm going to kill you! I'll shoot you!'," says Toad. It was Soldjy, and the man who the gun was pointed at was someone else that Toad knew, called 'Chicken George'. "Now I'm no angel," admits Toad (it's a fact he repeats often during our conversations), "But if that was happening to me I would like someone to try and save me." So he stepped in.

It turned out that all the argument was about was that Soldjy wanted to stand where George was standing against the wall. George didn't want to move, so Soldjy had started leaning up against him. "I'm not a pole or a post, and I'm not your woman, so what you leaning down on me for?" George had said. It was then that the gun was pulled out as a forceful way of saying, "Move yourself".

After that, things started to move fast. "I pulled Soldjy away," says Toad. "He was ranting and raving but I held onto him saying, 'You just come out of jail. Hold it down, man. You don't need this.' By now Tiger is in the room and he's clocked this. So I say to him: 'Don't pay someone else to do your dirty work', and Tiger and I exchanged words. Now Soldjy started up again with, 'You're disrespecting my boss'. So I said it was Tiger that was disrespecting him by putting a gun in his hand when he'd just come out of prison. I told him to go outside and sort something out. But then Soldjy was looking at me saying he's going to shoot me. 'Shoot me for what?' I said. 'For what? I've got no girls, I've got no money. I'm just a sufferer in the ghetto'."

Then the first shot went off.

By now Toad is getting excited by his own account. We are in the sitting room of his brother's house and he is leaning forward in his armchair, eyes blazing (his prominent eyes are where his street name comes from) and knocking my leg regularly with the back of his hand to emphasise his points.

"Now I've been stabbed, I've had a brick in the head and I've been hit with an iron bar. But I'd never been shot before, so I didn't know what it felt like," he says. The fact was he didn't know he'd been shot at all. "I heard a bang and felt this 'Ping!', like something hitting my leg [another knock to my leg], so I thought they were just letting off blanks to scare me. Then I heard another bang and felt another 'Ping!'," he says, giving me yet another poke to get his message across. At this point he's almost laughing at the ludicrous scene he's describing. "I mean there we are, two shots have gone off but no one's dropped down and no one's running. The crowd is just standing there. Then the woman from the blues comes out and shouts, 'We don't want no shots. And no drugs in the place!' And there's me, still standing. I'm the one that's picked up two shots and I don't even know it!"

Now Toad is getting very excited. He's on his feet, describing how the second shot came from behind where Albert was standing, when with a flourish he suddenly drops his jeans to show off his bullet holes. The first is in his sizable right thigh, while the second goes right through his right calf muscle, from back to front. This graphically illustrates Toad's first piece of luck and why he felt so little. Both shots, from 9mm handguns at close range, had gone straight through his flesh, missing the bone. Otherwise he would have been crippled for life. The rest of this section of our interview takes place in the same curious position, with Toad standing in front of me with his trousers around his ankles.

"So now I've got Soldjy's gun to my forehead and someone said, 'Take him outside. Finish him off outside'. So I said, 'If I'm going to die, I'm going to die where I stand'. Then, I don't know why, I just thought that gun had been there too long so I grabbed onto it, holding it by the nozzle," he says. He certainly felt the third shot. "There was this blue and orange light, then smoke, then my hand started to hurt - a lot, man - then it went numb. I thought, 'The other two might have been blanks but this is for real. I've got to get out of here. Now.'"

By now the room was in uproar. Everyone else had also worked out that this was the real thing, women were screaming and people were "running about like chickens with their heads cut off." The air was thick with the smell of gunpower. "It took me weeks to get rid of that smell," says Toad. "Sometimes I can still smell it." He shudders.

Seeing a possible route of escape, he went for it. "I just got flat down on the floor, went through a woman's legs and then just pushed out everything in sight." But to get to the door he had to get past Tiger, who decided to add his own contribution. "He said, 'Hold that you fucker,' and let go another shot," says Toad. Again he felt little, and in his confusion thought he'd been stabbed. He kept running. In fact he had been shot in the other leg (he shows me that bullet hole as well) but miraculously this had also passed straight through.

Outside he ran up the road until he came to a high fence. Once over there, he thought, and he'd be safe. "I tried to jump up, but nothing happened. There was nothing from my legs. I tried again and again, but it was the same. Behind, I could hear them coming after me. There was shouting and more shots going off," says Toad, describing a scene from a classic nightmare. "When I looked down I saw that my blue jeans had turned red. I knew then I'd been shot, because I knew I didn't come out in red jeans. I didn't have any." Legs useless, he just lay down in the long grass by the fence and hoped it would hide him. "I was looking up at the sky with the whole world going round. I just kept saying, 'Jesus, don't let them find me. Please don't let them see me. I can't die like this.'"

His next piece of luck came round the corner at that moment, in the shape of a taxi. Straining his head up, Toad caught sight of the bumper and realised that it belonged to someone he knew. Still he couldn't move. Then he saw a panicked couple run towards the car flagging it down, and realised that he knew them too. "The girl was a school friend of mine so I called out her real name, not her street name, which not a lot of people would know. 'Who is it?', she said. 'It's Rudolph,' I said, which is my real name, and she held up the car. Somehow, I still don't know how, I got across the street and they put me in the back. The driver was a guy who runs a rank near where I live. I just said: "Keith, I've been shot. Hospital."

Toad near-where he was shot four times and hid in the grass

HE EMERGED three weeks later, only to find that he was still not safe. "Tiger went to Jamaica for a hit-man to kill me. He didn't want me to take him to court," says Toad.

Again, it was only by another astonishing stroke of luck that he knew this. The hit-man, we'll call him Captain, was drinking in a bar in Jamaica before he left, waving his ticket about and boasting about the job he had just been hired for. Someone who overheard him happened to be a friend of Toad's family. Proving what a good friend he was, the man dropped everything, caught the next flight to England and went to Toad's house to warn him.

"Captain was due up on the Wednesday, and on Friday I saw him sitting in a car as I crossed the road," says Toad. Showing what a brass neck he's got, Toad did not run away. "I just went up and said, 'So you finally reach'. The guy started saying that he had heard the whole story and didn't want no part of it, but I didn't believe him. I thought he was just trying to get me off my guard. After that every time I saw him he kept trying to buy me a drink and talk to me, but I was having none. In fact it turned out that he was being genuine," says Toad. As is often the case when dealing with this world, just when you think you know what's going on something new turns up to throw you off again. In this case, it seems, it was something like honour among thieves.

Tiger, meanwhile, was not a happy man. He'd paid out for Captain's ticket, reputedly paying him £1,000 a week while he was here, but was getting nothing for his money. So what do you do when your hit-man won't hit? Tiger changed tack and started sending messengers to Toad saying he would pay him to drop the charges. The price eventually got up to £25,000, but Toad was not impressed. "I know a woman who was offered a similar deal by Tiger. She dropped her charges and is still waiting for a penny," he says.

As things turned out, Tiger need not have worried as he was never convicted. Soldjy got two-and-a-half years for his part in Toad's shooting, with a further three years for the shoot-out with the home boys the night before.

Toad is not happy about the outcome and the competence of the justice system. "What are they saying? Because we are black we must kill off each other? 'Oh, it's only another nigger, leave them to it. Less paper work?'" he asks. "At the end of the day this is my country, I was born here, and the law has a duty to defend me. It's a joke."

We are walking though the streets of Handsworth, and talking about the shooting has clearly got Toad riled up. It is a cold January day and he is also physically reminded of the ordeal by stiffness in his legs and in his left hand, which has a permanently disfigured and useless middle finger. In this mood I see a different man to the one who was previously discussing the ghetto 'runnings' with calm detachment. This is the 'no angel' I have heard so much about, and it is very convincing.

"People can't believe I'm just walking about doing nothing about that guy," he says, referring to Tiger. "But I tell you, he might not be in jail but he's a prisoner in his own house and in that fucking Jeep he drives around in. He can only go to dances out of town and God forbid I run into him at one."

The voice is now pure, cold menace. "I'd stab him up proper," he says. "And I wouldn't fuck around stabbing him in the stomach either. I'd stab him in the head, in the eye, in the face, everything. Then I'd lick the blood off my knife so he becomes part of me, and his spirit can't come back and give me no trouble."

TOAD is now 32, and has been 'on the street' since he was 13. Such education as he had, he says, comes from there. He still has trouble with his reading and writing, but on the subject of ghetto life and the rising power of gun culture he is more than eloquent.

"It's fashion, man. It's just fashion," he says. "The youth like it. It's something new, a new trend, a phase. It's a new thing, a fashion thing and everybody wants to be part of the fashion. It's an up-town kind of thing, you know what I mean?" And then we're back to training shoes. "It's like if you're not wearing Nike you better be wearing Fila 'cos those are the two top names. It's Top Tens, and if you're not in the Top Ten you're not in the charts, man, you're not saying nothing. You're just a shadow, not a figure, you're just a shadow passing through, you know? Like a breeze that's passing through, you know? To be known you've got to be in with the scene, you know? You've got to be updated, you've got to be IN."

Like Cherie he has watched this deadly trend come up at first hand. He was also a crack user, and he used to be quite a dealer in his own right. He shakes his head in sadness when he remembers staying up all night, for days on end fuelled by crack, gambling away thousands of pounds. It was a habit that cost him a relationship with the girl he loved. Then he will also shake his head with laughter, recounting tales of narrow escapes from the police when his pockets were stuffed with crack and cash. He does know what it's like to be caught, however, having served a five-year sentence from 1983 for robbery, wounding and possession of cannabis. This was the last chapter in his life of crime and punishment that went back to approved school at the age of 13 and included probation, borstal, and a 'short sharp shock' at a Detention Centre. "I'm not really a bad lad," he laughs.

Only the birth of his first child, just over a year before I met him, finally straightened him out, he says. He had worked as a lavatory cleaner just before that Christmas, in order to earn some 'clean money' with which to buy the child's presents.

Also like Cherie, he is in no doubts where the gun fashion came from. "It was the Yardies, they brought it here. The English people adopted it and now they're trapped in it, like a crab in a barrel," he says. "They brought it here, star, and it's really fucked up the area. It's turned the community upside down. It's turned people against each other. Like there's people used to be friends of mine I can't talk to no more because they're with the Yardies."

Part of the impact they have made is on the local girls, whose heads are turned by the promise of champagne and big money. But before she knows where she is, says Toad, such a girl finds that the Yardie has moved in, she's paying all his bills and is stealing to support him. Meanwhile much of his money is going back to Jamaica, to build himself a nice house with a pool and buying him a big Jeep so he can go back and show off to all his friends how the streets of Britain are 'paved with gold'.

"I know guys who have gone round to see a girlfriend, and here's one of these geezers sitting there in his dressing gown, wearing his slippers, saying 'I run things here now,'" says Toad. "And on the coffee table is this big gun, his power. What are you going to do?" The Yardie might have six such girls for security, so no one knows where he is staying, and the girls do nothing because they are terrified of his 'murderer' reputation.

Toad is the first to admit that there were plenty of things 'going on' before the Yardies arrived in such strength. But then it was more 'behind closed doors' and when youths got into a 'tiff' they would go up against each other with fists or at worst pull a knife. Even then people would jump in to stop it, and no one would suffer more than the odd cut. It hardly sounds like heaven, but it was a lot better than what is currently happening.

"Now it's just the gun. Everybody's put down the knife and everybody wants a gun, because with a gun you've got more power," says Toad. "It's like money. With money you've got power."

Neither is he saying that all Jamaicans are the problem. His mother is Jamaican, his family is Jamaican and he has visited the country often. "It's like anywhere, there's good and bad," he says. Even the real bad men he has met there are of a different order to the Yardies he comes across in Handsworth. There, they are "real, loving people," he says, who use the gun to impose some order on their chaotic communities. They do not walk around the street showing off their guns, terrorising people, because if you are caught with one by the Jamaican police then you are as good as dead: "They shoot first and ask questions later," he says. Yardies here just "take the piss' because they know the police are not armed and there is nothing they can do about it.

He has a similar view on the influence of the 'gun rap' music that booms incessantly from DJ's and black pirate radio stations. In Jamaica its understandable, he says, because that's where it's from, 'the heart', and is a reflection of what's going on, of what the singer might have seen the day before. But then it crosses the water and the local home boys get hold of it, and again it becomes fashion. "These people adopt it and think, 'Yeah that's me man, I'm going to be that man',", says Toad. "They're just following. Wannabes. 'I wannabe, I wannabe.' They don't want to be themselves because they've got nothing. But they need to stop fantasising. Get back to reality."

He is not optimistic. Partly, it's those training shoes again. "The kids have got to have the latest. So they're saying, 'If my mum can't give it me or my dad can't give it me, then I'm going to go out there and get it'," he

says. "And no one wants to go and earn hard-working money again. It's all got to be easy. That's also from Jamaica. It's fashionable to be a bad man, 'cos to be a bad man you get anything."

Then there is a more general collapse of family structures in parts of the community. Toad describes himself as a 'black sheep', but he comes from a stable, church-going family background. Pride of place above his brother's mantelpiece is a huge picture of his mother on her 60th birthday, surrounded by her nine children. Plenty of others are not so lucky. "You've got youths growing up now who've never seen their mum or dad do anything constructive. They see their dad off to some other baby mother, or their mum on crack. There's nothing there to make them fall into line. They've no respect for anything," says Toad. His vision becomes positively apocalyptic when he starts quoting from Revelation about "mothers sleeping with their sons, and fathers sleeping with their daughters", and talks about how living in the ghetto can feel like living in the Last Days.

Even here, though, he sees the influence of the Yardies, in particular those who started to appear in Handsworth from the mid-1980's. "They've got no morals, they've got no respect. All they want is money, money, money, money, money," he says. Many of them can't even go back to Jamaica, because they would be "shot out of their shoes". But even if they did, their legacy of the gun would remain.

"Now because of them fuckers they are going to have to arm the police. So then you'll have people say: 'Because I'm a black man the police are going to be after me, I'm going to have to get a gun too. It's either you or me.' They've got that mentality," says Toad. "I tell you, man, we ain't seen the start of it. Better ain't to come, worse is to come."

So what is he going to do? In a macabre, but legitimate, way he'll just go with the flow. "If I get some decent compensation for my injuries, I'm going to invest it in a funeral parlour," he says. "You think I'm joking? I'm serious, man. We're all going to die, and round here we're not going to be dying by natural causes. The way we live our life now, it's going to be the gun. So I'll just sit back and take."

Chapter Three

GOING OPERATIONAL

" LIKE gripping jelly in your hands," was the verdict of Roy Ramm, the first senior police officer in Britain to try and tackle the Yardie phenomenon. It is a fitting description of the difficulties faced by police trying to infiltrate and control this closed, alien underworld – or indeed to understand it in the first place. The story of their attempts, however, is not on the whole a happy one - characterised by high-level ignorance of the nature of the problem, leading to frustration among those trying to tackle it on the ground - while inherent difficulties have been compounded by constant changes in direction.

Ramm, then a Detective Chief Superintendent, was given charge of Operation Lucy, set up by the Metropolitan Police in 1988 to investigate 'Black Organised Crime'. The broad task given, as with names of a succession of later units, was a thin disguise for the real, far more focused target: the growing threat from Jamaican criminals. The operation was founded after three months of press hysteria about the coming of a 'Black Mafia', and no one was fooled. The nickname 'Yardie Squad' became accepted to such an extent that switchboard operators at Scotland Yard cheerfully used it when putting through calls.

The fate of Operation Lucy, disbanded after less than 18 months, and that of a number of other initiatives show a police force trying to tackle an immensely complex law enforcement problem while trying to remain sensitive to the wider questions of racial politics. It is a tension that remains today, and which has consistently hampered police operations. Together with a paucity of necessary expertise, and an unwillingness for many years to properly harness that which was available, this has been a significant factor in the growth of the crisis.

Hindsight, as they say, is a wonderful thing. But it can be fairly argued that the guns and the fear of guns that now hold sections of Britain's inner cities in their thrall would not have gained such a hold had the nettle, or jelly, of Yardie crime been grasped sooner.

ANY SUCCESS that has been achieved against the 'gangstas' is due largely to the efforts of a small group of dedicated, some would say obsessed, police officers and their opposite numbers in the customs and immigration services. For years much of their work was carried out in spite of, rather than because of, official policy and in many ways they had more in common with each other than with their immediate colleagues. All got a slightly manic glint in their eyes when on the subject of Jamaicans, the term Yardie

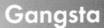

is rarely used, and they shared intelligence information in a way highly unusual between agencies which traditionally hold each other at arms length when not actually at each others throats. Informal meetings took place several times a week in what was affectionately known as 'the office', a small pub down a back-street in Southwark, south London, when policeman spake unto customs officer and the man from immigration spoke to both. Ideas were thrashed out in bewildering exchanges of street names, reminiscences and lager. For most of the time since the Yardie threat first emerged, this was the nearest thing to a national, co-ordinated response. Most of this irregular crew are now gone.

I was first introduced to the workings of this irregular crew at 7.30 on a cold February morning in 1992. The previous summer I had been on an attachment with The Gleaner newspaper in Kingston where I had become fascinated by the 'Posses', as the Yardie gangs are known there and in North America. Since then I had been trying to find out more about the real story of their impact in Britain and the people who were trying to deal with it. Contacts made in Jamaica pointed me in the right direction, and after weeks of delicate negotiations through Scotland Yard I was given unlimited access to spend a month with the main players. It was an experience that taught me much about both the efforts required and the frustrations involved in chasing the Yardies.

Big players seemed a more apt description for the two officers that welcomed me aboard at a north London police station that morning. Detective Sergeant John Brennan, an imposing 6ft 3ins figure with a shock of blond hair and a background as a professional footballer and a Physical Education teacher; Constable Steve Barker, who stands 6ft 5ins in his socks and is an international korf ball player, a Dutch variation on the theme of basketball. Size, despite what people may say, is a distinct advantage in this line of work, not least for getting yourself noticed and eliciting the all important 'respect'. This formidable-looking pair quickly showed, however, that a certain finesse and a detailed understanding of Jamaica and Jamaicans are infinitely more important than muscle in their highly specialised field.

WE ARE standing on the bare, concrete landing of an old block of council flats half an hour later, surrounded by the usual smells of decay and urine, hammering on a new unpainted front door. The previous one, it is explained, had been smashed in during a drugs raid some weeks before.

Our target is 'The Jackal', a former political hit-man in Jamaica, a notorious member of one of the biggest American posses, and a convicted killer in this country. He and Brennan are old adversaries, after Brennan pursued him to New York some years earlier as part of a murder investigation and brought him back to Britain to stand trial. After serving 18 months for manslaughter Jackal was released and deported, but informants had recently said that he was back, armed with a sawn-off shotgun and dealing crack.

The flat is home to an old girlfriend of one of Jackal's known associates, and Brennan and Barker are keen to see if she will come 'on-side', in other words give them information about where he is living. Their way through the front door is a warrant for her arrest on a minor outstanding cannabis charge, but they do not smash it in, or 'bosh' it in police parlance, like the previous official visitors. Rather they begin a curious kind of courtship ritual involving exaggerated politeness, a little string pulling on her behalf and a lot of time spent ferrying her backwards and forwards to court. It's an hilarious process, with everybody knowing exactly what is going on but it never being openly stated, carried off as if this was the standard level of police service.

The prolonged banging brings no response except from an ageing, concerned neighbour and a noisy dog downstairs. The two policemen whisper while crouching to peer through the letter box:

"What do you think?"

"She's definitely in. Her keys are still in the door."

Now shouting: "We know you're in love, I can see your keys in the door. This is the police. Can you let us in?"

Eventually she appears, we'll call her Jose - big, sassy, obviously straight out of bed and not at all amused. She lets us in amid loud complaints, and the charm offensive starts. The officers apologise for the inconvenience, assure her it is only a minor matter that they have to clear up, left up to

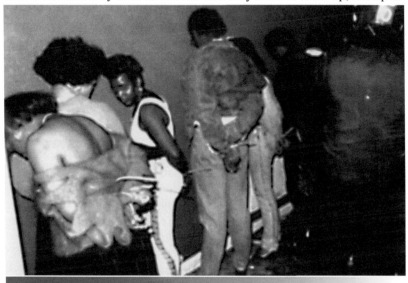

Police line up suspects during a Yardie raid in Clapton, London in 1988

them . . . etc. They even compliment her on the new decorations in the largely bare flat. A nervous man hovers in the background bedroom, until he too is assured there is nothing to worry about.

She re-emerges dressed but still complaining, an orange comb stuck defiantly in her hair, and we leave for court with her, of course, taking pride of place in the front seat. The tactics start to pay off on the way when, visibly more relaxed, she starts to drop little bits of information. Nothing which on its own would prove anything or allow the police to take action, but which adds little extra pieces to the intelligence jigsaw. To the uninitiated the conversation sounds like gobbledy-gook, with Jose regularly lapsing into Jamaican patois and the rest involving a litany of street names.

These are the vital stock-in-trade of Yardie-hunters, for while a gangsta will have as many identities as he needs passports, his street name originates from the ghetto and stays with him. Even then, gang members can have two or more, and a lot of time goes into building up a picture of who the street names actually relate to, and who are the associates of whom. Some are slightly exotic, like 'Jackal', 'Chinna', 'Early Bird' or 'Ratty', others more prosaic, like 'Bighead Pete'.

"Why is he called that," I ask Barker one day. "Because his name's Pete and he's got a big head," comes the answer. Obvious, really.

At court, quiet words are had to boost Jose up the list of waiting defendants and the lead magistrate is clearly impressed when she wheels in accompanied, apparently, by three large detectives. Jose, comb still in place, almost manages to be respectful, and gets away with a moderate fine.

Outside, I find myself involuntarily losing my passive-observer status when she decides that she has taken a shine to me. "You're nice," she says, subtly, "You don' look like a policeman at all." I smile, sheepishly.

It all, apparently, helps. On the way home Jose lets slip the street name of Jackal's current girlfriend, we'll call her Sandra. She also gave a chilling insight into the man we are looking for. "'Im sometime go crazy, an' 'im give her kickin' in the stomach. He bring baby-mother from Jamaica to live in her flat, and Sandra have to go out stealing to keep 'im happy."

This spot of domestic strife, however, pales into insignificance when one looks at the man's background. For the Jackal has the classic profile of what can be called the first generation of Yardies or posse members. A detailed explanation of the Jamaican political background appears in the next chapter, but his career gives a flavour of how the situation developed.

Born into a left-leaning People's National Party (PNP) stronghold in the Kingston ghettos, he was among those sent to Cuba during the 1970s for firearms training and returned to Jamaica as a member of a group of para-military gunmen known as the Brigadistas. He was active throughout the political strife of the 1970's, and was credited with 17 murders from the 1980 election alone. When the PNP lost that election and the advent of the eradication squads made the situation too hot at home, he fled to America to become a drugs dealer and a leading member of the Spangler posse.

His story continues with the vicious drugs war that then erupted for control over large sections of the American trade, waged between the Spanglers and the former JLP (Jamaica Labour Party) gunmen of the Shower posse. Jackal was operating in Florida when, in 1984, he was cornered by a group of Shower members who beat him, shot him and drove over him repeatedly in a four-wheel drive vehicle. Some Spanglers then arrived at the scene, raked the vehicle with automatic weapons, killing everyone inside, and dumped what was left of the Jackal outside a Miami hospital. He miraculously survived, but still bears hideous scars from the ordeal.

Brennan first came across the name in 1986, when he was part of the team investigating the murder of Innocent Egbulefu. The not-so-innocent Innocent was a Nigerian conman and drugs dealer who was foolish enough to sell a batch of fake 'weed', made up of herbs and tea leaves, to a group of four Jamaicans for £150. On realising they had been conned, the men returned to his eighth-floor flat in Islington, North London, smashed down the toilet door behind which Innocent was hiding, and in the following struggle he was thrown out of the window. After a 90ft fall he was, in the words of a policeman quoted at the time, "squashed like a flat-iron. Like in Tom and Jerry." It all happened so fast that Innocent was still clutching the television remote control panel when he hit the ground. In the ensuing inquiry, one of the street names to come up was that of the Jackal.

The case is significant in that it was the first time police identified a distinct group of Jamaican criminals sharing the same background and similar ways of operating. In Britain, it was, in short, the first officially recognised Yardie murder. It was also Brennan's entrée into the world of the Jamaican criminal. In the three years that the investigation ran, he travelled to Kingston and New York in search of the Jackal and his accomplices.

The experience and the contacts he made during that time formed the basis of a thesis he wrote for an MPhil degree in Police Studies at the University of Exeter, completed in 1991. This in turn was the first attempt to formally map the elements and the structure of what he terms The Jamaican Crime Group, and for a while at least it made him the acknowledged police expert on the subject. He was recruited to Operation Lucy when it was formed by Roy Ramm, and was prominent in some of its most high-profile operations.

Brennan's reputation in the north London areas of Hackney and Stoke Newington also brought him a street name of his own, 'Blondie', of which

he is clearly proud. Barker, for his part, had then spent 15 years on the streets of Brixton developing his own expertise and fame. There, and increasingly among Jamaican criminals in the US and Kingston, he glories under the name of 'John Wayne'. It was to Barker's 'ground' of south London that we moved in the next stage of our renewed search for the Jackal.

SANDRA, the Jackal's much put upon girlfriend, was already known to the police for her career in shoplifting. Barker also knew her mother, who lived in a council flat with Sandra's three children, all from different 'baby-fathers'. We visit her one afternoon to see if she can tell us where our man is hiding out.

If the Jackal is a photo-fit example of a 'bad-bwoy' and Sandra is a stan-dard-issue gangsta's baby-mother, then Granny, as we'll call her, is the classic God-fearing Jamaican matriarch. Her flat, in the middle of a depress-ing south London residential estate, is spotless. The children, while boisterous, are well disciplined and respectful. One word from Granny and they immediately fall silent and go out to play. Settled over a cup of tea in her lounge, the approach is to play on her devotion to the 'pickney' and her obvious concern about the kind of company her daughter is keeping. Brennan keeps stressing how long he has known Jackal, and how he is a 'very bad man'.

He has hit the right mark. After patiently listening to the pitch, nodding her head sagely and assessing her predicament, Granny starts to talk. "I know, I know. I know 'im no good," she says. "He come here a few time, wi' Sandra, and I don' like him round de pickney dem." She doesn't know where they are living, but coaxed a bit further she reveals that Jackal uses her flat as a mailing address. She has nothing at the moment, but it's a start.

Later that week, things start to 'come on top'. We learn that one of the things our man has sent to Granny's address is his mobile phone bill. This could be gold dust. A mobile phone, like a bleeper, is a drugs dealers life-line - anonymous, difficult to trace and virtually untapable. Long before British Telecom went down the same road, bills for mobiles were always itemised, and so getting hold of one gives not only the suspect's number, but also those of all their regular associates. Checks through intelligence data-banks can identify who they are, and an accurate picture of their busi-ness can be built up. We also learn that Granny has demanded that Jackal comes and picks it up. Following our visit she has become nervous and doesn't want anything more to do with him. He is bound to show, the theory goes, for if she were to dispose of the bill in disgust and his phone was subsequently cut off for non-payment, then Jackal would be out of action until it could be re-connected. The bill, in short, is the perfect bait for a trap. And that, as they say in the force, is a result.

THE TRAP is set for the following Saturday, and we turn up early at Brixton police station for a briefing. Despite the fact that our target is known to be armed and extremely capable, there is no back-up from armed police. This is a pattern that is to become familiar, where unarmed officers routinely crash in on raids looking for weapons and on arrests of known gunmen. It is a scenario that leaves foreign policeman gaping in disbelief, particularly in the US and Jamaica. Going out onto the street without a gun is bad enough, they say, but to try and forcibly take an armed man..? At that point the conversation usually trails off into silence.

Teams of specially-trained firearms officers are, of course, available, and can regularly be seen in the television coverage of sieges or anti-terrorist operations in Britain. To get such a team, however, requires approval from a senior level and paperwork in triplicate, street officers say. If a tip-off has to be acted on immediately there simply isn't the time to set it up. These specialised units, SO19 in the case of the Metropolitan Police (the Met), have their own set of procedures that must be followed for the safety of their own men and the public, and so they demand control of any operation in which they are involved. A reconnaissance of the site has to be carried out beforehand, for instance, and planning meetings held to discuss every move in military detail. Again, where a tip-off from an informant may only be fresh for a matter of hours there isn't time for all this, and preparations are likely to alert suspects in tight-knit communities. Officers also worry that drugs and other vital evidence may be destroyed by the targets before a building is secured according to the book. Most, then, prefer to take their chances with a bullet-proof vest and a lot of 'bottle'.

While being equipped with vests for this 'job', the black humour also associated with these occasions starts to show itself. I struggle into mine, the first time I have ever worn one, and it is heavy and awkward. Also, being long in the body myself, it barely reaches to my midriff.

"Are you comfortable with that? Does it make you feel safe?" asks Brennan, in a serious, concerned voice. I nod my assent. "You'll look well if he shoots you in the bollocks though, won't you?" I look down with the reflex reaction of someone who's been told their flies are undone, and everybody falls about laughing.

The plan is for Brennan to take position in a tower block opposite Granny's flat to observe the proceedings, with Barker waiting in one car round the corner. A second car, containing myself among others, will wait around a different corner to cover another exit from the estate. An 'area' police car with uniformed officers is also to be on patrol nearby. Once Jackal has made his pick-up and driven away, our cars will 'follow him off' for a respectable distance, after which the uniformed boys will pull him over. It will look, so the theory goes, like a routine stop, after which a bunch

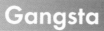

of Jamaican experts will miraculously appear to make the arrest. This is to save Granny from being implicated in the operation.

I share a car with Brian Fotheringham, or 'Fothers' to his friends, the aforementioned man from the immigration service and another vital member of the informal team. A wiry, chain smoking Glaswegian, who spends more time in the other 'office' than most, he is the undisputed joker in the pack. He is also in possession of a compendious knowledge of Jamaican criminals and their associates, which he carries around in his thinly-covered head. This is a data bank that has proved its worth in many a cell interview, where Fothers can cut through a tangled web of false identities spun by a suspect to establish just who he is talking to, and to make ever-more obscure connections in the shifting structure of Yardie gangs.

Like most people I have met who spend their time chasing Jamaican criminals, or 'Jamokes' as he affectionately calls them, Fotheringham has an enduring fascination for his adversaries. On the subject of respect, he has all but gone native, regularly reminding police colleagues that his Home Office rank is the equivalent to an inspector and half-seriously demanding the 'respek due'. It doesn't often work.

What his position does give him are powers of arrest that can sometimes far exceed those of the police. Immigration officers can detain anyone they suspect of being an 'illegal', and this can buy precious time for the police to run checks and assemble evidence on an alleged gangsta. Where such evidence is not available, and as Yardies almost invariably travel on false documents, a final resort is to put them on a plane back to Jamaica. This at least takes them out of circulation until such time as a new passport can be acquired. "Often this is little more than an inconvenience for them, and we get the same people coming back time after time. But at least it is some kind of deterrent," says Fotheringham.

In between our serious conversations while waiting for the Jackal, Fothers fills the car with garrulous accounts of dering-do and, occasionally, repeats from the previous night's curry. Still, however, the time begins to drag. This is not unusual on such surveillance jobs, or 'sit-ups' as they are known, particularly when one is contending with Jamaica Time - the rule of thumb which says that anything involving Jamaicans will run at least half-an-hour late, unless you are expecting it to. More than two hours after the appointed time Brennan goes to find out what is going on. After a further half-hour the police radio sparks into life, but it is only to tell us to pull off. The job has gone 'pear shaped'.

We rendezvous at a cafe nearby cafe where Brennan is frustrated, but amused in spite of himself. So what happened? We learn that Granny had gone out to a phone box to call Jackal, and strong woman that she is, had given this renowned urban guerrilla a severe tongue-lashing. His explanation? He had been out dancing until five that morning, and had simply slept in. He was still in bed, and very apologetic. The best laid plans.....Jackal 1, Met Police 0. The final indignity was that someone, no names, had locked his keys inside one of the cars and the uniformed officers had to be summoned to break into it.

And so it went on. After weeks of tracking and cross-checking intelligence reports, after many further hours spent on sit-ups in the less fashionable parts of south London and after another carefully planned sting, the Jackal managed to slip the net. We never did find him. A year later, a man known as Jackal was arrested, almost by chance. It was the wrong Jackal, bad but not that bad, who for some time had been wondering why an entire police force appeared to be chasing him. Such are the problems involved in fighting the Yardies.

IN THE LATE 1980's, when the first high-level moves were being made to tackle the Yardies, the main problem facing British police was that they didn't know exactly who or what they were looking for, even though the name had been in circulation for years.

The first tabloid press reports - warning of the emergence of a 'Black Mafia' which was running protection and prostitution rackets, drugs rings and illegal gambling dens - date back as far as 1983. Around this time vice-squad officers were filing their own vague reports that West Indian pimps they were watching seemed to be part of some kind of organisation. Over the next year, community liaison officers and those working for local criminal intelligence units started to hear rumours about extortion rackets among the black communities in east and west London. More reports were filed to senior officers, but nothing was done.

Later still, Brennan was working on a murder inquiry in Stoke Newington, north London, when he and his colleagues found themselves getting nowhere because of a total lack of information or evidence from the public. It seemed like the kind of wall of silence associated with organised crime, but there didn't seem to be any obvious 'Mr Big' co-ordinating criminal activity. He placed a request in the National Drugs Intelligence Unit (NDIU) Bulletin asking for information on similar problems, and from that came one of the first meetings of British police officers specifically on the subject of Jamaican criminals. "We didn't know anything about these people or where they came from, and had no idea what they were capable of. But from that meeting we realised that this was something big that had been developing almost unnoticed. It was a real eye-opener," said Brennan.

In July 1986, the London Evening Standard newspaper reported that a drugs war was being waged in south London by the 'Yardies' for control of the growing cocaine market. It claimed that there had been six related

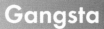

shootings, including two murders, in the previous eight weeks alone. "It's getting like the Wild West down here," was the quote from one drugs squad detective, "Some of these Yardies are armed with automatic weapons and seem to enjoy using them." The article gave accounts of the two murders: one where a 31-year-old man was standing outside a pub in Brixton, when a gunman got out of a blue Mercedes and shot him through the head with a sawn-off shotgun; the second where the doorman at a nearby night-club was also shot through the head for trying to stop a gang from entering the club and shooting their real target.

It was to be almost another year, however, before press hysteria really started to pick up, following the murder of Michael, 'Mickey' St George Williams, from Stoke Newington, who was found slumped over the wheel of his car after it had crashed into a tree. He had died from shotgun wounds to the chest. Ostensibly Williams, 31, ran a baby-clothes stall in east London's old Whitechapel market, but his ownership of a Porsche, his use of safety deposit boxes and his ownership of several properties suggested that this was not his only source of income. Williams had left Jamaica at the age of three, and at the trial of his killers it emerged that the shooting could have been over the division of jewellery spoils from a £100,000 armed robbery. At the time, however, the Yardies got the blame.

Press reports from this period were still referring to the Yardies as a single, "ruthless gang of organised criminals", or a "black, Mafia-style crime syndicate". Some claimed, half correctly, that the gang had backed the left-wing politician Michael Manley in the 1980 election and were now on the run. Others fancifully spoke of them having 'distinctive short hair', and the Daily Mail newspaper even described them as a 'cult'.

If the press was confused, it was only reflecting the state of police knowledge at the time. In the summer of 1987 the NDIU, based at Scotland Yard, had circulated a report to police forces throughout Britain warning of the new menace. It said that the gang were believed to be connected with 14 unsolved murders, owed its power to the extreme violence used by its members, and that it was out to control all West Indian crime in the country, as well as trying to move into the black music industry. The Yardie's ultimate aim, however, could be the domination of all criminal activity in Britain.

"In that event, a fearful situation would ensue, with a full-scale bloody confrontation undoubtedly involving the indiscriminate use of firearms," said the report. Heady stuff indeed. But there was more. The Yardies, it claimed, had already made contact with the IRA, Angry Brigade terrorists, and even with Israeli criminals, and drug profits could be going back to Jamaica to buy arms for the overthrow of politician Edward Seaga.

On more solid ground, the report identified over 20 possible 'members', mostly living in north and east London, giving their addresses both in Britain and in Kingston, their street names and even descriptions of their lifestyle, including where they played football. Areas of "North, East, West and Central London" appeared to be under Yardie control, it said, with the Stoke Newington and west London's Notting Hill areas being two particular strongholds. Elsewhere in the country, outposts had already been established in Bristol, Birmingham, Nottingham and Sheffield: "The inescapable conclusion has been reached that their domination is, or will be in the future, nationwide."

The report is a strange mixture of sensible analysis, emotive half-truths and apocalyptic vision. So it goes right to the final summary: "At the present time the Yardies are not highly organised. They are what may be described as an "embryo organisation" with tentacles spreading to many parts of the United Kingdom and affecting, in the main, the criminal elements of the West Indian community. So far, largely, so good. Then: "The most disturbing aspect of the Yardies concerns the future, namely when they have achieved - and there appears to be nothing, certainly at present, to prevent them - their aim of total domination of the aforementioned community, will they turn their attention to the domination of all criminal activities, irrespective of who controls them?"

Evidence in the report was later said to be largely anecdotal and unsubstantiated, and some of its more extreme claims were no doubt influenced by the visit of NDIU officers to Miami that July for discussions on international co-operation with the US Treasury's Bureau of Alcohol, Tobacco and Firearms (ATF). American estimates at the time held the 'posses' responsible for 500 murders in two years. For all its faults, however, it did at least have the virtue of taking the situation seriously. As well as being sent to police forces, with the request to monitor the situation and gather intelligence, the report was circulated to Home Office ministers and to customs and immigration officials. One theory is that it was meant to shock senior police officers into some kind of action, which had previously been resisted.

If that was the case, then it worked. Late in 1987, Scotland Yard appointed Roy Ramm to the job of collating the available information on the Yardies for a more thorough assessment of the threat. Recently returned from a three-month course on organised crime at the FBI academy in Quantico, near Washington DC, he was then a staff officer in special operations with a background in criminal intelligence. Clearly he was the right man for the job, and he quickly brought a sense of reality to the situation.

"I'm absolutely convinced that there is no such thing as a Black Mafia or a Black Godfather operating in this country," he said in one press quote after a month in the job. "I would admit there is a problem with serious

black crime, but there is no organised Mafia." His own report followed consultations with senior officers covering areas in London, Birmingham and Bristol with large black communities. It warned that Yardies could try to establish 'no-go areas' as a cover for their operations. It also, prophetically, identified them as being responsible for the increasing use of cocaine in these communities.

The perceived situation was clarified in a statement by Deputy Assistant Commissioner Simon Crawshaw, head of Scotland Yard's serious crimes branch, on February 24, 1988. Again, there was no black mafia, he said. "There is, however, a concern, notably amongst the black community, that a limited number of criminals are seeking to exercise control, using violence and drugs as their weapons, and that a further number of young criminals are using the name of the Yardies to exploit the black community." The occasion was to announce a new initiative, and the emotive language continued: "We intend to operate against this cancerous growth by the formation of a dedicated squad," said Crawshaw. Operation Lucy was born.

THE FIRST serious move against Jamaican criminals had actually been taken the week before, when 60 officers, including armed police, raided the New Four Aces club in Dalston, east London. Local intelligence had established that suspected Yardies were to hold a meeting there to discuss the importation of a fresh batch of cocaine. In the weeks before, suspects had been tracked through Heathrow airport as they had made trips to and from Florida. The press were invited along for the fun, and the raid was considered a success in showing that the police were actually doing something about the situation. Three hundred packets of cocaine, valued at £6,000, were seized and 14 arrests made - among them three men identified as 'Yardies'.

It was a high-profile approach followed by Operation Lucy when its officers launched their own first offensive two months later. The target then was Errol Codling, known as 'Rankin' Dread'. He had first been identified as an important figure by the NDIU report, and in the prevalent spirit of hyperbole was subsequently dubbed 'The Godfather' of the Yardies in a number of press reports. Though never named, he was described as a suspect in 33 murders, including that of two Jamaican policemen. One potential witness against him was said to have been shot, and he was reported to have twice been questioned over alleged rapes. Outside police and criminal groups he was best known, bizarrely, as the singer of a reggae version of the chart hit 'Fattie Bum Bum' in the early 1980's.

His background, indeed, was fearsome enough. As a political gunman in Kingston's Rema ghetto during the 1970's, he shot 'Trinity' Gardner, a famour Jamaican police officer, in the mouth. In an interview with the

Sunday Mirror in 1990, he described himself as: "a firebrand recruiter for the JLP. I was involved in many outbursts of violence - sure I was a hitman," he said. For a man with supposed total control over an organised crime syndicate, however, his experience in London was surprising. In the early hours of one morning in 1987 he walked into Tootsie's shabeen, or illegal drinking den, with the intention of carrying out a cocaine rip-off. His huge reputation did him little good on that occasion, as he found himself on the receiving end of Jamaica-style machete attack. "They chopped me up real good. They chopped me 18 times in the head. There was blood all over the place, people screaming and shouting. It was a real mess. I thought I was a gonna," said Codling, in the same interview.

The raid to net him, and to close down what police described as "a focal point for serious and organised black crime", took place at 5.30am on April 14, 1988 in Clapton, east London. The target address was a semi-derelict detached house, where a loud, illegal 'blues' party had been going on all night. Again, about 60 officers took part - from Operation Lucy, from the local division and from the recently formed Territorial Support Group - with a large detachment of press in attendance. None of the officers were armed, following intelligence reports that there were unlikely to be guns on the premises but, otherwise, the full panoply of new police equipment was on show.

As the front door was smashed in, revellers

Suspects arrested at the Clapton 'blues' party are led away

were dazzled and disorientated by Dragon floodlights with 1,000,000 candle-power beams. The support officers wore Kevlar body armour, to protect against bullets or knife-thrusts, riot helmets with anti-acid visors, and flame resistant overalls. After the 70 people inside, half of them women, were ordered to lie face-down on the floor they were secured by new, lightweight plastic handcuffs. After a long night of beer, weed and reggae, it must have been an awesome experience. Little resistance was offered. It emerged that the team had been practising the raid for weeks by storming a copy of the house erected on a site in west London.

Weapons recovered included a 2ft long machete and a lock knife with a

6in blade, while sniffer dogs found three bags of marijuana and smaller amounts of cocaine. Mr Big, in the shape of Codling, was among the 20 people arrested. After the raid, a cautious but satisfied Ramm described it as "a significant blow". A local police superintendent was more ebullient. "A man commonly regarded as one of the Yardies who could be billed as a godfather was among those arrested," he said. "He is a major figure and is possibly not only the top Yardie in Britain but in the world."

The supposed big fish, however, got away. Codling was one of five people eventually charged with drugs offences from the raid, in his case for possession of cocaine and cannabis with intent to supply. On November

7 he appeared at Snaresbrook Crown Court in east London to stand trial, but the Crown Prosecution Service offered no evidence on the grounds that he was due to be deported to face more serious charges in Jamaica. In the ensuing confusion he was re-arrested on immigration offences and expelled from the country the next day. While being driven to Heathrow airport, handcuffed to two detectives, he was reported to say: "I've had a good run, I've had my fun. I won't be coming back."

Codling was re-arrested as he arrived in Kingston, where he was questioned about a number of offences including the killing of a policeman in a shoot-out. But the farce continued when he jumped bail and fled to Toronto. There he was arrested again, following a tip-off from British police, but claimed political asylum. When

One that tried to get away during the Clapton raid

that application came to nothing, he voluntarily flew back to Jamaica. He was never convicted of any offences there, and in 1995 unconfirmed sightings had him living in Birmingham. Perhaps, after all, he did come back.

THE MEDIA spotlight remained on the activities of the 'Yardie squad' and their gangsta adversaries throughout 1988, and in August the story took a leap forward with the murder of Rohan 'Yardie Ron' Barrington Barnet, 26, in Harlesden, north-west London. He went down in a hail of fire from at least three different handguns in the early hours of one Sunday morning, outside a house where a blues party was being held in honour of the forthcoming Notting Hill Carnival. Police found nine bullet holes in the door of the house, and in the street recovered spent rounds from a 9mm, a .45 and a .455 - very heavy artillery. Here was a perfect illustration of the predicted nightmare, a Wild-West shoot-out in a London street, with black gunmen exchanging indiscriminate fire from high-powered weapons. One neighbour, returning home late, had to dive behind a dustbin bunker to avoid the flying bullets; another was shocked from sleep when a wild shot smashed through her bedroom window. Other Yardie trappings were also in evidence. After the shooting Barnett was seen lying under a white Mercedes. He was picked up in his own grey BMW and rushed to hospital in Notting Hill where he later died from his wounds. Traces of cocaine and cannabis were found in his blood.

"We believe the shooting was part of a feud," said the police officer in charge of the investigation. "It appears that several people came out of the house and the shooting began as Barnet arrived at the party. At least ten shots were fired, and it looks as if the victim managed to hit two men."

The picture was completed by what relatives later described as a conspiracy of silence from potential witnesses. No one at the party would admit to seeing anything. At the inquest, a cousin, Norma Jackson, was asked why this should be: "Because if they give evidence then the killer has got friends who might shoot them," was her simple, frightening reply. Those close to Yardie Ron had already had a taste of this reality. Two days after the shooting, his girlfriend's next-door neighbour's flat was gutted in a firebomb attack. Someone had got the wrong flat, but the warning could not have been clearer.

In September, the chance arrest of Devon 'Foodhead' Plunkett took the story on further. A routine stop by a uniformed constable in Clapham, south London, led to the discovery of a half-kilogram of cocaine under the driver's seat, but the officer had to chase Plunkett for half a mile before making his arrest. At the time he was operating under one of at least six false identities, which had already done him good service. He had been removed as an 'illegal' the previous March under the identity of Adrian George Price, but had come back soon enough to be one of those held after the Clapton raid. In the confusion of the night, and then calling himself Frederick Gordon, he was allowed to walk free.

Now, however, sitting in a police cell facing cocaine trafficking charges, he was identified by Brennan and Fotheringham as Foodhead, a notorious member of the Shower posse and wanted for questioning in America over 12 drugs-related murders. The ATF had him listed as one of the 12 most wanted criminal suspects in the country, implicated in arms and cocaine smuggling. He was finally given away by a distinctive facial scar.

The case was handled by Operation Lucy, and Plunkett got a seven-year sentence, reduced to five on appeal. When he was released, the American authorities declined to have him extradited - too many of the witnesses

that might have convicted him there had been killed in on-going drugs wars.

As another element to the big picture he was very important, a hardened Jamaican criminal who could apparently come in and out of the country at will on false passports and who was, allegedly, a hit man for one of the most violent posses in America. His significance was sharpened by a series of alarming reports from across the Atlantic about the speed and the ruthlessness with which these gangs had established their influence in such cities as New York, Miami and Dallas. The FBI at this time estimated that the posses had been responsible for 800 murders since 1984.

Even more chilling than such bald figures was the detail contained in a confidential memorandum sent to Lucy detectives from Robert Embleton, second secretary at the British Embassy in Washington, about the situation in that city. "There have been several highly-publicised gang executions and brutal murders carried out by the posses, which must have struck terror into the hearts not only of the local drug dealers but also potential witnesses," he wrote. "Many District [of Columbia] residents are frightened to go to the police: their immediate inclination is to lock the doors, draw the shades and claim they saw nothing. The posses have been implicated in over 60 drug-related killings.

"However the DC police's greatest concern is the phenomenal firepower of the posses. 410 weapons have already been seized, with more than 30 per cent of them being automatic or semi-automatic. The weapons favoured... are the Uzi sub-machine gun, the Mac 10 and the Tech 9. It is hard to believe that a semi-automatic was found on a 12-year-old after his arrest for drug peddling."

Part of the predicted nightmare, then, appeared to be coming true.

CONVINCED that they were on the right track, senior officers at Scotland Yard decided to expand the 16-strong Operation Lucy by up to a further 14 officers. At a time when limited resources were increasingly on the law and order agenda, it was a good measure of the alarm which the developing situation was causing.

In October, following this announcement, Ramm gave a detailed briefing to the Daily Telegraph newspaper on how far understanding of the Yardie problem had progressed in the eight months since Operation Lucy was established. Surveillance of 200 Jamaican suspects, based largely in London, Birmingham and Bristol, had given a detailed insight into the pattern of Yardie drug trafficking.

His first point was to re-iterate that the police were not facing a 'Black Mafia'. "It is a loose association of violent criminals bent on making profits from drugs and then spending them as quickly as possible," he said. Unlike the Mafia or the Colombian cartels, the gangs opted for a 'little and often' method of importation rather than large-scale smuggling operations. A typical cocaine deal would be of one or two kilograms, struck on the telephone between a Jamaican in this country and his contact in America. Two phone bills seized during more than 60 raids carried out by the squad illustrated the extent of these transactions. One was for £14,000, almost all for calls to New York, Miami, Los Angeles and Kingston. The other was for over £9,500.

"What we have is a small number of men with personal contacts with Jamaican drug traffickers in America. They go to black areas of American cities, do a drugs deal, probably paying up front but leaving empty-handed," said Ramm. "Later they will send a courier, often a prostitute or drug user, to pick up the drugs... If the trafficker sends enough couriers, some are bound to get through and as he can make £100,000 profit on a single kilo he can afford to lose a few for every one that succeeds. There is also a very small chain once the drugs are in the UK. Often the trafficker will also be the dealer."

On the subject of firearms, he conceded that the extent of their armoury was not then known, adding that the Yardies were a long way from having the influence or firepower of their American counterparts. By then the estimates of Yardie killings had been revised down to six since 1986, together with a number of non-fatal shootings and stabbings and the assumption that many others would have gone unreported. Ramm, however, added a warning: "Jamaican gangs took over a large part of the American cocaine market from small beginnings. We need to remain vigilant to make sure the same cannot happen here."

It was a sane, straight-talking assessment of the situation, much of which remains as accurate today as it was then. Over the years it has become distilled into a phrase used by many officers working in this area: 'disorganised, organised crime'.

THIS PERIOD, however, proved to be the zenith of Operation Lucy's influence. Less than a year later, the squad was disbanded. The reasons for this, like much in this story, are complex and show the authorities trying to jump in many directions at the same time.

One factor is thought to be the very conclusions that Ramm had outlined so candidly. In playing down the level of organisation behind the Yardie threat, he unwittingly gave ammunition to those who were unhappy about the operation in the first place. "If we are not, after all, facing an international plot to take over the whole criminal enterprise in Britain as-we-know it, do we need to commit such resources to opposing it?" was the drift of this argument. As the months went by with no obvious explosion of violent crime, it gathered weight. There was a shoot-out with armed

police in December, following a tip-off to the squad about a planned raid on a post office in Acton, west London, when two detectives and three gangstas were wounded. On Christmas Eve, a gun battle between feuding factions left a man dead in the back seat of his car. But, denied its Mr Big and unable to put 'Black Mafia' in the headlines any more, the media's interest was on the wane and these incidents received less attention than the earlier stories. Senior officers were by this time asking: "Aren't these just another bunch of small-time, if violent, crooks, better dealt with at a local level?"

The second, more powerful argument involved the thorny question of race. Heavy-handed, or 'racist' policing of predominantly black areas had been held at least partially responsible for riots in London, Bristol, Birmingham and Liverpool earlier in the 1980's. Yet, here was a special unit effectively targeted at what Sir Kenneth Newman, the former Metropolitan Police Commissioner had described as 'symbolic areas', and employing a lot of heavy back-up in its operations. Nervous senior officers did not want a repeat performance of rioting on their records, and indeed that fear had been the main factor in their initial slow response to the problem. Again, if the threat was less ominous than first thought, was this action still justified?

It was a point quickly picked up by those concerned to protect black people's rights. Diane Abbott, Labour MP for Hackney North and Stoke Newington, had expressed her disquiet in an interview in the black newspaper 'The Voice' as early as September 1988. "I am very concerned about the way the whole Yardie myth is being promoted by the Metropolitan Police and the way the press is colluding with it," she said. "The black community both here and in Jamaica is concerned that this is going to damage community relations."

The fact that the black community was on the receiving end of the violence, and that its less organised nature meant more, not less, efficient intelligence was needed, was apparently lost on both parties.

Operation Lucy's demise, however, was sealed by the emergence of a new public enemy number one - the potent cocaine derivative known as crack. Its increasing prominence should have strengthened the hand of those in pursuit of Jamaican criminals, but instead it was to send the powers-that-be off at a tangent. This, together with the other two factors, proved an irresistible combination. For years, the Yardies were to become a half-forgotten myth.

THE CATALYST for this change of direction came on a summer afternoon in 1989 when the most senior police officers in the country sat down to listen to the latest reports from America. The occasion was the annual drugs conference of the Association of Chief Police Officers, which represents all those from commander rank right up to chief constables. The speaker was Robert Stutman, head of the Drug Enforcement Administration (DEA) in New York, and his text was crack.

Here was another apocalyptic warning, delivered with great passion and backed by a 'personal guarantee', that Britain would have a serious crack problem by 1991. To illustrate what this would mean, he hammered out bullet-points of horror from the experience of American cities where whole communities had been devastated by the drug. Mothers abandoning their children in search of another hit, huge increases in drugs related violence and robbery - all spread like wildfire even to what he called "the heart of conservative middle America". Most powerful of all was his assertion that crack had previously unheard of addictive qualities, to the extent that anyone taking just three hits of it would be hooked.

Stutman's central theme was a disarming admission of American failure in seeing the crisis coming before it was too late, and a plea that Britain would learn from its mistakes. "We have screwed up enough times to write ten thousand books but I would hope all of you don't have to go through the same thing that we went through. Don't be like the people of Kansas and Texas and California, who said: 'It can't happen here'." His argument carried extra clout because he had been one of the few who had issued early warnings. In 1986, the year after crack had made its first appearances in New York, he had predicted that America would be swamped by the drug within a further three years and that 1986 would then seem like the good old days. He was proved right.

The speech had a galvanising effect. "It was a tremendous presentation - it made us all sit up and take notice," said one officer who heard it. But the impact went higher than that. Douglas Hurd, then the Home Secretary no less, admitted to Stutman's address making "a deep impression". Within weeks he was sufficiently inspired to make his own speech to European foreign ministers, warning that the spectre of crack was hanging over Europe, and Douglas Hogg, then a Home Office minister, was dispatched to the US to assess the situation there.

The press, not surprisingly, went wild, deluging a bemused public with headlines like: "Crack: 10 times more powerful than cocaine"; "Crack crazy - evil gangs spread drug through Britain"; "One hit to be hooked - next stop the morgue." This was a bigger story than Yardies had ever been. There had been nothing like it since the outbreak of AIDs hysteria, also fuelled by the American experience, two years before. As the summer progressed, public hatred was directed towards a new set of ogres - the 'evil' Colombian drug cartels and their scheming 'barons'.

The basis of Stutman's prediction was not new. This was that the US had become saturated with cocaine and that, in his memorable phrase: "there ain't enough noses left to use the cocaine that's coming in." So, the theory went, the cartels would be looking to Europe for its next market. By the time he made his speech, this was already common currency. I had been given a briefing to that effect by Peter Spurgeon, the Home Office's chief inspector of drugs, months before when conducting an investigation into the emergence of crack in Britain for The Sunday Times. Nevertheless, in a process that became known among drug treatment workers as 'The Great Hype', a whole series of new initiatives were launched by the government to combat the new menace. These included the announcement of an international drugs conference, to be held in London in April 1990, opened by the Queen and hosted by Margaret Thatcher. Her esteemed guests would include the UN secretary general and the President of Colombia.

On a more practical level, the police also acted fast that summer, dispatching Commander Roy Penrose, head of Scotland Yard's international and serious crimes squad (SO1), to America to make his own assessment of the situation. He visited New York to see the devastation, and Boston to find how that city had managed to prove the exception by keeping crack at bay. His report recommended that a thorough assessment of the emergent problem in Britain was the immediate priority, and in October Peter Imbert, the Metropolitan Police Commissioner, announced the formation of the Force Crack Intelligence Co-ordinating Unit (FCICU).

THE NEW unit, which quickly became known as the Crack Squad, was to be led by Detective Superintendent Chris Flint, a Cambridge graduate and Yard high-flier. His brief included working with those in the drug treatment centres and voluntary agencies to find what was the true penetration of crack at street level. Towards the end of the year the Home Office set up a separate joint task force of customs investigators and regional crime squad officers who were to target the cocaine traffickers feeding the demand for crack. In taking on these daunting tasks, in the full glare of government and media expectation, the new units had two important pointers as to where he should target his resources - from Stutman himself and from the experience of Operation Lucy. The answer in both cases was: Jamaicans.

After making his general point about Europe being next on the cartel's shopping list, Stutman had a special message for Britain. Jamaican criminals had taken control of crack distribution across much of the United States, utilising Jamaican ties in New York to spread the drug to many other cities. Britain had a large Jamaican population, was his general point, therefore Britain had a problem. "You have a large number of Jamaicans in this country, many of whom have relatives and friends in New York and none of whom are very stupid if they are dope peddlers to start with," he said.

"These guys don't have to be geniuses to realise, 'I don't have to import crack from the United States'. I can go out and buy a baby bottle at a department store. You certainly have water here, so I can make my crack right here in Great Britain, and I can increase my profit, if ratios are the same, by something like 300%."

This part of his address was not well received by the racially sensitive Brits, any more than the conclusions of Roy Ramm had been. Stutman's view on the situation in America, however, was to be borne out by the statistics. In September 1989, a report by the ATF estimated that Jamaicans controlled over 40% of crack sales in the US. Equally, by this time there was evidence that his hypothesis about Britain was already becoming fact.

The first dealer to be convicted of selling crack in this country was given a six year jail sentence in November 1988. He was Paul Matheson, who had been promised £500 a week to sell the drug - and he was recruited in Jamaica. The court heard how he had sold £105,000 worth of the drug in under six weeks before being arrested in a raid in Peckham, south London that summer. Days before his conviction, police were reporting bloody street battles being fought over control of the new trade, citing six shootings, including that of Yardie Ron, in the preceding months. In one case a man had staggered into a police station and collapsed with serious chest wounds.

The raid which caught Matheson was the first of an increasingly high-profile series against what became known as 'crack factories' - fortified council flats on some of the cities most deprived council estates where the drug was being produced and sold from behind heavy steel-plated doors. This exactly followed the pattern of operation that had developed in American cities, and again, a high proportion of those arrested were Jamaicans.

Roy Ramm described the scene: "One flat had an outer door protected by a steel plate with a letter-box sized hole in it. Behind that was another heavy door reinforced with steel which had a least eight bolts on it. The dealers used to sell the drugs through the letter box while they were safe inside the flat. They never opened the outer door." Special measures had to be developed to gain fast entry into such places, including the use of hydraulic rams and thermal lances supplied by the Fire Brigade.

After smashing their way into these places, police found the simple detritus of crack-making later referred to by Stutman. All that is needed to produce the drug is cocaine hydrochloride (powder cocaine), a source of heat and water, bicarbonate of soda or baking powder and a heat resistant container (Stutman's baby bottle). The crudest method involves 'cooking up' the crack in a frying pan. The process purifies the powder cocaine by extracting the hydrochloride and renders it into smokeable 'rocks'.

Both the purity and the method of taking this kind of cocaine, rather than 'snorting' powder through the nasal membrane, produces the instant and intense 'high' that accounts for its addictability. With a single rock then retailing at about £25, it was also a much cheaper way of entering the cocaine market. Again, this was the most important factor in the drug making such an impact on the poor, public housing projects in American cities. The short-lived nature of the high, however, and the equally intense depression that can follow it means that users are soon coming back for more and more.

By January 1989, when I was researching The Sunday Times article, the drug had achieved such a grip on one estate in Deptford, south-east London, that it had already acquired the sobriquet of 'Crack City'. A visit to the estate by a colleague and I at this time was an enlightening experience. As we approached the pub in the middle of the concrete blocks, a known centre of dealing, a group of black youths outside averted their gaze and shuffled uncomfortably. As we sat at one end of the L-shaped bar, we witnessed the amusing spectacle of almost the whole clientele evaporating through the door, until we were left sitting in an empty pub with one old Irishman. So much for our attempts at undercover investigation. The local youth had obviously taken us for police officers.

None of these lessons were lost on Flint and his squad, which carried on where Lucy had left off by concentrating its efforts on housing estates with large black populations. Some continuity was also assured by the transfer of some Lucy detectives to the new unit. In February 1990, just over a year after our visit, the same estate in Deptford was the target for the biggest-ever crack raid. After weeks of undercover surveillance of an open-air crack market there, 130 officers burst from removal vans, smashed down the doors of suspected dealers and searched everybody on the street. They seized 135 rocks of crack and made 11 arrests, while a nearby garage yielded a quantity of ammunition. The month before, a similar operation in north Peckham found 70 rocks that had been made in a local flat.

In April 1990, when Flint wrote an interim report on the first six months of the FCICU's work, it had a very familiar ring. "Where Jamaicans have cornered the crack market, as in south-east and west London, cocaine hydrochloride is becoming increasingly difficult to obtain in retail form," said the report. "Whilst the available information depicts a rather disorganised market place scenario, it is becoming increasingly clear that the promotion of retailed crack is the calculated intent of the dealing networks. The principal organisers behind these operations are male Jamaican nationals who are illegally in this country."

It also gave a fascinating insight into the modus operandi of the gangs and further evidence of parallels with the American experience. "They adopt many of the characteristics experienced in the United States of the Jamaican posses. For example, when moving into a new area they tend to target single black females who are used to secure, in their names, accommodation, vehicles and other necessities for facilitating a localised operation. These women are often used as couriers for the importing of cocaine hydrochloride which will invariably be converted into crack locally."

If policy-makers at the Yard were worried, or even grateful, for this confirmation of earlier conclusions, they had a funny way of showing it. A few months later the joint police/customs task force was abandoned, having been judged a failure. Part of the reason for this was the traditional rivalry between the two services which can be very bitter. A friendly mid-ranking police officer once told me that the one group of people he hated more than journalists were customs officers. Others dismiss the efforts of customs investigators as 'amateur', pointing to the fact that many are recruited as university graduates and so lack the street experience of a copper whose done his time on the beat. One reason I have heard for not liking the revenue men was simply because they 'aren't policemen'.

From the customs side, they pride themselves on a more intellectual approach and have been known to refer to the police as 'plod'. However petty or unjustified all this may be, here it caused real problems. One officer remembers attending a task force meeting when the customs men sat on one side of the room and the police on the other, apparently reluctant to share anything more than hostile glares. More seriously, they did discover that crack, as crack, was not being imported into Britain in large quantities. Or put another way, they had failed to find any at all while significant quantities of powder cocaine were discovered.

Metropolitan police figures for 1989, which did not include the proceeds of the big raids on Peckham and Deptford, had already told a similar story. The force's forensic laboratory reported that over the whole year just 58 grams of crack had been seized, as opposed to 58 kilos of cocaine powder. In comparison, total customs seizures in that year for other drugs were: 331 kilos of heroin, 424 kilos of cocaine, and 50,000 kilos of cannabis. Scepticism generated by these figures was backed up by evidence from drugs treatment centres and street agencies, who continually stated that the main problem they encountered was with heroin. Even the few cases of crack abuse that they had encountered were in the context of 'polyuse' in conjunction with another drug, usually heroin.

Some workers were openly agitated about the prominence being given to crack which they thought was distracting attention from other more pressing matters, particularly the growing problem from amphetamine abuse. One doctor at a drug dependency unit dismissed the idea that

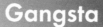

Britain was about to be devastated by crack as 'absolute crap'. So what had happened? In the words of a later police report, was the story of crack in Britain - 'Explosion or Myth?'

The first obvious answer was that, in 1990, it was just too early to say. Even Stutman had said it would be two years before the problem would fully show itself. More importantly, the whole strategy following his speech can be seen to have been pointing in the wrong direction. The emphasis - led by the British Government and followed by both police and customs - was on the threat from the drug itself, from the 'product'. In following this line, they were diverted from what had already been identified as the real problem: the people who were involved in its distribution and the violence that this trade brought with it. This confusion was to hamper police activity right up until the Crack Squad itself was disbanded in 1993.

Yes, crack was to become a problem in terms of users, but arguably no more so than any other drug. Indeed, crack dropped from top billing in the drugs headlines when the panic over Ecstasy began to take hold. Yes, as the detractors rightly said, there were differences between British and American societies that would prevent the taking of the drug from wrecking communities in the same way it had in the ghettos of New York and Washington. The tragedy is that one of those main differences, the relatively small numbers of firearms in circulation, has started to be redressed, and a major reason for that are the people who control much of Britain's crack trade - the Yardies.

So is it fair to blame the police and government for not seeing this situation developing? Much of the evidence, as we have seen, was already there. In Chris Flint's 1990 report there was more to be had. Police crime figures do not differentiate between nationality, but offences are collated by ethnic group using a series of identification codes known as 'IC's'. So, 'IC1' means White European; 'IC2' is Dark European (e.g. Greek); 'IC3' is Afro-Caribbean; 'IC4' is Indian/Pakistani; 'IC5' is Chinese; and 'IC6' is Arab or Far Eastern. Flint's report contains such a breakdown for the Met's arrest figures for possession of crack-cocaine between October 1989 and April 1990. For IC3's (Afro-Caribbean), the figure was 129. The next largest grouping was IC1's (White), and that corresponding figure was six. Crack Squad sources confirm that of the IC3 total, almost all were Jamaican.

One persistent reason for not taking this evidence on board was the police's wish to avoid accusations of racism, as already mentioned. Even now, senior officers simply will not confirm that they have officers dedicated to tracking Jamaican criminals. Another reason, I would suggest, was a lack of first-hand knowledge about where these criminals come from – a lack of understanding about the ghettos of Kingston, Jamaica – the 'Yard'.

Chapter Four

GHETTO RUNNIN'S

THERE is no question but that this is a border. There is no red-and-white pole, there are no customs checks and you don't have to produce any papers, but this is a dividing line as rigidly enforced as any since the fall of the Berlin Wall. If you are the wrong person, or if you cross at the wrong time, it could cost you your life.

This is the infamous 'Gully', a concrete sluice about 10ft deep and 10 yards wide which carves through the ghettos of west Kingston, dividing areas loyal to the governing People's National Party (PNP) from those supporting the opposition Jamaica Labour Party (JLP). It is as good a place as any to see the reality of Jamaican political life. It is also runs through the heart of Yardie country, the sprawling slums of Jamaica's capital which have spawned some of the biggest and baddest criminals to have made their mark on the Western world during the past 15 years. Here the law is gun law, as practised either by the police or by the local exponents of alternative systems of justice.

The Gully at this point has a few inches of stagnant water in the bottom and is strewn with rotting rubbish sacks. It is also a popular place for dumping bodies - victims of the on-going political war or those who have offended against the unwritten codes of the area, by being police informants or by committing other perceived crimes against their communities.

We cross it on a still, hot Saturday afternoon, walking across the wooden bridge which divides PNP Hannah Town from the 'Labourite' housing developments of Denham Town. Nobody is to be seen for some distance on either side of the bridge, even though the concrete blocks of flats go almost down to the edge of the Gully, for this is not a place to hang around. Nothing happens, no one reacts, but we are aware of being watched closely.

My guides on this visit are Sheila, a local journalist who has written an MA thesis on the youth gangs of Hannah Town, and Leroy, who lives in one of the blocks over the border. He can move freely between the two areas as he is not perceived as a threat, and Sheila gets by with the tactic of showering everyone she meets with rapid-fire bursts of patois conversation. Having a white man in tow, however, is entering uncharted waters for both of them and our nervous chatter is punctuated by frequent assurances to me to relax and to act naturally.

To slip unnoticed into areas like these is an impossibility, and to attempt it would be to arouse even more suspicion. So we had gone to the other extreme of loudly announcing our presence as soon as we entered Hannah Town. Our first move was to check in at the local police station, a decaying

wooden building close to the front line, surrounded by heavy metal grills which give the appearance of holding it up. One of the grills was locked with a pair of police handcuffs. Behind the deserted front desk, which looks like a 1960's coffee-bar, an ancient police truncheon was hanging from the wall. While much bigger and heavier than its counterpart elsewhere, neither it nor three others lying on a dusty chair looked as though they had seen action for some time. Bullet holes in the reinforced glass doors and windows showed that the era of simple strong-arm confrontation with local criminals has long-since passed. The station is regularly shot-up by youths on the rampage, when the police have little choice but to take cover and wait for the trouble to die down.

A World Cup football match was playing in the background, while the ubiquitous domino board was set up ready for a game in the ramshackle police rest room. We found the duty sergeant sitting outside in the shade with two of his officers, and he merely smiled sheepishly and raised his eyebrows when we told him where we were going. Next, we re-joined Leroy in a nearby bar where I swapped beer and jokes about Soho in London with a toothless old man who had been there many, many years before.

Once over the bridge, we buy some roasted corn from a group of watch-ful women, while Sheila makes a fuss over somebody's baby. The mother might just have been 16. Graffiti on a nearby block shows that we have indeed crossed the political divide with 10ft portraits of two dead JLP posse 'dons' shown holding guns either side of a racy motorbike. The caption reads: 'Jim Brown and Jah T, we will remember and love you for ever'. Next to it is a huge head and shoulders representation of Edward Seaga, the JLP leader, over the legend 'Peace in the Hood'.

As we round the next corner, the scene opens up dramatically. On the left of the road, the concrete blocks continue into the distance, each with stripes of colour painted round them as the only distinguishing feature. On the right is a area of low, wooden shacks known as 'Board Villa' - "because it's made of boards", explains Leroy. Later we are told that this is where many of the local gangstas live, and that earlier in the week an army patrol had shot and killed a man there while he was recovering his gun.

We approach Leroy's block by leaving the road to walk across a stretch of broken waste-ground and find ourselves the subject of close scrutiny by a particularly dangerous-looking young man, leaning on a corner by himself. "Talk to this guy, he knows more about it than anybody," said Leroy, before disappearing into the gloom of the block's central yard area. This was Robbie, his still-young face heavily scarred, or 'marked up', about the eyes and in front of one ear. Most worrying was the way that when he frowned his forehead would pucker into a crazed mass of vertical lines running up from between his eyebrows to his hairline. After talking to him for hours, I still couldn't work out whether this was the result of more scarring or whether he was just someone who frowned a lot. Whatever, he is frowning deeply as we walk up to him. Together with a shaved head, leaving only a small tuft of hair on the top, and his eyebrows cut into patterns, he is a formidable figure.

Earlier, Sheila had warned that if I tried to deceive or 'bullshit' any of these characters about what I was doing they would probably blow my head off. Now, true to her word, she abandons all standard journalistic practice of approaching a delicate subject gently and pitches straight in with breath-taking candour about how I was writing a book about 'bad bwoys' and Yardies and how we had been told that he could help us. I brace myself for a brush-off at the very least, but Robbie shows no surprise. He relaxes, leans back against the wall, and asks me what I want to know. In visits over the next few days he and his friends give me a detailed account of 'ghetto runnin's', or the realities of ghetto life.

"LIFE in the ghetto is very hard, man, very hard. You can't sleep properly because every little noise makes you jump up, because it could be the soldiers or someone coming for you. All the time you have to be looking out, looking out to check what's going on," said Robbie. "Every day it's like flipping a coin. It comes down heads, you're alright. It comes down tails, you're dead. That's what it's like."

Once over the preconceptions, initial culture shock and endless warnings not to go there, however, the over-riding feeling about this part of the ghetto is one of peace. It is noisy, it is chaotic and it is dirty, but compared to many other parts of Kingston it is remarkably unthreatening. The constant watchfulness which, as a visitor to the city, you have to adopt because of the perpetual hassle, or threat of hassle, slowly evaporates after a few hours hanging out in the ghetto. People are curious to the point of fascination about what a white man is doing there and they stare from a safe distance until you meet their gaze when they shyly turn away. But nobody tries to 'hit you up', that is ask for money or anything else. No one hisses or shouts racist abuse, which is a constant feature of walking around the 'down-town' business area. No one tells you to go home. Children gather in giggling groups behind me, occasionally running up to touch me as a dare, while the bolder ones play with the hairs on my arms and tell me, "You are pretty". Amazingly, it would seem I am one of the first white men they have seen venturing there. They scatter with a sharp "Goway!" from Robbie, only to re-assemble a few minutes later.

To paint this rather charming picture of the ghetto is not to say that Robbie and his friends are exaggerating the dangers or the pressures of living there. My relaxed reception has everything to do with the fact that

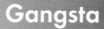

for the duration of my visits I am in their company. For Robbie is the 'area leader' for this block. He is the block 'don', responsible for protecting the people in it from the 'enemy' across the border and for administering the harsh internal justice which keeps the place just about liveable. His authority comes from those higher up the ghetto hierarchy and it is backed by guns. Robbie is 23 years old.

His domain is one of the concrete blocks that make up this part of Denham Town, known as his 'corner'. Like many of the local terms in this story, it is a word that means different things in different contexts. The corner is literally the corner of the block where he and his 'crew' hang out, chatting, drinking beers when they have any money and smoking cigarettes and 'weed', or marijuana. It also denotes his area of influence, the patch of ground and people which he controls. Theoretically, anything that happens within that area is his business and anyone who steps out of line has to answer to him. So, if he is talking to the strange visitors, then no-one else has got a problem with us being there.

The block itself is actually two parallel blocks of small apartments each six storey's high and built about 20 feet apart. Each has a walkway running the length of each floor and these are linked to two open stairwells. The space in the middle is the 'yard' and this is the focus of life for the community. Physically and psychologically it is a closed world.

In the yard men sit around a table playing dominoes in the way that only Jamaicans do, with a gusto that has made the game a national obsession and brought it to just one step short of a full contact sport. In a heated game, each move is a little theatrical event involving a wind-up of taunts and laughter directed at the other players culminating in the domino being brought down with a huge crash and a 'there, I told you so' kind of cackle. This is a serious business, played for money, and bad moves or someone having to miss a turn are greeted with howls of derision. Elsewhere, kids play football with anything they can find that will represent a ball. Girls stand around and gossip, women go about their business of keeping body and soul together. The flats have running water but when this fails (often) water comes from two standpipes at the end of the yard. Naked children play in and out of these with the same giggles and squeals of children anywhere.

One of the ground floor apartments serves as a shop, selling food, beer and soft drinks. The door is protected by a heavy metal grille and, whenever possible, transactions take place through this without it ever opening. Money and the order are passed through it into the gloom inside, and goods and change are then fed back by the owners who are clearly taking no chances. The likelihood of credit being available seems slight.

The conditions are fairly primitive, but the people living in blocks like these are the lucky ones amongst Kingston's ghetto-dwellers - beneficiaries of the political power games of the 1960's and 1970's.

JAMAICA'S first public housing project was envisaged by Seaga, then a leading member of the JLP government, in the early 1960's. Called Tivoli Gardens, it was to replace the notorious slum of 'Back-a-Wall' which bordered the harbour area of west Kingston and whose shanty dwellings of wood and corrugated iron represented, as its name suggests, the end of the line. Seaga's motivation in hatching the scheme, however, was far from being entirely philanthropic. The idea was to use the new estate, and the jobs its construction would create, to build a solid block of support in that area. Put at its simplest, the jobs and the housing went only to JLP supporters. People in the area would owe everything, including the roof over their heads, to the party and, with Tivoli Gardens, Seaga laid the foundations of the cult of personal support which can still be seen in the graffiti daubed on the walls of JLP areas.

Politically, it was a brilliant move. At the time, shortly after Jamaica's independence from Britain in 1962, the government was the major source of wealth and opportunity in the country. The economy was still largely based on the colonial plantation system, with its foreign earnings coming from the export of sugar and bananas, and the control of the new government over allotting large blocks of capital was virtually absolute. To get on meant getting on with the government, and the opportunities for political patronage seemed boundless. The long-term result, however, was the politicisation of the volatile ghettos into opposing and increasingly armed power blocks, which became known as the 'garrison constituencies'.

In common with cities in other third-world countries, Kingston was at this time experiencing the mass-migration from the rural areas of people in search of a better life, and these found their way to the fast-growing ghettos. Small-time street gangs had already started to emerge, fighting over 'turf' and over localised control of the illegal marijuana trade. But the input of party power created the conditions for the leaders of these

Edward Seaga, JLP leader, hugs 'Bigga' Ford, a famous front-line policeman.

gangs to become political warlords backed by heavily armed gunmen. Their successors still run the ghettos today, while others from this background went on to become the Yardies and 'posse' members who have made such an impact on the criminal scene in the USA, Canada and Britain.

Following his initial success, Seaga, now the JLP leader, had plans for

other housing schemes to extend the scope of his influence. In 1972, however, he lost the general election to the PNP, and Michael Manley became Prime Minister. Manley was elected on a socialist slate, and his government instituted a programme of radical reform, but the lessons taught by his predecessor were well learned. He set about building his own power base in the ghettos with the creation of Arnett Gardens, the 'Concrete Jungle', a carbon copy of Tivoli with the same use of patronage in providing jobs and housing. Over the next few years PNP support was consolidated in other important areas of the ghetto, such as Tel Aviv, while the JLP strengthened its grip on areas adjacent to Tivoli, such as Denham Town. The battle lines over which future elections would be fought, in the case of 1980 with the ferocity of a civil war, had been drawn.

THE JOB of policing those lines today comes down to people like Robbie. Large pitched battles are mostly a thing of the past, even at election time, but border skirmishes and raids resulting in minor 'wars' are still a regular occurrence. "We just form a group, a syndicate of mine. We protect people, old and young, so that the enemy don't come on and do us nothing," said Robbie. "The enemy is the PNP, and we's the enemy for dem."

The youths, or 'yout', of both sides are largely confined to their own territory. "Sometimes we go on the bridge and we stand up and look across, but we don't go and look for trouble. We just go look and view and take a fresh breeze. Then sometime dem come here but, when dem come, dem come and give trouble," he said. This conflict is no different from any other in that it is always the enemy that is mostly to blame for violence and atrocities. It is a recurring theme in conversations on both sides of the divide.

"Dem come and pick a war 'gainst people. If dem see a man they don' want see, dem just touch him [kill him] and gone. So we now, we have to see that dem ting never happen. If dem come over here wi' dem guns, me go there wi' my gun and me tell dem to jus' hold back dem ends [stay on their side of the line]." Such negotiations take place at the bridge: "We stay at the border and dem stay at the border and we talk. So we jus' say: 'Yo friend, jus' stay over dat side ya na, and jus' cool, and we jus' stay over 'ere, so we na look for trouble wi' na man, ya na." If things stay 'cool' in these confrontations, they will just go away, said Robbie. Otherwise they might "pussy we up, so we jus' pussy up 'dem back", that means, roughly, that insults would be exchanged. Finally, shots might be fired.

The last time gun battles had taken place was the month before, over the issue of a stolen bicycle. Two people from his side were shot, one with a serious chest wound, and an all-out war was only averted by the intervention of the police and army. These wars are most often caused by things being stolen by one side or the other, especially bicycles. People have been killed on their way to work just to steal their bicycle. "We jus' defen' it back. We get back the bicycle and jus' kill someone for it," said Robbie.

Inevitably, again, it is the other side that takes the blame. "Most of all, it's 'dem mostly pick all the trouble. If dem see a yout' go pass dat over here 'im come from, dem jus' shoot 'im. Dem jus' lick out all 'im head back." The last phrase, it was explained, is the term for when someone is shot in the face, the bullet goes through the brain and takes out the back of his head.

The quotes given above are in patois, the Jamaican dialect that is the everyday spoken language for much of the country's population. Although the conversation was suitably toned down for my benefit, it nevertheless gives some flavour of the authentic voice of the ghetto. Future quotations will mostly be recorded in standard English.

Robbie and his 'crew', he says, have access to five guns - an M16 rifle, known simply as a '16', a pump-action shot gun, a Tech-9 automatic pistol and two .45 calibre automatics. Such automatic weapons are collectively known as 'machines'. The guns are carefully hidden and are generally shared within the group and also with other crews from the same neighbourhood. These crews take their names from their corner areas such as Regent Street, Tivoli or Rema with others, such as The Bronx or New Jack City, calling themselves after areas of New York where Jamaicans have made their mark. "Every street you go on, you will find a syndicate of youth," said Robbie. There is no trouble between these different crews from the same side, with members as well as weapons being sometimes shared, and there is freedom of movement for all crew members within the JLP-held zone.

'Crew', or 'Cru' as it is sometimes written in graffiti, is another of those terms which means different things to different people at different times. Some will tell you that a crew is nothing more than an innocent association of like-minded friends from the same area, who do nothing more sinister than hang out, talk and drink beer. This is as opposed to a 'gang' or a 'posse', which stand for violence and criminality. For Robbie, however, the terms are largely interchangeable, depending on what the group is doing at any given time. "You see the crew now is a set of youth that sits on the corner, play dominoes, play their tapes, enjoy themselves. A gang and a massive is going out and looking for trouble. Like one man touch you in this gang, you gang that man and deal with it, like you chop him up, stab him up. A posse is warfare," he said. "It's just the same thing, it's just one word means a lot of things. The gang is the same crew, the crew is the same thing, it's the same thing."

Within a crew the 'Rankin', or important, gunmen such as Robbie have guns of their own. "I have one for myself, a 45, with 10," he said, meaning a

Gangsta

.45 automatic with 10 shots, "And I have an extra clip." These represent the ultimate currency in the ghetto. They are not for sale and will only be loaned to very close friends, or 'brethren', who can be trusted, because while a man might hold a gun, it was given to him for 'community use' and he would only lose it once. "If I give it to a friend, I'd say, 'I beg you, don't let anything happen to it, because if anything happen to it, it's going to happen to me," said Robbie, "If a man give you a gun and it's dashed away, you're going to lose your life for it." He would not say who had given him his gun.

We are standing on a corner, listening to a tape, drinking beer with the crew. The beers are all bought by me, at about 50p each from behind the grille but, as already said, no-one asks for another unless I ask first. Even here, where death and deprivation are a daily fact of life, there are such things as manners. It has just got dark, in the yard the domino game is in full swing and the area feels even more peaceful than earlier. In the distance, the lights of prosperous New Kingston twinkle, including the land-mark blue sign of the Government-owned Pegasus hotel where the local rich and visiting businessmen pay US$160 a night for a room. It is a little over a mile away as the crow flies but in a different world.

Suddenly, youths start coming up to us, slowly walking by with lowered eyes and voices saying: "Robbie, soldiers." An army patrol is on its way through the area. The police will only come here with army protection during the day, on what is known as the joint 'Rat Patrol' which cruises the ghetto areas in jeeps. At night the soldiers come on their own, and they come on foot. The local intelligence system is working well for it is another five minutes before we see them, moving down each side of the street in classic urban patrolling formation. They are in full camouflaged combat gear, complete with steel helmets, and their rifles are at the ready.

Not wishing to arouse suspicion, Sheila suggests we make ourselves scarce until they are gone. Robbie grins, puts his arm round my shoulders and says: "No, man. It's cool. They're not going to shoot us when we're with the white man." A youth is selected from the street at gun-point, pushed against a wall by one soldier and thoroughly searched. Others crouch on either side, making use of the available cover, rifles pointed outwards, looking nervous. One is pointed our way, but music plays on and we drink some more beer. It is a scene from a tropical Belfast, without the comforting normality of familiar street furniture.

They have come back, it is explained, to try and repeat the success of the past week when a gun was recovered in the nearby 'Board Villa' and its owner was shot dead. No one seems unduly concerned. "They find nothing. That was the only one there," says Robbie, with confidence.

PRECISELY how Jamaica came to be so dominated by the gun is a long and complex story but the basis of it is again political. Having established their respective power bases in the ghettos, both political parties sought to consolidate their positions there with the use of local gunmen and gang leaders. Buying votes with jobs and housing was a good start, but an effective whip could also be imposed on the local electorate through the use of intimidation and violence. Attacks could also be made on the opposition, most crudely on the basis that if three people were killed in, for instance, a PNP area, then that would be three less votes for Michael Manley. The exact involvement of the party leaders in this development has been protected ever since by a mutual cloak of silence and denial, but it is well established that the early 1970's saw the beginning of large numbers of guns arriving on the island.

The process was given a boost by the input of Cold War politics after Manley's first government swung further to the left and increasingly allied itself to Fidel Castro's communist regime in Cuba. Folklore stories from the time talk of Cuban troops exercising in the hills of Jamaica, and fears grew, however fanciful, that the country was on the verge of a communist takeover. In the standard procedure of the time, the USA sought a proxy champion in the form of Edward Seaga, and former JLP activists tell of how the CIA built remote airstrips to import the hardware to support him. The PNP for its part was getting its guns from Castro. It was also sending large numbers of its supporters to Cuba under the guise of training courses in construction work. What at least some of these young people also got, however, was expert training in the use of small arms, and they effectively became a para-military force known as the 'Brigadistas', based in the PNP areas of the ghetto.

Open gun battles at the boundaries between rival neighbourhoods became commonplace, and Manley was forced to respond. In 1974, he declared a state of emergency, introduced the draconian Suppression of Crime Act and set up the special Gun Court for the holding and trial of people guilty of firearms offences. The act allowed any police officer or member of the army to enter any building or to stop any vehicle or person merely on the suspicion that a criminal offence had either been committed or was about to be committed. The power of the gun court covered even those found in possession of a single bullet, and sentences, even for a first offence, ranged from one year to life.

In an operation that has parallels with the introduction of imprisonment without trial, or 'internment', in Northern Ireland around the same time, large numbers of gunmen were simply swept off the street and held in the Gun Court. It was a move largely responsible for the election of 1977 passing off relatively peacefully, and for Manley's re-election. This proved,

however, to be only a lull in hostilities. The build-up of weapons and the escalation of political violence continued, and the powder keg exploded in the 1980 election when martial law was declared at least 800 people were killed.

This time the victor was Seaga who, on assuming power, tried to bring the situation under control by offering an amnesty for anyone who handed in a gun. But the genie was out of the bottle, the gangs had tasted the power that guns could bring and they were reluctant to relinquish it. Few took up Seaga's offer and the guns were turned to the service of crime, particularly the emerging and lucrative drugs market. The dons increasingly used the control of the ghetto areas for their own benefit and as a source of willing recruits for their enterprises, both at home and abroad.

THESE twin themes of control and crime are still the dominant forces that govern the ghetto today. When Robbie is not using his fire power to fight the political fight he is using it to enforce the area's own harsh concept of law and order and, at least in the past, to carry out armed robbery and extortion.

"If people have troubles, they come to me and we solve it. If somebody trouble them or somebody beat them up we deal with it," said Robbie. "If a man rape we just discipline him. He'd have a broken foot (leg) or we'd kill him. Beat him and break his foot, shoot him in the foot or in the tummy or some part of him. Rape is against the law. He could take my mother, my sister or my baby and rape them, so we must protect against that."

As a rule, he said, people preferred things to be done this way rather than going to the police who were slow to respond and not as effective as what he half-seriously called his 'community policemen'. Once given a description of a thief, for instance, they would find the guilty man and, initially, give him a caution and demand that he return the stolen goods. If he refused or began to 'bad it up' against them, that is argue or show disrespect, then he would be dealt with. "We put him in his place. If he can't hear, we make him feel," said Robbie. Other available sanctions include knocking out someone's teeth or breaking their hands.

If a 'case', as he calls it, was too big for him, such as where somebody both asked him to deal with a situation and called in the police at the same time, then the matter would be referred upwards to the 'bigger man'. Currently this is a young man called Dudas who is the latest in the local dynasty, the son of the dead Jim Brown and the brother of Jah T. "We call him the Don. Anything we can't manage we put it to him and anything he suggests we do it. If he tells us to leave it out we leave it out, if he tells us to go along with it we deal with it - serious sah." There is even a cell in the community, he said, where people can be held, tried and sentenced just like a normal court. Again, it would be the don who would decide what to do. "Him just pick sense out of nonsense," said Robbie. "We just know what to do and how to do it. We don't make people bawl after, we make people glad."

Like any pillar of a community, this old man of 23 is worried about the state of modern young people: "Most of all, the youth here don't care a dam. They do anything they feel like doing." And like any lawman, his can be a thankless task. Sometimes, he said, the people can rebel against a decision or an action he has taken, where upon the matter would go to a vote or be referred upwards.

The penalty for getting it wrong and offending the powers that be is, predictably, severe. Earlier that year he had received a severe beating himself for exceeding his authority and attacking two young men who insulted him. "One time some yout' gwan wicked 'pon me, ya na, they pussy me up and call me a fool and dem ting there. So I jus' got ma knife and jus' juk, juk dem up, stab them up," he said. "So they go down there an' mek complaint an' a bad bwoy call an' we go down to the cell there wi' two other yout' an' dem start beat dem now, an' the man start lick me an' and lick me on ma head back and on ma face and knock me out and revive me back. See dat now? Dat happen to me."

The punishment was meted out by 'community bad men', friends of the don, who had thought he was getting too big for himself. It's all part of the system, he said. "Dem say me should not do that. 'Cos I stab dem up bad, ya na. Some go to hospital, critical. Some lose all dem lungs. Yeah."

These rules only apply, however, within the community. 'Out there', that is anywhere else, all bets are off and almost any kind of criminal activity is condoned as just being what needs to be done to get by. "That is the wicked part of happenings. You have to know how to do crime if you are to survive. You go out there, you go on the road, and take what you have to take, but you don't trouble poor people for their things. You just take what you have to take," said Robbie. In the past this has included robbing banks and shops at gun point.

A VISIT to a bank in down-town Kingston shows that this is no idle boast. I arrive to cash a traveller's cheque just as a pay-roll is about to issued, and a large security guard, armed with a pump-action shotgun and revolver and wearing a helmet with a visor, is standing vigilant outside the main door. Just inside, the bank's own armed guard is sitting on a chair, while another pay-roll guard is stationed half-way down the banking hall. Two others, one of whom also has a shotgun, collect four large clear plastic bags stuffed full with banknotes and slowly, watchfully, they make their way out to the waiting armoured van. The pay-roll guard from the banking hall follows up the rear.

While customers and staff appear to be going about their normal business as all this happens, there is a perceptible air of tension that goes, like a sigh of relief once the pay-roll has safely departed. Fear of being caught in the indiscriminate cross-fire of a raid is a very real one even though the bank is only 200 yards away from the main East Queen Street police station. To the outside eye, the show of force seems a bit excessive. That same afternoon, however, a guard was shot dead outside another bank just four blocks away.

Robbie explains how such a raid might take place. Five or six men would meet to plan the 'ting' (thing) when it was known a pay-roll was coming off, draw up a map and go down to the bank with their full armoury. "We just go there and watch for police. If there is no police then we just go juk the man with a gun, say 'Freeze, it's money we come for, if you move you're dead' and we just take the money from him." Simple, really. I point out that the odds I had seen at the bank seemed pretty formidable, but he said that would not present a problem. "We go there with blood in our eyes. We don't laugh with people. If I juk out my gun you can't move, you know. The first thing that comes into my head if I tell you don't move and you move is that your intention is that you want to disarm me of my gun. So me going to shoot you down."

The problem in the ghetto, he said, is that there is no work and you can't rely on anybody to give you anything, not even for food. This is the harsh reality of 'community' life. "They say a hungry man is an angry man. I've proved that, I've proved that many times. If I'm here, and I've got nothing, and I've got no food, and worse my kid is bawling at me for food and I can't get it and I've got nobody to turn to, and you mess with me, I'm going to lick it down hard," said Robbie. "When you deal with it out there you deal with it wicked. You don't pet people, you know." He said that he hasn't been involved in robbery for some years, and that now he only gets his gun out if there is 'warfare' or if it is needed to discipline somebody. This is partly because the police are getting better with more money, more equipment and more cars. Mostly, however, he has given it up because of having children. Robbie has four, by three different women. One child lives with him, and another is away living with the mother in New York.

Like most young men from the ghetto, Robbie's ambition is to get out and go abroad. This desire, and the ability to fulfil it through the easy availability of false passports and papers, is the basis of the problem experienced with Jamaican criminals in the USA and Canada, and more recently in Britain. Hard to trace, because of multiple identities and forged paperwork, and brought up in this climate of violent crime and gun law, they present one of the biggest challenges currently being faced by western police forces.

Robbie tells the story of a cousin who went to London and who, until recently, was making a lot of money from selling cocaine and 'weed' and from robbing other drugs dealers. He got there on false papers, acquired 'on the bandulu' from the British High Commission in Kingston by bribing someone who works there with J$50,000 (about £1,000). The process follows a classic pattern, where someone already in the country, in this case the man's mother, sent an invitation letter to him together with supposed proof that she could support him on his stay there. He took these, along with his bribe, to the High Commission and got his Jamaican passport stamped with a permission to visit Britain for up to five years.

His drugs dealing activities are now at an end, however, having been caught by the police last year, and he will spend the rest of his time there serving a five-year sentence for drugs offences. After that, he will be deported. He cannot expect any sympathy or a warm welcome when he does return home, because he has offended against another unwritten rule by not sending back any of his money to help his relatives. "He bought a car, the latest model car, he was making lots of money, but he sends me nothing. That's a bad man," said Robbie. "If he thinks he's going to get rich and come to Jamaica and model for me [show off] with a bitchin' ring and rental car, then he makes a sad mistake. I'm going to take away his things. I'll use my gun, take off his chains, take off his ring, take away his money, take away his car - take away all his girls. Then I'll run him away, kick him up the backside and say 'Goway!'. Somehow, I believed him.

AFTER this brief journey into ghetto life I found it hard to come to any consistent conclusions; the place is so full of contradictions which prompt diametrically opposed reactions. On the one hand, these areas are desperately deprived and the hard life goes on under the constant threat or reality of horrendous levels of violence. On the other, however, there is a sense in which the system works and the impression that were it not for the gunmen and the tight sense of a community under siege, then things could be a lot worse.

These contradictions were most obviously evident in the personal shape of Robbie, whose story is fascinating and valuable not because he is a major player on the criminal scene, which he isn't, but because his life is a microcosm of almost every aspect of 'ghetto runnin's'. He metes out violence in the name of law and order, but has also been on the receiving end when it was thought he had gone too far. He is a gang leader and one-time serious criminal, but he is also a doting father with a great sense of responsibility towards his family and those who see him as a protector.

Initially, I was very sceptical about this rosy view, assuming that all the

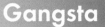

talk of being a 'community leader' was just a gloss over bare-faced gang-sterism. But after spending hours in his company and that of his friends, it was impossible not to be struck by the honesty with which they discussed their lives or by the courtesy and sense of humour which existed alongside the frankly admitted capacity for extreme 'badness'.

One of his lieutenants, who we will call Dermot, joined the edge of one conversation, gently spoken, apparently shy and making his contributions by talking to the ground in an accent that was even harder than usual to decipher. When he finally did raise his head, it was easy to see why. He had a scar running up from the left corner of his mouth to just below his ear, with the stitch-marks still showing. He too said that he had given up armed robbery some time before for the sake of his two children. He was 20 years old and explained that the children had 'just happened'.

Our first meeting with Robbie was, again, instructive. After Sheila had approached him with such terrifying frankness about what we wanted, she went even further by making jokes about his appearance, rubbing his 'marked-up' eyebrows with her thumb and asking if these were real scars or just affected to give him a more fierce appearance. Clearly knocked off balance by this feminine assault, he just coyly turned away and muttered something modestly. There was also the respect with which he was clearly held by other people we encountered in the block. Anyone who passed would call out a greeting which was graciously acknowledged with a nod of the head.

If they were frightened, however, they didn't show it. One young girl took a particular shine to me, or at least the contents of my pocket, and in her outrageous advances was the one exception to the rule of people asking for nothing. I bought a round of soft drinks for her and her friends after which she wouldn't leave me alone, including frequent interruptions to one interview I was having with Robbie. He just sat back and smiled indulgent-ly, later even offering to 'sort 'tings out' with her if I so desired, on the grounds that I was obviously shy and didn't know how to deal with such women. I politely declined but commented on the two very different sides to his nature. He explained that growing up in the ghetto meant he had been exposed to a lot of 'experience' that had made him wise beyond his years, adding: "Me easy. When you go easy me easy, when you go hard I fierce hard. I don't have no mercy." In the course of this statement his expression and tone changed from benevolence to menace in a disconcert-ingly short time. Again, I was inclined to believe him.

One fact is clear, that this is a distinct and isolated society and it has to be understood as such if any wider understanding of the crime wave that has swept out of Jamaica, or more exactly out of these blocks and shanty-towns, is to be achieved. It may sound presumptuous but much of Jamaican society is scarcely any wiser about the ghetto than their British or American counterparts. People rarely talk about it, and no one in their right mind ever, ever goes there. It has achieved an almost mythical status of evil within the Kingston élite, as well as being a huge embarrassment, while in the countryside it is viewed simply as a place full of 'mad people' whose actions are incomprehensible. Educated people in Kingston expressed horror at the idea of my planning a visit, and astonishment that I had come out alive.

Sheila Watson, my guide into this world, faced a similar reaction when she floated the idea of studying street gangs for her MA thesis. "When I told a number of my peers that I was going to do a study on gangs in Hannah Town, they all laughed, because they thought it was a joke," she said. In the time I spent working at The Gleaner, Jamaica's oldest and biggest newspaper, in 1991, she was the only journalist I found who had any interest in such low life. Even she, however, had never been unaccompanied into one of these areas before starting her study, and that's after nine years working as a reporter in the Gleaner offices - just half a mile from Hannah Town. On my last visit, one very experienced broadcaster did speak the unspeakable by stating that those who most would regard as common criminals were, in their own communities, seen as protectors. He added, mischievously, that people in Tivoli slept safer in their beds than those in some of Kingston's more prosperous suburbs.

There are signs, however, that the acknowledgement of such realities may soon be forced into the open, as the systems that held the ghettos under some semblance of control are starting to break down. Politicians may have been instrumental in setting up the Dons, but with the growth in the size and the profitability of the Jamaican-based drugs trade, particularly cocaine, the balance of power has already shifted in favour of the gunmen. Observers say that local politicians can only operate in some of these areas with the permission of the dons, rather than the other way round, and disillusionment with what can be achieved through the political process, overt or covert, is widespread.

This disenchantment was clearly voiced by Robbie and his friends. "I don't mix up with it any more. They are not helping me, not giving me nothing. Nothing at all," he said. "The politicians, they've used us. They send the guns, come give you. When they come give you and you go out there, you push out all the strength out there, they give you nothing. I'm tired of it." They did not get the guns direct from politicians' hands, he said, but people knew where they were coming from.

In the past, there were community 'elders' who would help people. If people weren't working they would find something to give you, they would give money to old people. The greatest of all, he said, was Jim Brown who

he described as a worldwide leader, but who is more generally known as the 'don dadda'- the big daddy of them all. "He gave old people work, he sent youths to school, give them their lunch money, give them uniforms, shoes, everything for them. Every weekend you can go there and he give you money." Wherever the money came from, said Robbie, he put it to use. "He was the only man who do things with his money. He didn't have it an say he's not giving it. He spread it." But these things don't happen any more. "Those times are done with in the late 70's and the 80's. Some of the elders are dead out. Some have gone abroad to live. The ghetto is run by the youth right now," he said.

The picture emerges, then, of a violent generation brought up on the use of guns but without even the forces of control or motivation that helped restrain, however imperfectly, their predecessors. It is a frightening prospect. The simplest and bleakest vision came from Dermot. Asked what the future held for a youth from the ghetto, he said: "GP [General Penitentiary] or a pretty casket."

Lestor Lloyd Coke, aka Jim Brown

JAH T's pretty casket wound its way through the streets of west Kingston in February 1992, accompanied by an estimated 30,000 mourners. A report in the Gleaner said that only the funeral of Sir Donald Sangster, a former premier almost 30 years before, had rivalled this procession for size in the country's history. Men and women turned out in their best clothes to cram the church and the surrounding streets where the funeral was being held, and to follow it on its way to May Pen cemetery, the final resting place of so many 'bad bwoys'.

Mark Coke, alias Jah T, had been 22 years old when he was shot on a ghetto street corner two weeks before. The son of the 'don dadda' Lestor Lloyd Coke, aka Jim Brown, he was then the don who ran Tivoli Gardens and the surrounding JLP areas. He had taken over the reins of his father's fiefdom after Brown had finally been arrested and was awaiting extradition to the USA to face charges of drugs trafficking, money laundering and murder associated with the cocaine smuggling empire this supposed building contractor also ran out of Miami. Jamaican police had previously tried, and failed, to charge him with 14 murders, including the 1984 killing of seven JLP defectors.

After he was shot, Jah T was taken to Kingston Public Hospital, on North Street on the fringes of the ghetto, (scene of a recent TV mini-series:

'Jamaica ER') and as the news got around a crowd of hundreds gathered in the hospital compound and on the road outside. Young women cried, while both they and the youths with them hurled insults at the hospital staff for not having responded quickly enough to the emergency. Police tried to restore order, but the situation was getting worse as more and more of the don's people arrived to keep vigil.

At 6.20pm Jah T was pronounced dead, and the community immediately erupted into violence. Road blocks of burning tyres were set alight, people screamed for revenge, and a barrage of gunfire went up, presaging the full-scale reprisal war that was about to break out. Some of the crowd were too stunned by the news to believe it: "No, him no dead. A lie dem a tell," screamed one distraught young woman outside the hospital gates. In the next three days, seven people were killed as the war took off.

Two weeks later, on the day of Jah T's funeral, the hospital was again the scene of rioting and gunfire - this time over the death of Jim Brown. News that there had been a fire at the General Penitentiary, where Brown was being held awaiting his extradition the next day, started circulating around the funeral crowds early that evening. As people rushed to the prison to find out what had happened they were met with a strong show of force in the area with police and soldiers stationed on top of buildings, on street corners, taking cover behind lamp posts or even lying on their stomachs on the pavement, all with guns poised. One eyewitness said he had been drinking at a nearby bar when he had heard shots and seen soldiers running up and down outside the prison, followed by two warders who emerged from inside and shouted that Jim Brown was dead.

Eventually a doctor arrived at the prison, followed 10 minutes later by an ambulance. The doctor re-emerged and drove away, and shortly after that Jim Brown was brought out on a stretcher. His face was not covered, adding to the speculation that he was badly injured, but not dead. Police were alerted to take up positions along the route to the hospital, and to be ready for combat. The ambulance with Jim Brown inside was escorted by four police vehicles and two armoured vehicles belonging to the army. By the time this convoy reached the hospital, a large, angry crowd had already gathered, most still dressed in their best clothes from attending Jah T's funeral hours before. In an attempt to calm the situation, police told them that Brown was not dead but that he was receiving treatment for smoke inhalation.

News that he was in fact dead, however, reached the crowd through television and radio broadcasts, and police and soldiers guarding the hospital compound had to run for cover as they were sprayed with fire from automatic weapons. Women and children joined the attack by throwing rocks and anything else they could find at the security forces, shouting:

"We want Jim Brown," and "We love Jim Brown". The police fired a few shots to try and disperse the crowd, but these were answered with a barrage of fire from the direction of the ghetto and the rioting continued.

Most businesses in down-town Kingston remained closed the next day, as the city braced itself for more violence but blanket security by police and army prevented serious trouble. A week later, west Kingston witnessed another huge funeral when Jim Brown was given his send-off. Edward Seaga, who had described Brown as the 'protector of Kingston's poor', was amongst the chief mourners.

Such was Brown's standing that even after the funeral rumours continued to circulate that he wasn't dead at all, that the body was too badly burned to be recognised, that it was a substitute and that Brown had been spirited away to Peru or Panama. That issue was settled for most people at his inquest when it emerged that the body's fingerprints had survived and did match those of Brown. A leaked picture of the victim on the mortuary slab also clearly identified the body as that of Brown.

Many other questions, however, remained unanswered. The inquest could only record an open verdict as to how exactly he had died and afterwards his lawyer told reporters: "If you believe that Jim Brown just burned to death, by accident, in his jail cell, you'll believe in the tooth fairy." Just how a prison cell could suddenly burst into flames has never been explained, nor why it took at least 15 minutes after the first alarm was raised to open the cell door, nor why it took nearly two hours to get him to the hospital which is only a few minutes' drive away. In evidence to the inquest, one prisoner claimed that he had been told to cover up for warders who had left their posts while Brown's cell burned. Speculation, not surprisingly, was that he had been killed in order to ensure his silence. The enduring question, however, remains who had the most to hide and so the most to fear from him appearing before an American court? For a man with his connections, on both sides of the law, any number of answers are possible. Another theory was that he had become simply too big for everyone else's good. The laws of the ghetto, it seems, go right to the top.

Jim Brown's burnt body lies on the mortuary slab

Chapter Five

GHETTO COPS

MY FIRST visit to the ghetto had been in 1991, some three years before I met Robbie, when I was shown how the area looked from the other side of the law and order divide. On that occasion I was driven into Rema, the area of Trench Town bordering Denham Town to the north west, by Assistant Superintendent Keith Gardner - better known by his street name of 'Trinity'. He is one of the all-time stars of the Jamaican Constabulary Force (JCF), a member of a select band of policemen who during the 1970's and 1980's established reputations as formidable as those of any local don. Again, these reputations, or 'reps' were forged in the battles of the ghetto wars and Trinity, like the rest, is known as a man with 'many notches on his gun'.

His fierce image proceeded him, so at our first meeting I was surprised to find a large but softly-spoken man who greeted me with a beaming smile and exaggerated courtesy. The walls of his office hung heavy with certificates and photographs but pride of place went to two pictures - one of his graduation from police college in Harrogate, Yorkshire, and the other of him, rifle in hand, storming across a Kingston street during a shoot out. He was full of praise for the British police but modest about his own mythical status as a 'fearless crime fighter'. It was a reputation enhanced by his one-time position of personal body guard to Edward Seaga, and by the fact that, two years previously he had been acquitted of the murder of his wife on the grounds of self defence.

Since then, it was said, he had discovered religion and most recently he had been studying to become a lawyer. On the subject of gangstas, however, his tone hardened. "These people are ruthless, and they must be pursued with the same ruthlessness. I don't think any of them have heard of conscience, they will kill infants in the street," he said. "I'm sorry to say it but these people are not human beings, they are animals."

As we drive into Trench Town he winds down his window and tells me to do the same. People in these areas like to see who is passing through, he explains, otherwise they become nervous. The word 'nervous' is suddenly charged with a menace I had never previously noticed. 'Sensitive' is another such word, as in: 'this is a sensitive area' by which he is not referring to a high density of local poets. Certainly this is anything but an undercover operation as Trinity folds himself out of the car on one street and draws himself up to his full height, resplendent in immaculate police uniform.

He is not wearing a gun, explaining that it was not necessary because

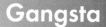

he was so well known in the area, although friends who know him later speculated that he probably had at least a small revolver tucked into an ankle holster, just in case. Women and children rush up to greet and touch him as though he were a visiting pop star, calling him 'Mr Trinity', and he smiles back beneficently, fussing over the children and even allowing one to wear his hat.

He shows me the burnt-out remains of a Chinese store, saying that such shops had once been the mainstays of these communities but that they had now all closed due to theft, vandalism and being caught in the cross-fire of local disputes. It then emerges how he knows the place so well. He takes me through collapsing fencing and yards containing the odd scrawny chicken to the door of a one-roomed wooden hovel with a beaten dirt floor. This, he revealed, was where he was born and brought up, and we chat to a rheumy-eyed old man who is the only current occupant and who Trinity describes as an 'uncle'. I don't understand a word the old man says.

Other famous people also come from this part of town, explained Trinity. "I could name you three or four big posse leaders in the States who come from this very area. It's a major recruiting ground for the posses." Young men from the ghetto are sent for by these leaders, he said, and taken on as 'soldiers' in the big American drugs operations. They are drawn by the promise of fast money which is fuelled by stories from those who have gone before. They are also, increasingly, going to Britain where it is seen as easier to gain illegal entry. "Some go as stowaways, but mostly they go with fraudulent travel documents arranged by the posses," said Trinity.

"The common denominator in these gangs is money. Greed for money has transcended every other ethnic or political consideration to the extent that political boundaries no longer really exist, particularly in the US. It is a lust for money." If deported, these youths usually return to Jamaica completely broke, because nothing they acquire while abroad can be legally registered in their own names, but they do bring with them the habit of hard drugs abuse which is now having a serious effect. "I have seen what this crime has done to systematically eat away at our society, both through its distribution and use. It is damaging the current generation, and if something is not done about it the next generation will be very, very seriously damaged," said Trinity.

He has not escaped unscathed himself. As we cruise by some of Rema's concrete blocks, he points out the one where he and a colleague were both shot and almost killed in a shoot out with Rankin' Dread, Britain's first Yardie 'godfather'. He then opens wide his mouth to proudly show where a bullet from that exchange went through his face and knocked out four of his teeth.

Another block on the edge of the estate is surrounded by high walls and razor wire, and watchtowers manned by policemen with machine guns stare out over the wasteland beyond. This part of the housing project was requisitioned by the police as a holding centre for gunmen arrested during the 1980 election 'war', and is now a permanent 'lock-up' or prison as well as the local fortified police station. Further down the deserted road we encounter a 'Rat patrol', and are waved through by an army officer who stands by his jeep, covered by the assault rifle of the steel-helmeted police-man perched in the back. It is reminiscent of a scene from Beirut but without the bustle and local colour.

WHEN Trinity said that hard drugs abuse had been introduced to Jamaica from the USA, he was alluding to an idea that has taken a firm hold over the thinking of many senior policemen and government officials. That is, that much of the country's horrendous crime problem has been imported from other places, especially America, and meaning that Jamaica is as much a victim of the guns and drugs crisis as it is an originator. It is an idea with obvious attractions for a country desperately trying to improve its image and it is repeated often enough for it to have become an official line.

In the area of hard drugs, particularly cocaine, there is clearly a lot of truth in the argument. While the use of marijuana is endemic in some sections of Jamaican society, but only some, the arrival of cocaine is a rela-tively recent phenomenon. The trade in 'ganja', as marijuana is known locally, reached a peak in the 1970's when tons of the stuff was cultivated in the remote Jamaican hills and plane loads were being flown to the USA on a daily basis.

The hulks of old Dakotas and light aircraft which rot around the perime-ter of the Norman Manley International Airport in Kingston were seized during this period and stand as a memorial to it. Under intense pressure from the American government to do something about the problem, and with a large injection of US dollars for the purpose, the Jamaicans institut-ed a marijuana eradication programme in which the army used helicopters and huge amounts of manpower to search out the ganja plantations and destroy them.

This still goes on, and any trip through parts of the island's interior will encounter armed troops engaged in slash and burn operations or one of their sweet-smelling bonfires. The trade also continues, controlled as ever by organised gangs and making fortunes for those in charge, but activity is seen to have stabilised. There was, and is, violence and corruption associ-ated with the ganja trade, but the violence at least was not on the same scale as that which has become associated with cocaine. As a huge gener-alisation, the tools of this older trade were more likely to have been knives and machetes rather than Uzi sub-machine guns or M-16 rifles.

Cocaine started to make a big impact on the country in the 1980's, as the American market for the drug exploded and the possibility for astronomic profits became apparent. With a geographic position perfect for the purpose, lying between South America and the USA, Jamaica became a major trans-shipment point for the drug on its way from the Colombian cartels to the hungry consumers. Jamaican gangsters already established in America took full advantage of this situation and seized an increasing slice of the action through sheer force of arms and ruthlessness. On its way through, some of the cocaine stopped off in Jamaica and a home market for this, and for its potent derivative, crack, was established. The illicit flights associated with the bulk end of the drugs trade are now firstly coming from southern or central America. Consignments of tens of kilos at a time are either brought in to the many secret airstrips that still operate in the Jamaican hills or they are dropped off the coast to be collected by expensive speedboats or fishing boats. After storage they are then taken on to the USA, either by ship or on other flights. To that extent, then, the escalation of the drugs trade, and the problems of violence and lawlessness that it brings with it, are things that have been brought into the country from outside.

The most contentious question, however, is the extent to which the personnel involved in this trade and its associated crime are also imported. How, in a sense, they are not really Jamaicans at all, but semi-aliens who have learnt their evil ways elsewhere and who are now visiting a terrible plague on the country. The question is at its most politically sensitive over the issue of deportees, criminals who are sent back to Jamaica in their hundreds every year from the USA, Canada and Britain.

I first heard the official line on this later in 1991, in an interview with KD Knight, the minister of national security in the PNP government, and deportees have been moving up the political agenda ever since. "What we are getting returned are the worst elements of those societies. Here we have people who have often spent the greater part of their lives in the country from which they are being sent, who really see Jamaica as home, but home only for vacations," he said. "They are sent back here with flimsy or no ties left in Jamaica and this necessarily causes a crime problem for us. When these guys return they are not going to return as angels, having lived crime. It puts a strain on our resources; it puts a strain on our ability to secure our people."

Even at that time, the figures on deportees were staggering. A total of almost 3,800 had been sent back since the beginning of 1987, according to Jamaican police statistics. The vast majority were from the USA, and were for drugs-related offences. American government figures, purely for those deported after serving a prison sentence for a serious offence, showed that almost one Jamaican a day was then being sent back in this category. Officials said at the time that these were by far the highest figures for any country. Of the 963 such cases over the previous five years, all but 57 involved drugs or firearms offences.

More recent Jamaican statistics show that the process is accelerating. The number of deportees per year more than doubled between 1987 and 1993, when a total of 992 were sent back. In the first six months of 1994, a total of 661 had already been returned. Of these, 404 came from the USA, 178 came from Canada, 50 came from Britain and 29 from other countries. All these are going back to, and originally came from, a country with a native population of around 2.5 million. It is as if former inhabitants of Birmingham were being shipped back to that fair city because of their criminal activities at a rate of a thousand a year.

Needless to say, the authorities in these other countries put rather a different interpretation on these statistics to that propounded by the Jamaicans. They see violent crime as Jamaica's least attractive export commodity which is causing them problems on a scale almost unknown among any other ethnic group.

In America, this has led to Jamaicans becoming demonised to the extent that law abiding migrants in Jamaican communities there, who form the vast majority, have found themselves suffering harassment and abuse on behalf of their criminal brethren. In Britain, police and immigration officers say that the figures for deportees from here are much higher than those recorded by the Jamaican police because it is only recently that information on all those sent back has been passed on to the other end. They also privately admit that immigration laws are regularly used to get rid of Jamaicans suspected of serious offences in cases where there is not enough evidence to mount a prosecution.

A full judgement on who is right in this debate must be made after a detailed study has been made of the development and impact of Jamaican criminal gangs in these other countries. A working conclusion, however, is that it is the propensity for extreme violence in pursuit of criminal ends, particularly involving firearms, that has been exported from Jamaica and which itself stems, to a large degree, from the country's turbulent political past. The link between gunmen abroad and the ghettos is a direct one and violent crime in Jamaica, particularly in Kingston, has been a constant fact of life for decades.

It is also true, however, that, once established in America, the gangs did develop their ambitions and the sophistication and scope of their operations with the money and hardware available, and through having access to the world's largest cocaine market. This expertise and firepower was then re-imported to Jamaica, enhancing the considerable capacity for

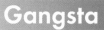

'badness' that already existed there, and confronting the authorities with a crime problem that is all but beyond their abilities to control. The response has been to increase their own levels of sophistication and to embrace greater co-operation with law enforcement agencies from other countries. One recent move was a law passed in 1993 which allows the Jamaican police to monitor closely all returning deportees for up to a year, requiring them to register at their local police station and report there regularly. Only time will tell whether this and other measures will be enough to stem the tide.

Until late 1996 the problem was in the hands of Colonel Trevor MacMillan, a former officer of the Jamaica Defence Force (JDF), who was appointed Commissioner of Police in 1993 with the brief to reform the much criticised force and renew public confidence in it. That he is an army man is no coincidence. It is a common belief that the JDF is the only organisation in Jamaica to be largely untouched by either corruption or political cronyism. I interviewed him after his first year.

A SMART, saluting police officer stands guard at the gate to an old colonial mansion on the outskirts of Kingston's city centre. Once inside, a sweeping drive leads to the building's entrance past a neatly clipped lawn. This is MacMillan's imposing headquarters.

Once inside, the atmosphere is less formal. The desk officer is reading the comic section of the afternoon tabloid and dance hall music is thumping in the background from a tape player. Above his head is a burnt-wood motto saying, 'Teach Us True Respect For All', and below that a yellowing, hand-written sign which states, 'Persons Going Upstairs Report to Leave their Firearms at the Front Desk, Thank You.' There is a security scanner-arch, which I eye nervously as I am carrying a bag full of camera equipment, but the officer merely asks, "Have you got any firearms in there?", I say I haven't and he gestures me through, returning to his comic.

MacMillan is not a large man for the size of the task he had been set but he exudes confidence and good humour from behind his huge desk and military moustache. He is also remarkably open and forthcoming about the problems he faces. This is a new phenomenon. On my last visit I had tried for three weeks to speak to one senior police officer in order to get clearance for the release of some information, involving a ritual phone call to his office every morning to be told by a bored-sounding secretary that he was 'in a meeting'. Eventually, I went over the officer's head but I never got to speak to him. The Colonel, as he is often referred to, is a very different kettle of fish who demonstrates his independence by being fairly rude about just about everybody, particularly politicians.

First, however, we have to deal with the impact of deportees on the local crime scene. "The Jamaican gangs' main mission in life, which goes hand in hand with cocaine and drugs, are guns," he said. Cocaine is the most important problem, and the level of violence from the gangs is largely dependent on how keen they are to expand their drugs dealing turf. But they also lease their services and weapons for other people to commit other crimes. "There is a major input into these gangs from deportees," said MacMillan.

"Hey look, we have simple Jamaican boys, uneducated boys, who get involved in crime here. They sell ganja, they become bad men, and then they seek alternative sources overseas. They go to the United States and Canada where they become really involved in more organised crime, and then become so difficult to handle that they are deported back to Jamaica. When they get back here, they are postgraduates," he said. "Our level of crime has increased, although it sounds rather strange, as a result of the education that some of these guys have got overseas. I maintain that our Yardies are no different to the posse members of the States in that a lot of them go to the UK and get involved in gangs and learn and develop techniques and systems which they bring back to Jamaica, having mastered them in a first world country. The level and sophistication of crime in Jamaica has increased in direct proportion to the return of these postgraduates from abroad."

I point out that the idea that Jamaican gunmen are learning their trade on the streets of London or Manchester is an interesting view on the problem, to say the least, and one which raises more than a quizzical eyebrow amongst British police - hackles would be a more accurate choice of metaphor. Who is teaching who what is very much to the point, they say, but from where they are sitting the exchange of information is absolutely in the opposite direction. This has meant the adoption of Jamaican-type methods and levels of violence by British criminals which has made everybody's life much more dangerous.

ANOTHER, less contentious, factor in Jamaica's crime malaise highlighted by MacMillan is the changing nature of the relationship between local politicians and the gangs. Again, this is connected to the high profits available from cocaine dealing and accords with the views expressed in the ghetto. "There have always been gangs but in the past gangs have tended to be politically orientated. There is not very much political orientation to gangs now in Jamaica except in Tivoli Gardens and some other areas. But even there I am not sure that the politicians have the kind of control they had two or three years ago," he said.

MacMillan traced the roots of this relationship back as far as the 1940's, where it began with the economic problem of limited resources. From that

time, he said, the politician was seen as the individual who could deliver the goods. "He was the man who could get you the house, which were in limited supply, who could get you the job, who could get you bread and butter for your children. In respect of the police force, he could get you promotion or get you a transfer," said MacMillan. Resulting rivalries began with people cursing each other at political meetings and moved from these verbal assaults right up to the 1970's and 1980's where guns became involved. Drugs, initially ganja, also joined in the cycle. "Narcotics trading, politics and guns were very closely associated in many ways," he said. As the situation evolved into one where cocaine became 'king-pin', that relationship began to alter. "Now, the money you can make out of cocaine and the changes in the political system in Jamaica makes the politician not as powerful as he used to be, and therefore in some areas the politicians no longer have control over what they used to control." Some are still clinging onto the gangs in the hope of using them to deliver votes in the next election, he said, but added that he sees it as one of his tasks to widen the split between them and so isolate the gangs through the use of an increasingly professional police force. He was nothing if not ambitious, the Colonel.

ONE OF the first jobs in creating a more professional force was to grasp the nettle of police corruption, including allegations that officers are heavily involved in the drugs trade. MacMillan's opening move was to be characteristically, and astonishingly, open about the problem: "The entire population of Jamaica recognised there was corruption in the police force," he said. "But the police never admitted it. The Police Federation, the union, always said, 'Well, we'll get rid of the bad eggs when we get the evidence'. But you don't get evidence against policemen from policemen, I don't think any police force in the world does that; it's basically very difficult." As well as talking about what he was going to do in the media, he showed he meant business by taking on a few sacred cows. "A number of people who allegedly were untouchable in the police force suddenly found themselves moving, found that they didn't do the same thing that they used to do," said MacMillan.

But that, was only the beginning. Armed with new statutory instruments demanded by a law passed in 1992, he determined to push the matter to the point of criminal prosecutions against corrupt police officers. The force now has an Office of Professional Responsibility, divided between the Police Complaints Division which investigates allegations of mistreatment by the police from members of the public, and the Internal Affairs Division which investigates corruption. There is also a separate Police Public Complaints Authority to provide an independent point of appeal on matters of malpractice with which, by law, the force must co-operate. Amendments to the

Constabulary Force Act in 1994 sought to tackle the related problem of political interference by separating the powers of the commissioner from those of the minister of national security. Not everybody, however, is convinced that the new laws will be enough to fundamentally change the practices of the Jamaican police. A leader article in The Gleaner which appeared on the same day that I met Colonel MacMillan, enthusiastically participated in the new atmosphere of open criticism. "For among the problems of Jamaica's police force are that it has for too long been subject to political pressure and that many policemen are blatantly partisan - as demonstrated in the infamous general election of 1993, where high-ranking officers did nothing to prevent flagrant abuses." It added, as almost a throwaway line: "Many policemen, including seniors, are known or perceived to be involved in drug trafficking and political patronage."

From MacMillan, there was more straight talking. "Ninety per cent of the corruption in the police force is the cocaine trade, cocaine and ganja," he said. At that time there were 80 to 100 files of corruption under investigation but the perennial problem was one of getting evidence. "So we have certain strategies that are now put in place and certain actions which we are taking which I hope within the next year will bear fruit. These have to be a different way of dealing with it, with different methods and different techniques," he added. He was understandably scant on details, except to say that this would involve an 'operational intelligence type of activity' and that it would be within the law. "I intend to catch some big fish," he said, with more than a hint of menace. Other people, it appears were also taking him seriously. Within months of taking office he was the target of an assassination attempt.

THE OTHER major image problem that the police have to contend with is their reputation for violence and a willingness of some to abuse their powers, and their guns. The first thing to understand here is that Jamaica, particularly Kingston, is a very violent place where murder is more than a daily occurrence, running at a rate of around 600 a year. As we have already seen, in certain sections of society guns are both an everyday reality and the ultimate status symbol and in these circumstances a different kind of policing is to be expected. In one room at the Office of the Commissioner, where paintings of all the incumbents of that position are hung around the walls, there is a Roll of Honour which shows the price that the Jamaican Constabulary Force (JCF) pays in lives lost. The year of 1980, for instance, has a column all of its own on this memorial with the names of 28 officers killed on duty during what was virtually a state of civil war. On the other hand, there are routinely more than 100 killings by the police every year. It is said in the ghetto that the reason a gunman will always put up a fight

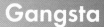

against the police if cornered is because he has nothing to lose. A man caught with a gun, it is said, is a dead man anyway so he may as well try to shoot his way out of trouble. The numbers of criminals held in the Gun Court, a prison specially built in the 1970's to deal with firearms offences, go a long way to disproving that as a solid rule, but it is true to say that the police are as much feared as they are respected.

During one week in 1991 as I was visiting the country, there was a murder every day but one - when there were two killings. All of these happened in down-town Kingston, an area of about one mile square.

One of these incidents perfectly illustrates both sides of the story. A street vendor, of the type common throughout the city, was selling water melons from his barrow while smoking a ganja 'spliff'. An off-duty police-man approached him, pulled out his gun and tried to arrest the man for this minor infringement of the drugs laws. Either believing he was being robbed, or unwilling to be arrested, the man stabbed the officer through the chest with the machete used for chopping up the melons, and ran off. The policeman managed to get several shots off before he collapsed and died, wounding the man in the leg. Within minutes another policemen arrived on the scene, and reportedly finished the vendor off as he lay in the street. Here were two additions to the grizzly statistics, both killed over virtually nothing. The story made the front page that afternoon but was forgotten about shortly afterwards.

A story that did make a sustained impact on the public imagination through its sheer senselessness, was the case of Donald Faulkner, aged 30, a one-legged motorcyclist who was killed by members of a bus crew in July 1994 for refusing to run a red traffic light. How Faulkner lost one of his legs is also instructive. It was amputated the year before after being smashed by copper bullets from a policeman's gun, following an argument over whether or not he was harassing tourists in the resort town of Montego Bay. He had returned to his home in Kingston for treatment and was living with his grandmother at the time of his death. That day he had stopped his motor scooter at a red light when a number 37 bus came up behind him and the driver tried to force Faulkner to ignore the signal. He refused and the two continued until the next stop light, when the bus again tried to force him through by smashing into the back of his scooter breaking the lights and throwing Faulkner off. He was trying to take down the registra-tion number of the bus in order to make a complaint, when members of the crew reportedly attacked him and stabbed him to death.

He was left by the side of the road while the bus continued on its route. The incident was so bizarre as to be almost comic for all its brutality, as was the response from a local police inspector. He said that despite warn-ings given to bus crews they had not improved their conduct: "The bus crews are under scrutiny just like the police," he added. Public sympathy, however, was widespread and PJ Patterson, the Prime Minister and Faulkner's local MP, was amongst those who donated J$10,000 towards his funeral expenses.

Later that month the Star newspaper ran a special feature highlighting five particularly horrendous murders, including Faulkner's, that had taken place in the previous four weeks, One involved a businesswoman who had her throat slit after an argument with her son, who was later shot and arrested by the police. Another was of a 10-year-old boy who was chopped to death by a man who was believed to be mentally deranged. A 21-year-old woman was beheaded by a jealous boyfriend who accused her of having an affair with another man, and the body of another woman was discovered after her crack-taking boyfriend had tried to dispose of her remains in a charcoal kiln. Operating in this kind of environment, it is not surprising that Jamaican police are not renowned for standing on street corners with a truncheon down their trouser leg, giving people directions or telling them the time.

MacMILLAN had his own theory on this climate of violence, while stressing disarmingly that he has: "No political, scientific evidence for this theory, absolutely not," which is that it arose with the steady economic decline of the country and the erosion of the value of its currency since the 1960's. At that time the Jamaican dollar had rough parity with the US dollar, indeed originally it was worth more. When things started to slide and a Jamaican dollar was worth only 20 US cents, people started to panic and were openly saying that if it ever fell to 10 to 1 then there would be riots on the streets. At the time of our interview, the rate was about 33 to 1. "We haven't had any overt violent reaction. We haven't had street riots, we haven't had major industrial unrest. What we have had is a significant increase in violence, person-to-person. I maintain that the hardships and frustrations and lower standards of living that come about when the dollar moves that much are being taken out by individuals against each other." How else, he said, do you explain the kind of murders described above? Between 30% and 40% of that year's murders were domestic and a further 30% and 40% were directly related to gang violence and the cocaine trade. "Both those factors are literally outside the ability of any enforcement agency to do anything significant. They have to do with the question of educating people and with social and economic conditions," said MacMillan. "So we are trying to carry out a police function in an environment which the police really have no control over. That's my unfortunate assessment," he said, candidly. "I can't hide behind a veneer of bull-shit."

All that being said, MacMillan was the first to admit, as ever, that this

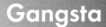

was not helped by police abuses, particularly in connection with the Suppression of Crime Act. "That created a number of problems by removing a lot of rights; for instance the police never had to use search warrants once they had a suspicion. Therefore any policeman in the force today with 20 years service can be someone who has never had to use a search warrant in his career. Also, you could detain people for unlimited periods of time. It was a powerful law, a strong law, required to fight crime, but it was abused." Again, he put this down to a lack or professionalism and a lack of proper leadership in the police as compared with the army over the same period, itself partly a result of abandoning direct recruitment of officers to the police in favour of promotion through seniority. The Suppression of Crime Act was still on the statute books, but is not routinely used any more, he said.

I encountered an example of the old-style interpretation of police powers on a previous visit to Jamaica, as I was being shown round one of the largest police stations in central Kingston. When my tour got to the 'lock-up', or prison where men awaiting trial were held, I asked to go in but the jolly sergeant accompanying me said this would not be a good idea. Prisoners were pressed up to the grilles on the windows of the blockhouse, shouting to anyone who went past while there was large scrum around the heavily barred entrance gate, elbowing each other for a chance to talk to the visitors standing outside. I asked how many men were in there and the sergeant shrugged: "Maybe 200 or 250, I'm not sure," he said. I asked if anyone knew, and he just smiled and shook his head. There could be prisoners who had been in there for years but who had simply been forgotten about, he said.

This old law enforcement world produced the Jamaican superstar policemen like Trinity, and others who glory under street names such as 'Ox', 'Bigga' and 'Spongie'. Men of undoubted courage and legendary power who are good with a gun, often very good, and who can be relied upon to 'deal with it' in their own way. Most are still around, but at the time of my interview with MacMillan, there was a definite feeling that, like the passing of the quick-fire lawmen of the Old West, their day may have been drawing to a close.

It could just have been wishful thinking on the part of MacMillan and his supporters, with their dreams of a fully 'professionalised' police force, but this change was an image he was keen to promote. In one move of outstanding bravery, or naiveté, the old army man even tried to smarten up his force's appearance. "We used to have a situation in Jamaica, and the public hated it, where you could not differentiate a policemen from a gunman. They were sloppily dressed, they were unkempt and they had their armed M-16s. I've said to hell with that, nobody carries an M-16 unless he's in uniform and detectives must be neatly dressed with their shirt and tie," he said.

The key to his future strategy was intelligence. A computerised Drugs and Firearms Intelligence Unit was established by K D Knight in 1991, with the help of British and American agencies, and was working well to provide part of the answer, he said. Almost more important, however, was the public relations onslaught MacMillan launched in order to get more information from the public, an exercise to "win the hearts and minds of the people of Jamaica." If more intelligence can be gathered in this way, the theory goes, then "we don't have to have the radical gun against gun", apart from when dealing with the "vicious animals" of the gangs and, of course, the deportees. He claimed that things had already started to move in that direction. "The more we get intelligence, the more we get people on our side, then the more successful we are which to me is evidence that the gung-ho, Rambo-type individual is not all that critical," said MacMillan, before adding quickly: "But you need him up your sleeve."

THE GIRL in dark blue fatigues and huge combat boots bursts through the door, a .38 revolver on her hip and a bottle of Red Stripe beer in her hand. She shouts something incomprehensible past my ear and then rushes down the path in the same direction, brushing by me as if I wasn't there. I take a deep breath and push the door open. This is the Special Anti-Crime Task Force (SACTF). This is what Col MacMillan had got up his sleeve.

It was set up in July 1993 on the direct orders of the Prime Minister, desperate to do something about the rising wave of crime in the country. Originally called the Anti-Crime Investigation Detatchment (ACID), it brought together about 100 of the hardest, most reliable officers on the force drawn from such units as the Flying Squad and the Drugs Squad and sent them away for special combat, marksmanship and fitness training at the Jamaican police academy. When they were released onto the street their impact was immediate, if not quite in the way intended. In its first week of operation, members of the new team shot and killed two suspects in the grounds of the Jamaica Public Hospital, in full view of dozens of horrified witnesses. Complaints piled up about indiscriminate shooting in pursuit of supposed criminals and opposition politicians condemned ACID as crooks and hoodlums, almost as bad as the people they were supposed to be chasing.

The image problem became so bad that after only a few months their name was changed to the SACTF, and some of their initial exuberance was reined in. At the time of my visit, however, they remained very much at the sharp end, the shock troops in Jamaica's war against crime and the most heavily armed and highly motivated unit in the force. This was then the

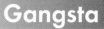

new home for some of the country's most famed and 'fearless crime fight-ers', including Trinity.

The man I have come to see is Superintendent Tony Hewitt, the detective in charge, who is as famous and reputedly fearless as any. His headquarters sit rather incongruously down a pleasant suburban street in New Kingston in a group of old chalet-type buildings set in their own grounds. Next door, within the same complex, is the police's community relations office. It is Friday evening at the end of a hard week, and the unit's motley collection of jeeps and cars are drawn up outside. The small bar, in a hut attached to one end of the building, is doing a fairly brisk trade with other blue-overalled police officers all with pistols on their belt, some with M-16 rifles slung casually over their shoulders. There is an interesting array of headgear, and the whole atmosphere is relaxed-military. Indeed, this could be mistaken as a base for some irregular army unit, were it not for the logo: 'POLICE S.A.C.T.F' emblazoned in large white letters on every-body's back. So far the new dress code is being strictly observed, all those with a rifle are in uniform. The detectives I meet later, however, seem less impressed by the requirement for collars and ties, favouring instead a range of casual sportswear with their guns stuffed down the backs of their trousers. Many of these automatic pistols have extended clips, giving more shots per re-load, protruding from the butt.

Inside, the atmosphere is equally relaxed. One man is cutting up a melon, which he then distributes to others sitting around in the small recep-tion area/common room, others watch the television or wander in and out with plates of food, guns and bottles of beer. There are a number of women officers in the room, and they joke and mess about with the men amid much laughter. I am asked to wait. Across the other side of the room, behind a low wall and blocked in by a table, another young man is waiting, but I don't think he has an appointment. He dozes on a chair with his hands above his head, handcuffed to the window grille. A door in the opposite corner bears the sign: 'DSP Hewitt's Office', and a constant stream of detectives go in for what is becoming a very large meeting. Occasionally, one will re-emerge, come over to me and report in a dead-pan voice: "The head of this outfit will be entertaining you soon."

Eventually, the man himself appears, walks over and stands in front of me without saying a word. He is about 5'6" tall, stocky with closely-cropped greying hair and the thinnest of moustaches traced along his top lip. Fortunately, I recognise him as we had met briefly some years before and I jump up, gibber on about our last meeting and what I am doing there this time, while limply waving my letter of introduction from the Commissioner's office. If he recognises me, he shows not a flicker but continues to fix me with what Paddington Bear would call 'a long, hard stare', still not saying anything. I am suitably terrified and the rest of the room looks on with hushed amusement. Finally, he says 'Come' and we move off to another room. This was not going to be an easy interview.

"Crime is the number one problem in Jamaica now," is his opening gambit. "There was an upsurge in crime about a year ago and that's why this team was set up. There was an influx of deportees at that time and the thinking is that they might be responsible." Ah, it is those deportees again. Hewitt speaks in short bursts with long pauses in between. It's very unnerving. "There is no other specialist operations team. There was a special operations team but it was disbanded. The flying squad is still involved in investigation. We are involved in investigation and operations. Road blocks and raids. We are extremely effective, especially in the recovery of firearms." Another word, 'effective', joins the list of those with a previously unsuspected ability to chill. A temporary thaw comes when, grovelling madly, I tell him that he is very famous. Another pause then he smiles a thin smile (the first of the day, I shouldn't wonder) and replies slowly: "People say it but I don't really know." Then, we're off again: "Local police ask for our assistance. We have the manpower and the firepower. We also carry out our own investigations that we initiate. Firearms, drugs, armed robbery and stuff. Murders. Hard core criminals. We deal with them." I believe, I believe. "Our main job is to identify the gangs. To target the gangs." I think: I know whose side I would rather be on.

After about 10 minutes of this Hewitt is called away and I am left to watch the Friday night festivities taking place right outside the window. The whole of the duty team is assembled for their end of week meeting, sitting around under an awning suspended from two tree's in the 'yard' at the back of the building where a tape player is thumping out dance hall sounds. As the serious part of the proceedings draws to an end, a detective produces two coolers of beer and starts to dispense bottles from behind a table. There is an immediate rush on this make-shift bar and hands and arms dart out from a very disorderly queue to grab a piece of whatever is going. At which point the detective draws his gun. Yes, he pulls out the automatic from the back of his pants and points it at the crowd. Surely not, I think. Surely not here, of all places, are we going to see a gunfight over a few bottles of Red Stripe? I need not have worried. With a deft and practised action, the detective starts to wield his pistol as a bottle-opener, flicking the tops off with his gun sight. When the beer runs out people have to make do with vodka and whisky, served up neat with blocks of ice.

I am summoned again. "Mr Hewitt will entertain you now," says the familiar dry voice, round the door. The entrance to his office, however, is barred by the biggest man in the squad, a towering specimen of overalls, gut and muscle. "What's your problem?", he demands in a less than friend-

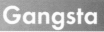

ly, protective manner but after more hanging around he ushers me into the presence. Hewitt is now lying on a patio couch in the corner of the room, a tiny pair of spectacles balanced on the end of his nose and a report lying open on his chest. It becomes clear why his behaviour has been a bit strange, the man is completely knackered. In a touching gesture the huge officer bends solicitously to Hewitt's ear and whispers my arrival, at which his boss, without opening his eyes, demands that he gives me a beer. The man apologises that the beer has run out, to which Hewitt, with an air of impatience repeats the order. The poor man looks bewildered and lost until he sees Hewitt pointing at the large fridge which dominates one wall of the office, at which the officer shoots me a look of complete respect and meekly provides me with a bottle from the boss's personal stash. Clearly, I must be someone of importance after all.

And there it sits, or rather there I sit, for another half-hour or so, while Hewitt sleeps - oblivious to both the blaring radio and the ringing telephone, the report still on his chest. At one moment he suddenly raises himself on an elbow and says: "I'm sorry but I'm just trying to catch five," checks that I did get my beer, and then goes back to sleep. With nothing else to do, except to read the newspaper again, I scan the office. By the filing cabinet there is a heavily tooled, Western-style gun belt. The desk is a mess of paper work and under it is an empty crate of Red Stripe. In the corner, there is an empty crate of Heineken. This observation is not meant to reflect on the level of alcoholic activity in the team, which doesn't seem to differ much from any other police force I have ever encountered. But it is still mildly significant, because in hard-line areas of Jamaica even the beer you drink can have political implications. Green is the party colour of the JLP, so Labourites drink Heineken which comes in a green bottle. Orange denotes the PNP, so the brown Red Stripe bottle (almost orange it you hold it up to the sun), finds favour in socialist circles. Even the colours remind you of Ulster. At any rate, the SACTF clearly passes the rudimentary bottle test on political independence.

THE REASON that Hewitt is so tired is that he has spent most hours of the past week trying to get a 'result' on another high profile case. The previous Sunday, a bunch of Kingston 'yout' had charged up to the north coast for a bit of profitable fun in a stolen Pathfinder jeep, robbed a few people at gun point and shot dead an American tourist who foolishly resisted in a bar in Runaway Bay. This is serious business. Only the month before another American tourist had been killed in a robbery, and his wife just happened to be an anchorwoman for a US television station. Her subsequent anguished account of the incident over the airwaves was entirely understandable, and probably great TV, but it was very bad PR for Jamaica Ltd.

Tourism, predominantly from America, is the country's highest foreign exchange earner and the business has been taking a battering over the past few years as the island's reputation for violence has received more and more publicity.

The need to show a strong response to such crime is, therefore, a matter of national importance and when news reached the police that Sunday that the gang was on its way back to Kingston, the SACTF was called out.

A force of about 40 officers set up a road block on the Washington Boulevard, the main western approach road to the city, but the gang refused to stop and one member was killed in the ensuing shoot-out. He had been riding a stolen motor cycle in front of the jeep and had fallen off, possibly shot, as it approached the obstruction. Travelling too close behind to avoid him, the jeep ran over the bike and its rider, lodging them under its front bumper, and both then smashed through the line of police vehicles and burst into flames. In the gun battle and confusion which followed, the other three gangsters got away down a nearby gully. Two suspects were arrested within two days and three guns recovered, but at the time of my visit the final gunman was still at large. What was left of the burnt-out vehicles were sitting round the back of the SACTF headquarters, bullet holes clearly visible in the rear of the jeep.

The morning after my strange meeting with Hewitt he has obviously benefited from a few hours sleep and is a different man. Dressed in weekend casual mode of a pink polo shirt and jeans tinged with purple, he sits next to the child of one of the unit's canteen workers, fussing over the little girl while watching a World Cup football match. He had previously described the necessary qualities of his officers as "Honesty. Integrity. Bravery", and now he introduces me to one. Constable Veryl Davis, 32, has been on the force for eight years and a member of the SACTF since it was formed a year before. He is a very motivated man. "These are tough guys here, you know, tough guys. And the girls too, very tough," he says. "It's like a family in here, we are always thinking about the welfare of one another. We all put our shoulders to the wheel."

Their main focus, he says, are the 'volatile areas' and their big problem is the increasing sophistication of the gangs. "The drugs situation is such that now the drugs gangs have the firepower to match our firepower. A few years ago it was enough for the police to carry an SMG [a British army issue sub-machine gun], but now the gang members have got M-16's, 9mm automatics, all kinds of stuff. We have to try and try to match them at least." He dismisses the risks involved as something that have always been part of the job but adds that you have to be on your guard all the time. "You have to have some respect for the gunmen or you're letting your guard down. You have to know what they are capable of. If you say: ''Im jus a fool', then

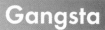

you're letting yourself down". The gunman will always put up a fight, says Davis, although his explanation for this differs somewhat from that given in the ghetto. "He will never just run away because if he puts up a fight and gets away with it then he can boast to his friends about it." Davis had been at the road-block on Washington Boulevard the previous Sunday and confirmed that the gunmen involved in that confrontation were no exception to this rule.

Quite apart from the dangers faced on a daily basis, he also indicates the other difficulties of being a policeman in this society where law and order is only one of the demands on people's loyalty. He is lucky, he says, in that he lives in a 'disciplined area' where it doesn't matter who knows what he does for a living. Others, however, have to keep it a secret. "Some guys live in areas where there are things happening around them but they can't do anything about it because there would soon be reprisals against them. It's not their fault, it's just the way it is," he says. "I think police should live in areas where they are free to say and do anything they want to with the knowledge that no reciprocal action can be taken against them." While faithfully repeating the Commissioner's views on the importance of building community relations, he shows how much work has to be done to achieve this and how wide the gulf has grown between the people of the ghettos and those of the richer residential areas which are perched on the hills surrounding the city. "What is alarming is that if a person from the hills gets killed, it is generally seen as more important than if someone is killed in the ghetto," says Davis. "If someone gets killed in the ghetto, it's like nothing happened. The unit aim is to prevent people in the ghetto or in the hills from getting killed." In this field of restoring public confidence, it seems, the SACTF is becoming a victim of its own success. "If something happens on the street people always call us, they have so much confidence in our capability," he says. "The people think only the Anti-Crime can solve their problem, they want us to be with them. We feel good to know that."

A SMALL example of this rather touching faith came during my last visit to the unit, two days later. I was sitting in an inspector's office, waiting to go out on a morning operation, watching through the open door as final preparations were made - vehicles being made ready and weapons being issued. A uniformed officer with magnificent moustaches was walking down the corridor when the magazine dropped out of his M-16, clattering onto the hard floor and spilling a number of live rounds. "Shit," he said, under his breath, before stooping casually to collect them up. Into the midst of this military activity came a little old lady and her daughter who sat nervously in the corner of the same office. Had they come to complain about gang intimidation in their community? Had they come with important intelligence about drug dealing or armed robbery? Not quite. As the inspector sat and listened, with great patience but also with an air of mild amusement, a complicated story emerged about how the woman had been trying to buy a house and how the deal had fallen through. A large deposit on the property had been paid to her solicitor so that he could complete the transaction on her behalf, she said, but now it was not going ahead he would not pay the money back. Months of correspondence was produced, together with a litany of the hardships the woman was suffering for want of her cash. Once convinced that he had got to the bottom of the matter, the inspector picked up the phone and called the errant lawyer, his tone changing immediately from that of an understanding family GP to that of a very unhappy detective of the Special Anti-Crime Task Force. It didn't take long. What did the solicitor think he was playing at? What was the problem? Oh, he was about to pay the money back? And when would that be? Next week?

How about today? That was now possible? Good. Down went the phone and away went another satisfied customer.

We reach the target address in a small convoy of two unmarked police cars and a bright red open Wrangler jeep, out of which the rifles of six heavily armed officers point at all angles. Again, this is anything but a low-profile operation. An anonymous tip-off earlier that morning had identified the house as a place from where drugs were being dealt and where guns might be found. This is not the ghetto, but a quiet suburban area west of the city called Duhaney Park in the parish of St Andrews and our arrival causes much low-key interest among the locals, who gather in small groups at a safe distance to watch the fun.

Almost before the jeep has stopped, the uniformed boys pile out of the back and rush into the yard to quickly surround the house and push guns through its locked security grilles, shouting at anyone inside to

Police open negotiations with suspects at gun-point

open up and come out. At first it is all an anti-climax as the house is totally quiet and no one seems to be in. Then one of the detectives bringing up the rear, in brightly patterned shirt and baseball cap, spots some movement and opens a loud, gun-point negotiation through a side window with a man inside. Eventually the rear door is opened and a quick search takes place but nothing is found. In a pattern that was to repeat itself throughout the morning, the uniformed officers, having delivered their shock wave but meeting no resistance, soon seem to lose interest in the proceedings. They drift off to the street to find some shade to stand under, leaving the three detectives to do the talking.

My minder on this operation is Detective Inspector Oswald Ayre, a large laconic man with a dry sense of humour and very little of the gung-ho urgency shown by some of his peers. He explains that they have had their eye on this house for some time and, while nothing concrete was found on this occasion, useful intelligence could always be gleaned from such high pressure interviews with suspects. It is a watchful approach that shows its worth as we round the next corner on our way to another job.

Ayre spots a white car with a woman in it parked in a driveway; there is a frantic burst of radio traffic, the convoy comes to an abrupt halt and everybody jumps out again. The woman is surrounded, her car is thoroughly searched and she is given a body search by the female officer who is part of the patrol. She expresses her bewilderment about what is going on, as she is bombarded with questions about why she is there and what she is doing. The woman, respectably dressed in skirt and blouse, claims she was visiting her 'auntie' who lived in the house, but starts to sound

'Auntie' is charmed by task force officers during the raid

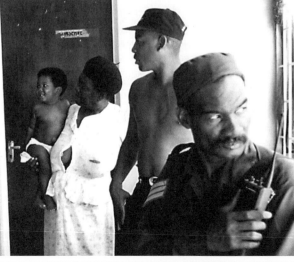

Ghetto Cops

Whitehall residents helping the Kingston police with their enquiries

less convincing when she can't give her supposed relative's name. "I say auntie, but that's all I know her as. Really she is just a wise woman who I visit from time to time. Someone I come to see for counselling," says our suspect without missing a beat. This is becoming interesting.

Inside the house another search is going on and 'auntie' herself is being questioned. She is much put out by all the fuss, a more downmarket character in a beret and button-through dress which is straining, with mixed success, to restrain its owner's ample bosom. Auntie is also unhappy about the photographs I am taking, an activity made more conspicuous by the fact that I am the only white man present, and demands to know who I am. Ayre deftly dodges the question and puts the ball back in her court: "Just because he hasn't the same pigmentation doesn't mean he isn't like you and me. Out of Many, One People," he says, sententiously quoting the Jamaican national motto. She grunts her assent and things calm down, to the point where one huge, bearded, gun-toting policeman starts to play with the small child she has balanced on her hip. The woman in the car is allowed to leave and we move off again.

"When we were at the other house, I saw her come by in the car, slow down for a moment and then drive off. The house where she was parked is also one we have targeted although we weren't going to hit it today," explains Ayre. "She is probably working for the guys selling the drugs and when she saw us hitting the first house went round to the other one to warn them. She thinks she has got away with it but now we have all her details and know who she is. Maybe next time." For all the guns and bluster, it seems, Jamaican policing is not as simple as first meets the eye.

The rest of that morning's operation was less subtle. We cruise back towards town through the run-down area of Whitehall where the streets are narrow dirt-track canyons between high walls of corrugated zinc sheeting and dense vegetation. Twice we halt, apparently at random, to 'have a word' with groups of the local 'yout' hanging around on street corners. This involves lining everybody up at gun point for more thorough searching although the process doesn't take long as most of the 'bwoys' are wearing only jeans or shorts. After initial sharp commands and a certain amount of attitude striking by the police, this all takes place in remarkable good humour. Clearly it is something that can happen to residents at any time and the amount of firepower being waved about just does not impress any more. One big 'dread' in bright yellow pants, a turquoise string vest and wearing a heavy gold chain, was particularly camera shy. Others, however, actually asked to have their pictures taken.

Suddenly, as we are driving along again, it all gets very serious. The radio is crackling on overtime, the convoy picks up speed and we go charging through traffic towards an obviously urgent destination. I fear for the safety of the officers perched in the back of the lurching jeep, while Ayre keeps turning his head alarmingly away from his driving to shout that there is a reported sighting of the third gunman from the weekend's shoot-out in Grants Pen. Without stopping, the vehicles divide to come down the offending street in a pincer action, the men with M-16s go jumping over a wall commando-style and I am advised to hang back for a moment. In the event we find two young women with small children in the house, again remarkably unfazed by the action (they also want their photographs taken) and after more questions Ayre concludes that this was not, after all, a serious call. "Some people call us in like that just to get back at their neighbours. It

Gun-point searches in the Kingston ghettos are routine

happens," he said. Neighbourhood Watch with a difference.

The final drive of the morning is the most hair-raising, after a senior officer turns up at the scene and orders everyone to follow him. This time our car, at the back, doesn't quite keep up. "Some of these guys are crazy," chuckles Ayre. "Me, I just take it easy, bring up the rear and pick up the pieces." After about ten minutes of this we arrive - not at a suspect's hideout but back at the SACTF base. It is lunch time.

Chapter Six

POLI-TRICKS

"POLITICS? It's poli-tricks not politics." It is a phrase you hear a lot of in the ghetto, from youths who feel they have been used for too long by a system which requires them to fight and die for political parties but which gives them little or nothing in return. While cynicism is running high, however, few know enough of the machinations of power to be able to pinpoint their grievances.

One man I met who does claim to know is Michael, a former PNP Don who for years operated at the top of Jamaica's gangsta heirarchy in close co-operation, he says, with local politicians. His story, which has never been told before, paints a picture of corruption and manipulation in parts of the country's political process that shocks as much as it fascinates. He has now fled the country, and believes that his knowledge will one day cost him his life. Michael is not his real name.

His life of crime started in the mid-1970's when he was a young teenager living in a PNP ghetto in central Kingston. Brought up in a caring family, he was bright, ambitious and a good student. His school, however, was in a JLP area at the time when these communities were becoming more polarised and he quickly found himself caught up in the growing atmosphere of political hatred and suspicion. Accused of spying for his local PNP gang, he was beaten up by JLP heavies outside the school. At the time he had no interest or involvement in gang life, indeed he had his heart set on being an accountant. Like any normal youth faced with the problem of bullying, he took it to his mother. Like any normal parent, she sent him back to school in the hope that the problem would go away. But it didn't. The taunts continued and in a second attack shortly afterwards he was stabbed. This time, he took the problem to the gang he was accused of helping and the response was very different. "We form up a group of about 17 men, all with knives, cutlasses [machetes], stick an' ting like that, and we go back to the school where I was attacked and start stab up and chop up man," said Michael. "From that day I don't go back to school. I just get deep in bad, now, because I don't have no other way out. If I'd gone back to school, then the third time I might lose my life. I just decide, I say: "Alright, they drew first blood'" Another criminal career had begun.

From small beginnings of petty theft and burglary, it was a career that quickly flourished. Michael found himself in a whole new world, with its own rules and it own career structure and a very long way from his life as a studious, khaki-clad school boy. The way he describes it, however, it was not without its attractions.

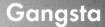

"In order to get recognition in a gang, you have to do things to attract the leader of that gang. In those days they call it 'Rankin', and 'fryers' were the lower class. I was a fryer," says Michael. "So I start to be forced to do things that I would never think of doing. You start from thieving, most yout' dem start wi' tiefin', and the more you tief, a man respect you 'cos 'im say you're serious." It began with him 'grab chain', meaning literally pulling gold chains from people's necks. This remains a popular pastime in down-town Kingston. On a number of visits to the prestigious Ocean Conference Centre on the city's waterfront, I have noticed female colleagues discreetly taking off their jewellery and hiding it in their bags before going out onto the street. The next stage was burglary where, like something out of Oliver Twist, the fryers were pushed through small windows of buildings by the older men. "When a man 'im push you through a building, 'im stand on one side and observe you. If 'im say you're brave, and you do this more than once, regular, then you start to focus the eyes of the Rankin'." Eventually it was clear that he had arrived. "After that, now, the Rankin' would hug you, we call that 'Hands and Gloves', like cherish you, and make you feel like a real gang member."

Then, he says, the Rankin' might give you highly-prized Clarks shoes to wear, or an Arrow shirt, the most expensive around at that time. He would also start getting you to run errands for him, like going to call up one of his girlfriends or to buy take-away food, known as 'box food'. "You buy a box food and the Rankin' eat and then pass it to you. And the other Rankins then know they can't molest you, because you are liked by the main leader of the gang." There might be eight or nine Rankins of different importance in the gang, says Michael. "But the major Rankin' is the most intelligent person, the man who can go out there and speak on your behalf, stand up for you and demand the things that you need. That is the duty of a Rankin'. He looks after his boys."

At this stage he claims that he still didn't really know what he was up to, except that the gang seemed like the obvious place to be. The almost nostalgic mood he conjures is like the early part of the film Good Fellas, which describes a young man's induction into an American Mafia 'family'. These were the guys with respect in the community. These were the guys who got to wear all the nice clothes, had access to all the nice women and who had all the money. Here was camaraderie, here was a defined struc-ture to work your way up; here was a paternalistic boss-man who took care of your every need. A seductive picture, indeed.

It was a scene that began to change as the 1970's drew to a close, and as the knives and cutlasses were replaced by guns. "When 1978 come up, then they start to give you firearms. When they start give you gun, then you start to go out and stick-up business place, and stick up pay rolls."

After the first three of those jobs Michael was moved within the gang to become a 'right hand' to a Rankin'. This effectively meant being his body guard, going with him wherever he went and always carrying a gun for his protection. "Well, from Claudie Massop dead now and all dem other Rankins start dead, and the violence start to take a different turn." As always, it was the opposition's fault: "The Labourites dem now, dem start commit more serious offences towards the PNP, and force the PNP to start thinking evil like them. Because JLP supporter more evil than PNP, up 'til today. They are the most cunning set of people on the face of the earth in terms of doing violence," says Michael. "I'm not saying that PNP don't cruel, but JLP are the ones that implement that kind of system."

Guns had been around the political scene in Jamaica since the 1960's, he said, but had been concentrated in a few hands in a few areas. On the JLP side these had been Tivoli Gardens and Rema, for the PNP they were Concrete Jungle, Dunkirk and the genuine bandit country of Wareika Hill, a bush area east of Kingston which was a known hide-out for serious criminals. These more powerful groups and constituencies would support the weaker ones, occasionally loaning a gun to 'deal' with something, but according to Michael it had never previously got out of hand. Records show the steady growth of political violence. The first State of Emergency was declared in Jamaica in October 1966, in the run-up to the 1967 election, and it lasted for a month. A second was declared in June 1976 as that year's election approached, but this time it stayed in place for almost a year.

"In 1979, coming up to 1980, that's when you find yout', no matter how small, start to shoot man," says Michael. "The question at that time is: Kill or be Killed." By the time of the election, he says, "Jamaica was on fire."

For him and number of other up-and-coming gangstas, disillusionment with the Rankins and their form of social control was already setting in. After a robbery, all the money was supposed to go to the Rankin', and then he would give a bit back to the bwoys who had carried it out. They decided they were not getting enough and started to skim money off the top before giving it up. Also, they began to object to having to give their guns back after every job because this left them unarmed and exposed.

"When you shoot a man, you have to look for his friends coming back. So when a man disarm you, 'im a leave you fi' dead. At that time, the Rankin' never really cared about dem soldier comin' up" says Michael. "At the same time, you are young and you are under the influence of those men, an' if you don't do it dem cut you up, or dem beat you, or dem rape off your sister. That was the duty of Rankin' all over Jamaica. Dem used to do as dem like."

In the turmoil of 1980, these youths started to 'break out' from this influence. "I myself, me start to do a lot of things. Me out of control.

Uncontrollable," says Michael. "The more you grow and get more mature, the more you realise that no human being should have that control over another human being. So you want to break away from that. So in order to break away from that, the more things you do, the more respect you gain. That's why so many things happen in 1980. So me start doin' a lot of things. A lot of things. Me start shoot people. Shoot JLP."

He was shot himself, when JLP gunmen came to his mother's house, but was lucky that the wounds were not too serious. After recovering from that, his personal war was really declared. He claims to have killed eight people during the election period. "Me jus' get serious now. Me say, bwoy, things jus' get from bad to worse. It was a day and night thing. Every day." He attributes his survival to the fact that he never shot a policeman, concentrating his efforts on the enemy. "Me always said, bwoy the JLP trouble me, so the JLP me a deal with, 'cos dem ruin my life, run me out of school and blight my future and sabotage my freedom. So me start take revenge out 'a dem, an' start kill people. Start kill them. Seriously."

Kingston policeman on patrol

ON THE question of where all the guns came from, Michael is emphatic. "The politicians bring the guns," he says. "The politicians are the ones that are responsible for all this violence." While this is a freely expressed opinion in the ghettos, and a softly-spoken one in more polite circles of Jamaican society, for Michael it is knowledge. He says he has done the deals, delivered the guns and used them. What he reveals is an unholy alliance between power-hungry politicians and money hungry gangstas using a network of corrupt police and officials. He also describes the origins of the Jamaican drugs-and-guns culture that is still plaguing its society today, and which has made its impact felt as far away as Anchorage, Alaska and Birmingham, West Midlands.

"You see the Rankin' for the area, 'im a big man. When the MP [Member of Parliament] come in a the area, 'im no deal with no body but the Rankin'. Dem mek dem deal," he says. "The MP say: 'Wotcha, me gon' give you nine 9mm, me a' give you four M-16, and me a' give you four Uzi an' ting. Come up country, please.' So you see the Rankin', now him either call me or the next man who is serious like me wi' respect, and mek we accompany him to go pick up the firearms. Most of the time when you get guns, it is in the country." The MP would then pay large sums of party money for the Rankins trouble and to keep him and his lieutenants loyal. A typical payment would be around J$50,000.

So where did all this money come from? "They do fund-raising and that type of thing, but that is just one form of how they get money," says Michael. Mostly it came from crime, from armed robberies that the MP's helped to set up, and later still it came from drugs. "You have politicians who work in a bank, you have politicians who work in an insurance company. Politicians work all about. Dem organise for dem pay-roll to get tek. Either dem rob the bank of half-a-million, or dem come tek pay-roll of 400-odd thousand." The backbone of this operation for the PNP was the gang from Wareika Hill, otherwise known as Rockfort, wanted men or escaped criminals under the command of renowned gangstas Tony Brown and George Flash. Some of the money would be used to keep their babymothers and children if they were killed or arrested while robbing for the politicians, says Michael. The vast majority, however, would go through a special man in the party who was responsible for distributing this slush fund among the constituencies and using it to produce yet more money. "Most of that money there, it buy guns, an' it buy drugs and smuggle drugs. Money bring money," he says.

The vital common factor in both these trades was control over parts of Jamaica's ports system. It was as true for the PNP as for the JLP, which used its hegemony of Tivoli Gardens to ensure free passage for its selected cargoes through the 'wharves' that run along the area's southern flank. "The same politicians control immigration, dem control police, dem control customs. So ganja go through 'a foreign and money come in. The more money they make, so the guns come in," says Michael.

This description develops the over-simplistic picture that one side got its guns from Cuba and the other from the CIA. Once the drugs-and-guns cycle got underway, both sides were getting illegal weapons from America. Indeed the first recorded use of M-16s, the standard-issue US Army rifle, by the gangs was by the PNP in what became known as the Gold Street Massacre. In August 1980 four PNP Rankins, armed with their new toys and backed by youths with petrol bombs, opened fire on a JLP fund-raising dance, attended by many important Labourite Rankins. The attack left five dead and 13 wounded. It was set up, so the story goes, by a JLP Rankin' who had been bought out by PNP gangstas, illustrating that in Jamaican politics at that time it was money that had the loudest voice.

When a politician wanted to bring in guns, he did it through a senior customs contact at the port, said Michael. "The box or the barrel with the

guns in, it come to a special man at the wharf. He knows when it left and when it come. It would be labelled with his name on it, and when it arrives no one else can touch it. When he has cleared it 'im just call the boss man and say 'shipment coming up'." It would then be picked up and moved to a country area. Following a meeting at a local hotel between the MP concerned, the area Rankin' and other party officials, a date would be set for the collection. Michael has been on several of these missions.

It was at this point that the police became involved. "When you bring them in, you have police who is loyal to the party and you carry him as an escort," he says. Sometimes there was even an escort of police cars for the gun shipment on its way back to Kingston. The guns were carried in the boot of the MP's car and sometimes in the boot of one of the ganja barons' cars. "If you don't deal with the right people it would never have come through, because there were road blocks on the street. When you get to the road block the policeman just say, 'Me control this', and they just let through the string of cars. That way you can move unnoticed." The police involved went right to the top sections of the force, says Michael. Guns also came in on the ganja planes which flew to America from country airstrips and returned with weapons bought with the hard currency generated by drugs sales. Again, they would finish their journey to the ghetto under police escort. He even claims to have hidden-out in politicians' houses when the pressure from non-sympathetic police and from his JLP counterparts became too intense.

AS THE fighting intensified by the day in the run-up to the election, Michael's personal body count rose, his respect grew and he became wanted 'Dead or Alive'. Like so many other young guns, he was arrested, charged with multiple murder and left to rot in Gun Court. When Seaga won the election, Michael was convinced he would "hang fi' sure". With so much dirty washing on both sides lying about, however, and with a need to get the country back onto some kind of normal footing, the post-election atmosphere was officially one of amnesty rather than revenge. Some big-name embarrassments were spirited away to America, allegedly with help from their respective parties. Others, like Michael, were left to cool their heels in jail.

While conditions in Gun Court were notoriously savage, it was the safest place for him - as many lower-Rankin' gunmen who stayed on the streets or who escaped from prison were to find out. For unofficially, the problem of the gunmen was being solved by the police 'eradication squads', charged with sweeping the ghettos clean of trouble-makers without the need for messy show trials where political affiliations would undoubtedly come out into the open. As ever, it is impossible to peg the responsibility for these operations back to Seaga or any of his senior ministers. But it was carried through with all the vigour of an officially-sanctioned policy. Recently published figures show that during the five year period 1981 to 1985, 1,320 Jamaicans, mostly ghetto youths, were shot down during alleged armed confrontations with the police.

As with most trends in the violent story of Jamaican politics, the idea of using state power to systematically wipe out political opponents or embarrassments was not a new one but only a development in degree. The foundations of the eradication squads had been laid in 1978, in a PNP-inspired operation that became known as the Green Bay Massacre.

With the constant raising of the political temperature, and the increasing polarisation of the once mixed communities of central and west Kingston, the competition for work and scarce resources had grown steadily more intense. Dr Basil Wilson, the Jamaican provost of the John Jay College of Criminal Justice in New York, traced the process back to the 1960's in a thesis 'Surplus Labour and Political Violence in Jamaica. The Dialectics of Political Corruption 1966-1976.' His argument, simply put, is that as the urban population grew and more people were chasing the same work, the political parties used the promise of delivering this work to its supporters as a means of building influence. As there were not enough resources to go round, however, the other side of the coin was the growth of 'political tribalism' and the victimisation of political opponents.

Jamaica, says Wilson, had always suffered from a 'surplus of labour' in what was a small country with a largely agricultural economy. This had traditionally been kept in check by high death rates, but the increasing quality of post-war health care had led to a burgeoning population. In the 1950's the problem was alleviated by the large-scale migration of labour, first to Britain and then to the USA, but immigration controls introduced in both countries in the early 1960's gradually saw this safety valve being shut down. Increasing industrialisation within Jamaica took up some of the slack, but led to a migration from the country to the city and the creation of a new, large urban population centred on west Kingston and the adjoining parish of St Andrew which the politicians had to court.

The expansion of the economy also meant a huge increase in the size of the Government's budget, and so its ability to engage in public works projects. Politicians, in short, suddenly found themselves wielding a lot of economic power which was translated into power of patronage.

A dependency on the local MP then grew up, as the man who could deliver work and relative prosperity by the placing of public contracts within his constituency. "Unfortunately, these necessities of life can only be delivered if the respective party is triumphant at the polls," says Wilson. "Politics then becomes a life and death struggle, since it is known that the

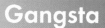

winner takes all and there are no spoils left for the vanquished."

As already mentioned, these developments took place alongside the increasing power of the urban gangs, and the resulting alliances between them and the local politicians created the pattern for political violence which first showed its developed face in the 1967 election and which has characterised country's political process ever since.

In reference to this period, Wilson re-iterates his point. "People in a desperate situation were literally fighting for their lives and the politics, especially in western Kingston and St Andrew, took on a violent complexion. The situation developed its own momentum to the extent that it became impossible to engage in political activity in that section of the urban complex without the support of the gangs."

By the late 1970's, Michael Manley's attempts at socialism had failed, the country was in a state of economic crisis and unemployment was again on the increase. It is into this context, as a microcosm of the broader picture, that the Green Bay massacre must be seen.

In late 1977 a PNP housing project in central Kingston was stalled because of fighting between the local gangs and the Rankins of the adjoining JLP area, known as Southside. Police in the area were unable or unwilling to do anything about the situation so a group of PNP officers from the Jamaica Defence Force decided to take matters into their own hands. This is one of the few occasions when elements of the JDF has been seen to take sides in the political conflict, and when the plan went wrong it severely tarnished the army's reputation for impartiality for years to come. The plotters were led by Major Ian Robinson, a small man with a big reputation for his abilities with a gun forged in many a shoot-out. His idea was simple, to lure Southside gang members with the promise of guns and security work and then wipe them out.

This dual bait proved to be potent, and there were no shortage of applicants when the word was put around Southside that men were needed for security work on the housing site and that the army would supply the weapons. These were eventually narrowed down to 10 men, all suspected JLP gang members, who met on the night of January 4, 1978. They were told that trucks would drive them to the army firing range at Green Bay, west of Kingston where their guns would be issued. On arrival they were led down to targets set up on the beach, and hidden machine guns opened up. Five of the men were killed immediately.

The other five, while wounded, escaped in the darkness and managed to get into police hands before army search parties were able to find them and finish them off. Their version of what had happened destroyed the army's cover story - that a group of soldiers, at the range for target practice, had been attacked and fired back in self defence. The inquest into the five deaths returned a verdict of unlawful killing but no-one was ever prosecuted and the plotters were spirited off abroad. Again, the level of knowledge and participation on the part of the PNP government was never established.

When news of the massacre hit the streets the day after, however, it sparked an immediate reaction from the gangs who were convinced that a political finger had ultimately been on the trigger. That reaction was not an escalation of violence, as might have been expected, but an outbreak of peace between the two sides, both shocked that the State's guns had been so overtly turned against them. The guns of the ghetto, for a few months at least, fell silent. The peace movement culminated in a 'One Love' concert at the National Stadium in Kingston in April 1978 when Bob Marley managed to get both Manley and Seaga on stage to join hands in a symbol of reconciliation, but the euphoria was to be short-lived. Police used the cease-fire to settle some old scores, and some dons and politicians saw in it a threat to their positions of influence. Slowly at first but then with gathering momentum, the killing resumed.

Dreams of lasting harmony were finally cut down the following February when Claudie Massop, the Tivoli don who had been instrumental in setting up the peace movement, died in a hail of police gunfire. In what is generally regarded as a politically-motivated murder, his body was found to have more than 50 bullets in it. The way was then clear for Jim Brown to take command of the Tivoli battalions and the scene was set for the battles of the 1980 election campaign.

THE LESSONS of 1978, however, were not lost on Michael and the new generation of gunmen that the election produced. Given the time in jail to consider their position, to mix with the opposition and reflect on how their Rankins and political masters had deserted them, they forged a new kind of radicalism. It hit the streets of Kingston's ghettos when the bulging prisons started to release their young charges around 1981-82.

"Use we and refuse we," is the phrase Michael uses to summarise the sense of grievance. It describes how the politicians and the Rankins who carried out their bidding where happy to use the youth when it served their purposes, but then had washed their hands of the young gangstas once they had been taken by the police, with MPs denouncing them as 'terrorists' and leaving them to rot in prison.

Disillusionment with the Rankins hold on money was another factor. "When the MP deal with the Rankin' and give him some money, the money was fi' share up in the community - amongst the gang man dem, the elderly and the disabled people - people that cast dem vote for the PNP," says Michael, "More than three quarter of them people they don't get a cent,

never get a cent yet, never, never." Right-hand men such as himself might get the odd thousand and the fryers even smaller scraps but most of the money was going straight into the Rankins' pockets.

"That is why after 1980 so many of the youth all over Jamaica turn round and start kill Rankin', use back the same gun wa' they give you and shoot dem down back," says Michael, "Because they use we, and refuse we."

Some, as he says, were shot, others were just chased out of the areas to run off to the country or abroad, and some sought refuge in the remaining strongholds of established power that were well enough organised to resist this minor revolution. In Tivoli, Jim Brown's authority remained unchallenged as did that of the major Rankins in Concrete Jungle and Rema. Together with the activities of the eradication squads, however, it was enough to shake the old order and, briefly, provide another opportunity for peace. Even the MPs of some areas were given short shrift and told they would receive no more support until money was provided to build better housing and facilities.

When the smoke cleared, Michael found himself as the new man of authority in his area. He was then 22 years old. "It's now 1982, and the first thing me go do then was to make peace with the JLP dem." he says. "We just call a peace truce and say 'Whatcha, we are black people and we young an' we no have nothing, we are poor people. Let us put the violence aside and put hands and heart together and see if we can build back the community like it was in the 1960's'." It was a brave attempt, but without the support of the big guns doomed to failure. It ended in Michael's area less than a year later, in traditional style. He was shot again by a Labourite gunman, and the war re-started.

THE WAR now, however, was being played by different rules. Cynicism about the politicians and their system had become deep-rooted, so that the levels of dependency between the ghetto communities and their MPs would never be the same again. Following the exodus of gunmen to Miami and New York after the 1980 election, the gangs also had their own contacts abroad with which they could set up their own drugs operations and import their own guns. At its most basic, guns supplied by politicians were used to steal weapons from security men or the police, giving the gangs another means of access to an armoury of their own, out of political control. As the gangs still held sway in the ghettos, however, their support was vital to any politician needing votes from that area. To some extent, then, the relationship of dependency was reversed.

In this new environment, even the terminology changed. Whereas the posses and the early gunfighters had taken their inspiration and many of their names from the classic Westerns, now it was Mafia movies that provided new role models. Rankins became 'Dons', 'right-hand men' gained the more straightforward title of 'hit-men' and fryers became 'foot soldiers'. "Jamaicans in their head are the Mafia," says Michael. "They adopt some of the Mafia style and then carry it one step further ahead." It is a claim that meets with scepticism in the 'disorganised-organised crime' school of law enforcement officers, but it is none-the-less an interesting insight into gangsta psychology.

Rigid divisions between areas of different political colours, at least at the highest levels, were also eroded. Aside from political cant, everything in the end was reduced to taking care of business, and this has bred some strange allies. Michael claims that the JLP's Jim Brown at one time ordered him to be killed because he was becoming too powerful as a PNP leader but that before Brown himself died the two had become firm friends. "Jim Brown, 'im love me like cooked food," he says.

It was in this new environment that Michael became a Don man, and from that position comes his claimed knowledge of the later machinations of 'poli-tricks'. The central relationship in the game is that between the MP and the local don.

"The first duty of an MP in any garrison constituency is to communicate with the most respected man inside that community. He has to try and impress that individual to the best of his ability so that in turn he can get his work done," said Michael. He stresses that an MP will only work with this one man, with whom a relationship of trust must be built, so that the politician can distance himself from what is done on his behalf and keep himself and his party out of trouble. Most importantly, this must be a man who can keep his mouth shut.

The pact is sealed with money paid to the Don from a personal budget set up by the MP for the constituency. This in turn would be financed partly from party funds and partly from the MP's own business interests, be they legitimate trade or drugs smuggling. In either case, the aim would be to generate political support, greater leverage and more money.

"Most of the MPs dem, they are in politics for personal benefits, personal interests - money," says Michael, "We call them opportunists waiting to get an opportunity."

Once this deal is underway the MP will start to ask the Don for favours. This would initially be to organise and mobilise the local youth to boost his own respect in the constituency to protect his power base from rivals. The Don would also be required to set rules and regulations to ensure a level of order in the area. "When the MP and the Don sit down they discuss all types of things," said Michael. "If the MP has a violent constituency, you have violent reasoning. Them start to find ways and means how to combat against the opposition. That mean them build an armed force."

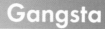

As already explained, this would involve the MP utilising foreign and local contacts to facilitate a shipment of arms and the arrangements for its transfer to the constituency. The Don would then be responsible for distributing the weapons, making sure they get into the right hands. If one of his men were to subsequently step out of line, it would also be up to him to take care of it.

"Take for example the man that shoot the police which an MP definitely would not support. After the MP deal with the Don, the Don would get that man, kill him and tag him and throw him out of the area," said Michael. To 'tag' someone is to put a notice on their chest or round their neck explaining why it was done. "It would say, 'This is the man that killed constable so-and-so,' and when the police arrive and find it they say 'Cha, long time fi' dead 'cos 'im do that. Foul play.' The case is closed, and nobody looks for the man that killed that man. Nobody can know who done that, only the Don knows, an' once it is carried out the MP don't want to know any more about it."

Where situations are more serious, threatening the whole smooth running of the constituency, the MP would become personally involved in issuing orders. This leads to one of Michael's more startling revelations: "Me deal with both JLP and PNP MPs," he said, explaining just how far the old battle lines can bend when it comes to a matter of expediency.

If a Don were lose control of his area, to the extent that crime levels within it were becoming an embarrassment for the MP, he would seek help from outside. Under normal circumstances he would go to another MP from the same party, who in turn would task his Don to go and sort things out. This would be a 'bigger Don' who carried respect beyond his own area, who would consult with the local Don man and deploy some of his own soldiers to help restore order.

"Say an MP in Spanish Town has a problem, it could be raping gwan too much and 'im want it cut out. The business people of the area might get robbed too much and 'im want it cut out. It's out of control and his own Don can't sort it out. He goes to his friend, another MP, who say 'Don' worry, my boy will talk to him'," explained Michael. It's a job he has been given on a number of occasions, he said.

"So when I arrive, now I call a meeting, they call it a board of directors meeting. We sit round a table, and if a man is to be disarmed or dead, it will come from that meeting. Then his soldiers and mine will combine together and deal with it," he said.

Throughout, the delicate dance of giving mutual respect must be maintained. The Don who is receiving help must not be seen to lose too much face or this would further destabilise the community. He must be seen to have asked for this support, so that some of the greater respect of the 'bigger man' rubs off on him and bolsters rather than undermines his position.

This is of utmost importance to the MP himself, for reasons that underline the nature of his revised relationship with the constituency Don. Again, it is all taking care of business. "Why the MP hold onto the Don man is that 'im can't afford to lose the Don man, because if the MP lose the Don man he lose the constituency. Remember me a' tell you that," said Michael.

In extreme situations, this can even mean a JLP Don being brought into a PNP area or vice versa. "It gwan, it happen. I myself have been out of town to mobilise the yout' in a JLP constituency. Everybody a' run wild so they need a man to get everybody together. Me 'a deal with both PNP and JLP together, because them live as one you know." said Michael. The logic is always the same, the maintenance of the status quo, of the system so that business can continue as normal. "This is really poli-tricks, but the only person who benefits is the MP who gets the constituency he wants."

The cross-party links do not stop there. Deals are also done between apparently opposing Dons if they feel their position is being threatened, whereby they would bring pressure to bear on their respective parties to cut out trouble in an area in order to keep their show on the road.

Most cynically of all, this shows itself in instances of 'Foul Play', already alluded to. At its simplest, this just means a gang killing but some variations on the theme could teach the Borgias a lesson or two. "The wickedest one, now - say a man out there disrespect me an' you and the man fi' dead, see? I jus' send you go kill 'im, and when you kill 'im now I jus' lick off back a' your head, same place. The gun you use to kill 'im I jus' leave it by you, so when the police come and see the gun that was used for the murder they jus' announce it as 'Foul Play' and it done. That mean no investigation," explained Michael.

If you can't be seen to be killing someone from your own side, help can always be brought in from a friendly neighbouring JLP Don who would sacrifice one of his own men for the sake of the deal. "You import someone from the JLP, an' after you kill back 'im. Foul play. And the gun used to kill your friend, you jus' make sure you put it 'pon the JLP when the police come. They jus' say it's a shoot-out, simple." The big question remains that, if all this co-operation is going on, how can a Don rally his troops against the 'enemy' when warfare breaks out? How can the opposition be painted as evil opposition if such deals are regularly being done. The answer, according to Michael, is equally simple. "Most men are dunce. They don' know what is going on. They have no understanding."

RELATIONS between Dons in some of the most notorious garrison constituencies can be very close, although they are not about to weaken

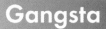

the siege mentality on which their power rests by telling everybody about it. Michael was no exception, he would meet regularly with the JLP Don from a neighbouring area. "Nobody don' know say that me an' him sit down and drink; nobody don' know say that when JLP in power he mek contract reach me. Nobody don' know that," he said. "But at the same time me, I tell my brethren 'Kill JLP', and he tell JLP dem 'Kill PNP'."

To the next obvious question of why this should happen, particularly the allocation of precious government contracts to the 'enemy', he answers that it is all about keeping the system going. Come the next election and a change in power, he would expect to do the same thing to prevent all-out war and total breakdown of the communities. Such a move would normally be approved by the MP's concerned. It is also about maintaining each other's power in a balance - if a Don is seen as the principle provider for an area, he must be seen to be providing something otherwise there will be a challenge and further disruption. "You see the Dons have a mutual understanding more than the foot-soldier, who don' know what's going on at the top."

We're back, as ever, to poli-tricks. "I tell you this, it is a very trickified game, an' if you don' know, you jus' don' know. A whole heap a' yout' who come up in badness between PNP and JLP, dem no really understand the significance of politics because dem don' reach to those heights," said Michael. "The reason why me know is because me was a player in the field, me come from foot-soldier until me tek over, that's why me know the game."

It is a game he eventually grew tired of, he says, with its constant threat of death or violence. He saw many friends shot down or stabbed to death beside him, and after a second stint in prison he decided that enough was enough and went to Britain to try and lead a normal life. He was speaking out, he said, because he wanted things to change in Jamaica. "If it continues so, yout' are jus' gwan be dead an' dead an' dead an' dead, and me want it to stop. Me wan' de yout' dem to open their eyes."

He quotes from a song by ragga star Half Pint: "Due to political fiction, man an' man gone in different segregation." Politicians banned the record from the Jamaican airwaves, he said, because it spoke too close to the truth.

MICHAEL is a confusing man. He speaks of the need for change and honesty, yet relates with obvious pride his ability to navigate the dark and dangerous waters of Jamaican poli-tricks and survive in it for so long. He talks of God and high principles, yet shows little or no remorse for his long list of killings. He paints himself as a much-loved protector of his community, and then in the same breath speaks with contempt about the lack of intelligence among most of his people. But then he comes from a bewildering world of mirrors where intrigue and treachery are a daily fact of life and where few things, except death, are quite what they seem.

Even at the height of his powers, he says, he could trust no-one. Everything was a deal, a balance, a calculation of risks. In one shoot-out his automatic pistol jammed and let him down. After that he always carried a revolver for back-up.

Vigilance cannot be relaxed for a moment. "Any time you trust a man, you're dead," he says. If you set up the situation properly, however, there are people in which you can have confidence. "Trust and confidence, it's two different things. It's two different things, star."

In his case these people were his right-hands, "the cruellest set a' hit man" who would literally watch over him day and night. Always one would sit outside his door at night, waking him at regular intervals to make sure he wasn't sleeping too deeply. "In Jamaica, every man 'im awake at four o' clock, every single man. Can't sleep," he says, echoing the words of Robbie, across the political divide. "If you're asleep in your bed at nine 'o clock, you're a dead man."

These bodyguards were men of proven loyalty, many of whom he had known since they were children and who he "treat like my son". But the numbers allowed to carry guns at any time were strictly limited. "The more gun you have, the more men you have amongst you, 'cos men follow gun. Me can confident two or three or four, but me can't confident the rest of man dem," says Michael. "So, say my loyalists consist of 12, out of them I select five who at all times oversee everything."

Even these are not above suspicion: "Like Saddam Hussein in Iraq, 'im have police over police over police, so me have operate. So my second, he have a man over him, who watch 'im. And the man who watch my second, he have a man over 'im," he says. "So down the line me have man who watch man who watch man, so at all time me always safe."

If this all sounds cold and calculating, it is what you need to stay alive, and Michael is the proof of his own pudding in that he is around to tell the tale. 'Cold' is yet another of those words that takes on new menace when spoken by the gangsta. It refers not just to the cool intelligence needed to stay one jump ahead but also to the vital attribute of a successful killer. The man who comes up and tells you that he wants to kill you is not a problem, says Michael, and tells stories of how he has 'psyched out' would-be assassins even though he wasn't armed at the time. This is not, after all, the Wild West of the movies with neat, honourable confrontations face-to-face in the street. The man who will get you is the 'cold' man who will "befriend you and fuck you", says Michael. Or it is the one you never see.

One night, in a corner of a crowded pub, he gives a demonstration. His animated face is instantly changed to the dull-eyed expression of a man

who has had a toke too much ganja, as he shuffles, head down, hood up, hands in pocket, across the room. Right up close, a hand whips out and a finger is extended towards my head. 'Bang'. That, says Michael, is 'cold'. That is how you do it. Pun intended, it is chillingly real.

Coldness and intelligence, then, are what you need to make it as a gangsta and, of the two, the latter is the more important. Too many have died, he says, because they never use 'this', indicating his head. "In criminality, if you na use this, yous a dead fucking dog," he explains. "If you do something, do it for a reason. Every'ting you do." Having opened his eyes and seen the waste and futility of it all, he has given up his Don's life. The only people he would fight now, he says, are the politicians.

Ultimately, though, he is unrepentant. "Me tell you again - an' I'm proud to say this you know - the bad bwoy that me lick down, me glad me lick dem down, because it was a kill or be killed, an' me no hurt innocent people," he says. "They say me gun bwoy, but let me tell you something, me don' like gun bwoy, me no like chucky, me no like people who brutalise people an' take advantage of people. That's why me no like politicians."

CONDEMNATION of Jamaica's political leadership and its role in the growth and maintenance of the gang structure, is not confined to the street or the ghetto. While many of Kingston's 'up-town' elite pretend or wish that the problems do not really exist, a few brave voices have constantly probed the relationship between the politicians and the Dons, and called for concerted action to tackle it. They have faced heavy criticism for their efforts, up to and including libel action and death threats. Their arguments, however, add intellectual weight to Michael's more colourful, first-hand account.

One such voice was Carl Stone, Professor of Political Sociology at the University of the West Indies situated at Mona just outside Kingston. Until his death in 1993, following a long illness, he was Jamaica's best known and most widely respected academic. He used a weekly column in The Gleaner to launch frequent attacks on political cant and hypocrisy and to issue dire warnings about the consequences of allowing the gangs to maintain or increase their grip on society.

A particularly outspoken column came in March 1992, during the warfare that erupted following the deaths of Jah T and Jim Brown, in which he predicted that the country was on the road to Colombian-style anarchy. It is worth quoting at some length.

"Jamaica is on the verge of developing a vicious level of narco-terrorism that could easily mature into the kind of Colombian situation where drug gangs operate as a state within a state and can dictate terms to governments, communities and whole societies. If we fail to take decisive action to wipe out or diminish the power of these gangs, that is where we are heading," said Stone.

Interestingly, he does not mention the influence of deportees on the problem. Instead, he cites the relationship between the gangs and national politicians as the most important link in the way that Jamaican gangs have developed.

"Similar gangs exist all over the world without any connection with party politics. They are simply creatures of social alienation, inner city poverty, the disintegration of family life and organised community life, lack of opportunity among the poorer classes and social doctrines that convince some poor people that their poverty is due to social injustice. In these circumstances violence is developed as a means by which the aggressive among the poor seek recognition, power and standing in the community," he said.

"What is different about Jamaica is simply that the gangs have been emboldened and empowered over the years by their connections with top political organisations that run the country."

The growing threat from the gangs, however, came from the fact that they were no longer under the control of even the most powerful politicians. Echoing the power-shift described by Michael, he said that the gangs had become stronger while the grass roots political organisation of both the JLP and the PNP in the inner city areas had become weaker. The idea that Manley or Seaga could now solve the problem overnight was dismissed as "Absolute rubbish".

National leaders in the fields of business, church, the professions and politics have preferred to pretend that no real problem exists, he said, while condemning people like himself who drew attention to it as being alarmist. He backs up this argument with a sad picture of the state of the country and a litany of inaction.

"When guns are fired in the precincts of a court, or a man is chased into a school office and shot in broad daylight, or school teachers' lives are threatened by bad boys for trying to maintain discipline, or managers are shot or threatened for disciplining workers or exposing corruption, or downtown commerce is disrupted for weeks after an election because JLP gunmen are angry with rural people for voting out Mr Seaga, nobody takes these issues seriously as signs of our drift towards anarchy, absolute disrespect for authority and a growing motivation by a few to intimidate the majority of us at gun point. We simply issue words of condemnation but do nothing decisive to deal with the root causes."

The responsibility, finally, lay with the politicians and the implications of this could hardly be wider, according to Stone. "The issue sharply brings to the fore the hypocrisy and paralysis of will at the level of national lead-

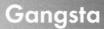

ership which has so far impaired our capacity as a country to solve problems."

The words are important in the context of this book because they come from a prominent Jamaican - not from a 'bad bwoy', not from 'racist' British police, and not from a white outsider such as myself. Carl Stone and dispassionate critics like him are not so easy to dismiss. When I interviewed him shortly after this column appeared he said that he had been taking heavy criticism for 20 years for voicing such views, by people who felt he should not be attacking the politicians so hard. "You have to knock them, you have to knock them," he said. "After a while the public develops a respect for your position because the fact of the matter is that ninety-odd per cent of the Jamaican people want peace, they don't want any violence so they are with you."

His prognosis at that time, however, was not optimistic. Given the involvement of certain sections of the police force in the drugs trade, their inability to penetrate the ghetto areas (itself in part due to the brutality they had traditionally meted out to poor people) and the overt political support that was given to the Dons in some of these areas, he could only see the problem expanding. Within reach of every middle class area in Kingston there was a little ghetto, and the gangs had by then established very strong connections with those communities - outside the established garrison constituencies. The Dons influence had also spread to towns outside Kingston like Spanish Town and May Pen, both east of the capital.

"It's a whole lifestyle, it's a whole set of values, it's a whole macho thing which is attractive to the males, and they're really caught up in it," he said. Neither the politicians nor the police were capable of handling it.

Quite apart from the political influence on the situation, he saw this growth as being a product of the recent social history of the country which had seen its economy stagnate and even shrink after early optimism in the years following independence. Again, his analysis echoes the experience of Michael and the other ghetto youths. "Jamaicans are strivers, they are very ambitious people, and in the past there were opportunities available through education to move up the ladder. With the problems of the economy over the past 20 years, opportunities via education are almost zero. Places where you could move up with education to get jobs are shrinking, like the public sector," he said "What I think is happening, quite simply, is that these drives for upward social mobility are blocked and people are finding alternative avenues." Even more simply and more controversially, he added: "We are an aggressive people."

The decisive Jamaican factor explaining the aspirant aggression is the country's long exposure to guns. "We've been into guns for 20 years," said Stone, using again his favourite time-frame. "Right now if I wanted to I could go and hire an AK47 or an M-16 for about J$1,000 a night [around £25 at the time], I could find somebody who would hire me one. We're at that level. You can pay someone a couple of thousand dollars to shoot anybody. That is where we are, and the rest of the Caribbean is way, way behind us, they haven't got there yet."

THIS IS serious stuff and Carl Stone was a very serious man. Curiously, however, much of his conversation was punctuated by chuckles and even the odd belly laugh. It is a common occurrence. Outside formal statements from some of the country's many church leaders, you don't find a lot of hand-wringing angst among Jamaican people when discussing their predicament. Statements like, "We are an aggressive/violent people," are also voiced often, if quietly, most commonly accompanied by an open-handed shrug of mock contrition and a wolfish grin. In part, no doubt, this is trench humour. People cannot function under an almost constant threat of violence by being timid, and an obvious relief is to laugh about it. But there is also, apparently, an element of pride in this idea, of the sort you might get from a military unit with a reputation for ferocity and high losses or, in a less extreme way, from old industrial areas of Britain with a reputation for being 'hard'.

Jamaicans pride themselves on being different, on being extraordinary, on making an impact on the world. At one time this showed itself in a willingness to go 'a' foreign' and establish a reputation for fierce hard work in pursuit of a better life. If changed circumstances means that this is now in part expressed through the gunmen, then at least it shows the country is not just rolling over and lying down in the face of adversity and injustice. These are very broad brush strokes, and as such fraught with the same dangers as any attempt at commenting on 'national characteristics' of any country. It is by no means the whole story. But again, as they are views expressed by Jamaicans themselves, they deserve recording as a contribution to understanding the wider picture.

The difference between Jamaica and the rest of the Caribbean, and pride in that, was what Stone was alluding to in his comment about the other countries being 'way, way behind us' over the question of guns. He was being ironic but for many this is an important part of the national identity. People from other Caribbean countries are dismissively referred to as 'small islanders' (pronounced 'smaaaaaall' to emphasise the sneer), while it is a commonplace, and another source of pride, that these people hate Jamaicans right back. I once asked a very professional, aspirant, church-going young woman about the cause of this antagonism towards her country. "Jealousy," was her sharp reply, stressing the importance of Jamaica in such areas as athletics and popular music. "Who else has got

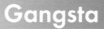

Merle Ottey? Who else has got reggae music?" she asked. "Who else has got the posses?"

For Stone the important connection was not that between Jamaica and the other islands, but the very close ties between Jamaica and north America. Migrant workers have been going to the USA and Canada since before the last war, doing everything from cutting sugar cane in the fields of Florida to working in the factories of the northern industrial belt, to attending college and taking up positions as lawyers and teachers or starting their own businesses there. On this high level of activity was the Jamaican reputation for hard work founded, often to the annoyance of sections of the local population. It also led to the establishment of large Jamaican communities, initially in Miami, New York and Toronto, but then with offshoots as far afield as Kansas City, Texas and Anchorage, Alaska.

Eventually, this has led to more than hard currency being exported back to Jamaica. "That strong connection with north America and the ghetto culture feeds back into our system," said Stone. "The value system and the whole kind of aggression we have is pretty similar to what exists in black America - in Detroit and Washington and so on. It's a similar kind of phenomenon, a similar syndrome of attitudes - of just tremendous anger and despair, and it explodes on itself, you see."

This connection was also a contributory factor in the failure of the police and other agencies to catch the gangs and limit their operations. "What we have is not a Jamaican problem or a US problem. We have a regional problem," he said. "Therefore there is a need for the law enforcement guys to share information and develop common strategies but that is not happening. It is only the gangs that are regionally linked and so they get away with it every time."

Not counting the occasional explosion of warfare, such as the one going on at the time, Stone said that the concentration of gangs on the drugs trade had in fact led to a reduction in certain categories of extreme violence. The big gun battles associated with bank robberies and pay-roll hold-ups, as described by Michael, were largely a thing of the past. "This is the paradox: the drug thing has really pacified the gangs because they are living well. There is relative peace," he said.

But this was no cause for complacency. "They have enormous caches of weapons, heavy weapons," he said. "I think that they have the capacity to really shut down Jamaica. We're playing with fire. We're playing with fire, man, we're playing with fire."

Chapter Seven

THE POSSES

ANOTHER cop car, another country, another climate. I am huddled in the back of an NYPD (New York Police Department) cruiser on a Friday night patrol of the 67th Precinct in Brooklyn, shivering. It is January, the famous New York winter is finally showing its teeth and we are hours away from the biggest snow dump of the year.

The weather might be a million miles away from the Caribbean, but this area of East Flatbush and Crown Heights is known by local law enforcement officers as 'Little Kingston'. This is where some of the ghetto's most serious gunmen moved next. It is one of the main birthplaces of the 'Posses', the name gangstas took from Western movies to describe their gunslinging activities in America.

These streets, and those of the adjacent 77th Precinct, were the stamping ground for Jamaican criminals who helped to re-write the already bloody American book on gang warfare and violence. They are also one of the places where crack was first 'cooked' and distributed to the desperate urban poor of surrounding apartment blocks and public housing projects. There are no plaques to commemorate the achievements of these pioneers of badness, but their legacy lives on.

It lives on in the eyes of dealers, hunched inside overcoats in doorways with ski masks hiding the rest of their faces. It lives in the thumping beat from the reggae music store, its sounds doing something to warm yet another set of crack peddlers outside, and it lives in the acrid stale-urine smell of the abandoned crack house. Most of all, perhaps, it lives in the bullet holes which pepper a local school sign. 'Children Crossing', says the warning underneath.

"THIS AIN'T actually the worst part of New York by any means," says Officer (pronounced "Awe-fficer") Jim Klewicki, cheerfully. He has been assigned to show me around the 67 (pronounced as quick-fire 'Six Seven', not 'sixty seven') with his partner, Officer Desmond Egan, who does the driving. Klewicki does most of the talking. "As you can see a lot of the property around here looks fine. Very respectable. But there's a lot of guns, a helluva lot of shooting," he says.

The 67 measures about two miles long by about a mile wide, and in that area there were more than 60 murders the previous year - mostly from shooting. It might not be the worst, but it is in the top five.

Klewicki is 'Polish', medium-height, thinning on top and an experienced street cop. He has a classic stiff-legged gait, weighed down by the equip-

ment on his belt, and a laconic turn of phrase. Egan is 'Irish', young and enthusiastic. "Here we go. Real time," he says with undisguised excitement as we take off, siren screaming, on a 'gun run' (suspected sighting of a gunman). They are both born-and-bred Brooklyn, and they could have come from Central Casting. They're great.

Klewicki says he is aware of the history of Jamaican bad bwoys in the area, but the details are for people higher up the chain of command. "All that stuff is handled by the detectives and the Feds. We're just patrolmen, the lowest of the low," is one of his most frequent, self-effacing refrains. "Am I supposed to be telling you all this?" is another.

Certainly, he is not racially discriminating as he goes about his work. In the course of the night we visit a Dominican 'numbers' joint, where the illegal gamblers gather behind a phoney shop front, and a Trinidadian 'weed' house, employing a similar technique, as well as staring from the wrong side of a two-way mirror protecting a Jamaican ganja spot. He hammers on the door with a metal slide-hole in the middle where money is passed in and drugs are passed out, but no one seems to be there.

We also attend a dispute in an apartment block where a Jamaican neighbour has attacked someone's door with a baseball bat. The dents are clearly visible in the metal plate protecting the outside of the door. The alleged - female - perpetrator ('perp') doesn't want to answer her door either.

We sit under the shot-up school sign watching the comings and goings at a crack house across the street. Nobody enquires after the nationality of the dealers who melt away into the darkness within minutes of spotting us. Indeed, no questions of any sort are asked, there is little point. Neither are any arrests made all night, it is just not possible.

Rules of evidence and arrest are so tight in New York that nothing we saw would have stood up in court. Our entries into the various illegal premises were all done without warrants and so anything we did see there would be inadmissible. We were just looking around. To close down one of these places would have required covert surveillance to identify suspects and then a series of 'buys' by undercover cops before the necessary warrant could be obtained. It is very different from Kingston.

"OK, put your hands on the counter, PUT YOUR HANDS ON THE COUNTER. OK, thank you," says Klewicki as we stroll into the numbers joint. "OK, everybody take it easy. We're not looking for you tonight. OK, relax. We're not looking for you tonight, sir. Thank you." He takes a numbers ticket from the man in the booth and hands it to me, as a souvenir.

Back at the station house for a quick break, we run into one of the undercover narcotics teams who have just completed an operation. The sergeant produces a vial of crack, containing four inoffensive- looking 'rocks'. This is what all the fuss is about. The other proceeds of his night's work are behind the bars of the 'pen', in one corner of the main desk area.

I absent-mindedly light a cigarette to help me warm up, forgetting for a moment that smoking is banned in all of New York's public buildings. "Aw, what the heck," says one of the officers behind the desk. "It's late and we don't get many visitors at the 67."

"Gi' mi a smoke, man. Gi' mi a smoke," says a voice from the pen. It is unmistakably Jamaican. Privileges, however, do not seem to extend to his kind of visitor.

"Be safe out there, now," says the desk sergeant, as we go off again in our bullet-proof vests. It is the standard NYPD farewell.

In fact the guys never have to draw their weapons. But the safety clips on their holsters do come off once when we visit another crack house, located in another dilapidated apartment block. There is a swift rush up the final flight of stairs and the door goes in. The place is empty. The smell has already been described and there is a stained mattress in one room, little else. Klewicki shows me the missing spy-hole in the apartment door. Sometimes people would come in to smoke their rocks, other times they would buy 'deals' through this hole from an armed man sitting behind it.

Later we are on the roof of a public housing project, watching other deals go down at ground level, among dim figures in a dark door-way. "We sometimes do surveillance from roofs like this, but you can see the problem," says Klewicki. It would be impossible to identify anybody in that gloom. "There used to be lights but they got wise and shot them out." I query him. "You know, shot out. Like with guns."

EARLIER that week I had visited the detective's room at the 67 where officers were investigating a different kind of shooting. Three young people had been killed at Legends night-club, a local Jamaican hot-spot, the previous weekend. The incident had taken place at 3am, and the youngest victim was a 15-year-old girl. Political pressure was clearly being applied to get a quick result and the detectives had been working round the clock to try and oblige.

The squad room looked like one from any TV cop show you'd like to mention, only worse. It was reached up a narrow set of concrete stairs and old wooden desks were clustered in the middle or pushed against the walls, with scarcely enough room to squeeze between them. Detectives were eating lunch at their desks, and drinking lots of coffee (pronounced cquaw-fee). Reports were being written-up on venerable typewriters, no high-tech here.

"We don't have your case, what can I tell you?" shouted a frazzled officer down the phone. Nobody was in much of a mood to talk.

One homicide detective, with a lot of years on the scene, was finally provoked into response by an inane question about his opinion of Jamaican posse members. "What do I think about those Jamaicans? I think they're no fucking good," he said. "They're wild, they're uncontrollable and they don't care who they shoot at. If one of those guys draws his gun, he's going to empty the magazine, no matter who is standing around or anything."

IT IS an image and a reputation that has been ingrained on the collective mind of American law enforcement agencies for years. It was, however, a long time coming.

Jamaican gangstas had been setting up serious operations in the USA from the mid-1970's when the ganja-for-guns trade, as described by Michael, was taking off and the atmosphere of political tension was building at home. An early indication of what was to come occurred in 1977 at what became known as the Palm Sunday Massacre. In a spill-over of violence from the previous year's election, four PNP men from the emergent Spanglers posse were found handcuffed together and shot in the head. Their murderers were said to come from Rema.

Even before that there had been a 'healthy' market in America for Jamaican ganja. Basil Wilson, who has watched the phenomenon grow for more than 15 years, sets the date for Jamaican drugs involvement in New York as far back as 1968, in the aftermath of the country's first real political violence during the 1967 Jamaican election. "In America, this was the time of protests over the Vietnam war and the whole '60's thing. There was a demand for drugs, mainly ganja, and the Jamaicans moved into the market as entrepreneurs," says Wilson.

Originally this involved linking up with drugs coming in from Mexico, but then the trend was to increasingly import 'home grown' ganja from Jamaica in order to boost profits. So evolved a largely self-contained drugs importation and distribution system with every stage of the process, right down to street sales, being handled by Jamaican nationals. This differed from most other ethnic-based drugs operations at the time which would concentrate either on the import, wholesale distribution or on 'retail' aspects of the trade.

The process was facilitated by the large existing Jamaican population, particularly in New York and Miami, which had been swelled since the 1950's by ambitious, legal immigrants from the island. Into these established communities, in places like Flatbush and Crown Heights, Queen's and the Bronx, the bad bwoy could easily blend and drop from view. A sad aspect of this story, not often reported, is that the only traditional animosity towards the existing Jamaican community was because its members were too hard working. A standing joke in the 1970's was that a Jamaican would take as many jobs as necessary in order to work 24 hours a day and improve his lot. It was an image and a version of the American Dream that was to be soured by the later influx of largely illegal migrants.

As the drugs market developed in the late 1970's and early-to-mid 1980's, first into dealing powder cocaine and ultimately into crack, the established network was to give the Jamaican dealers a commercial edge over their rivals. As a closed system, it also helped to hide them from the attentions of the US law enforcement agencies. Jamaican dealers were known about, but during this period the police and others called them 'Rastas', and saw them as small scale dealers in marijuana and so relatively harmless. "It was a very low law enforcement priority," said one officer. Respect for the established, law-abiding Jamaican community was also a factor. Attention was by then being concentrated on Cuban and Colombian cocaine gangs who were thought to be far more dangerous. It was to be a costly mistake.

The big change was brought about by the arrival of hardened political gunmen in large numbers - the fall-out from the 'civil war' of 1980. The refugees came from both JLP and PNP camps, the latter an embarrassment to Seaga's new government, the former in fear of their lives from the eradication squads. The ease with which they made the move, despite stringent US immigration laws, suggests some element of political involvement from both sides in the provision of acceptable paper work. In any case, none of these people saw working 24 hours a day as the way ahead. They had seen what the power of the gun could bring and set about applying this lesson with ruthless efficiency.

Elements from each group had a presence in both cities and trade between the two was brisk. As a rule of thumb, however, it can be said that the process began with JLP affiliates from Tivoli setting up shop in Miami as what was to become the Shower Posse. PNP gunmen from central Kingston, who became known as the Spanglers, based their operation in New York. The era of the posses was born but it was to be years before the American authorities fully woke up to what was going on. By the time they did, a loose network of terror had spread itself across much of the USA.

OFFICERS from the Immigration and Naturalisation Service (INS) soon noticed an increase in the numbers of illegal immigrants from Jamaica, both entering on false passports and 'overstaying' on visitors or migrant workers' visas, and by 1982 police and federal agents found themselves arresting hundreds of Jamaicans for ganja dealing and drugs-related murders. It wasn't until 1984, however, that the defining characteristic of these gangs was uncovered - guns, and a propensity to use them that had never been seen before.

This part of the story started on May 16 that year with the discovery of

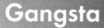

a cache of weapons at Port Bustamante on the Kingston waterfront. The guns had arrived in a container from Miami and consisted of four semi-automatic rifles with 40-round magazines and seven automatic pistols. Given the levels of violence at the previous election, this could not have been the first such importation. But it was the first to be found and it caused a political storm. Something had clearly gone very wrong. Somebody hadn't been paid enough to let them through or perhaps they were just doing their job properly.

The wharf in question was in west Kingston, and so the assumption was that the guns had been on their way to Tivoli before being stopped. Michael Manley, then leader of the PNP opposition, demanded a full inquiry: "We are concerned as to what is the possible link between the weapons discovered on the wharves and the weaponry available to gunmen from Tivoli Gardens," he said.

All the registration numbers had been removed from the weapons, but these were painstakingly restored at the JCF's forensic laboratory and Interpol was asked to trace them. The case went to the US federal Bureau of Alcohol, Tobacco and Firearms (ATF), the old 'Untouchables' of prohibition fame, and landed on the desk of Special Agent JJ Watterson in Florida. He is the man widely attributed with discovering the posses in America.

When he began checking gun store records he found that the weapons were part of a much bigger consignment of between 50 and 75 guns bought in Florida by Jamaicans. Many had given false addresses, but those who could be traced seemed to live in virtual fortresses. Outside, as often as not, were expensive Mercedes or BMW cars. Within months, guns from the same consignment had started to turn up in drugs-related murders in cities as far afield as Washington DC, New York, Detroit, Miami, Chicago and Los Angeles.

"It was an amazing scenario," said Watterson. "We had murders everywhere."

The discovery was significant as it was the first identification of the Shower Posse at work, and also for the involvement of the ATF. From this point it was to become the lead agency tracking the posses across the country, using the Jamaican's penchant for guns as the means of building a picture of their activities. Elsewhere in the US, other evidence of the emerging posses was not far behind.

THE EVENTS of August 4, 1985, were to provide the most graphic lesson in what became known as the Oakland Picnic shoot-out. About 3,000 Jamaicans in all their finery had come from many parts of the US and Canada for a celebration of Jamaican independence day at the camp grounds in Oakland, New Jersey - itself an affluent, suburban community that had never seen the like. Local shock was completed when the event turned into a gun battle.

Unknown to the vast majority of those present, the Spanglers had shot a Shower man in Manhattan the night before in the on-going feud that had followed the establishment of an extensive Shower Posse in New York. The gangstas who went to Oakland had tooled up for further action. It is not known what sparked the shooting but the party atmosphere quickly turned to blind panic when the 'machines' started to bark.

Three people were killed and 13 wounded, and police later recovered 30 discarded guns from the scene as well as large numbers of 'spliffs'. Among the dead was a Tel Aviv posse member from Boston but another victim was a bus driver who had nothing to do with any gang activity. Four days later, the continuing feud claimed its youngest victim when Christina Avala, aged 7, was killed by a stray bullet from a Spangler/Shower shoot-out.

Five years later, after the Oakland site had been sold for development and the surrounding swamp land drained, a further 15 guns were discovered. A few minor sentences arising from the incident had been handed out by then, mainly for possession of ganja. No-one, however, was ever prosecuted for the murders. Gunmen and witnesses alike just went back into the woodwork.

A MONTH earlier, an apparently routine murder investigation had started in Dallas which was to make its own startling discoveries. The victim, a 28-year-old Jamaican called Howard Gordon, had been shot at a Saturday night dance at the Kool Vibes Club, and detectives soon began to uncover a network of Jamaican drug connections surrounding the murder. By the time they had finished, the police had identified between 500 and 700 Jamaicans - many of them teenagers known as 'street worms' - involved in 27 different drugs rings that between them ran 75 crack houses and generated $400,000 in profits a day.

The gangstas were also starting to pop up in Kansas City in the heart of the mid-West, in the shape of the Waterhouse Posse led by Errol 'Dogbite' Wilson. Conspicuous by their accents and dreadlocks, Jamaicans there had been arrested in significant numbers since 1983, mostly on drugs charges and almost invariably with false passports and identification. The full picture, however, did not emerge until 1986 when an investigation into 15 murders involving Jamaicans revealed that the Waterhouse boys were running a string of at least 50 crack houses in the city. This was one of the first views of just how professional such an operation could be.

The posse had brought in about 450 Jamaican youths from New York and Miami with the promise of wages of $500 a week. By all accounts they

earned it, if it was ever paid, by working like slaves in the crack houses. The raw material of powder cocaine was bought in by Jamaican female couriers as often as six times a week, and at their height some of the houses were taking $15,000 a day.

In order to win and hold their market, the posse sold only the highest quality crack and gave it out in bigger pieces than anyone else for the same money. They even had the catchy marketing slogan of 'Stock up on Mother's Day', referring to the first of the month when welfare cheques were sent out. If all that failed, of course there were guns. Lots of them, and again only the best would do.

'Dog-Bite' Wilson was indicted on a series of drugs charges in 1987, but by then he had escaped back to Jamaica. He died there, in a car crash, in 1990.

BY 1986, the NYPD was finding that it too had a serious problem on its hands. The Spanglers had by then established themselves on Edgecombe Avenue, in lower Harlem; they had switched from dealing ganja to crack and were clinically disposing of all opposition.

Terry Quinn was a homicide detective working at the 30th Precinct, which covers this patch at the time. "We suddenly had this rush of homicides, 30-plus murders in a four-block square area," he said. "Every time we would try and do something about it we were faced with petrified witnesses. Most would say nothing and even those that did couldn't be relocated afterwards. Others reneged on their evidence after people had been arrested. We were stuck with an impossible situation." It was a scenario that was to recur again and again around the area: brutal murders allied to unprecedented levels of witness intimidation.

It is easy to see why people were so scared. One case featured a rival black American drugs dealer who had been gagged, shot and dismembered - or 'jointed' in posse jargon. The next morning, police officers found a local crack addict using the man's severed head as a football, the tape still secured over his mouth. Inquiries revealed that the dead man had tried to steal a $3 vial of crack from two of the Spanglers. When officers raided a nearby apartment for evidence they found that the bath tub had traces many different blood types ground into its surface, and informants told them that at least 15 people had been jointed in the tub that summer. Identification of the victims through further analysis of the blood samples proved impossible, however, because they were all mixed up with the remains of 'something else': the bath had also been used to butcher goats for the restaurant downstairs.

June 1986 saw the first cop-killing in New York attributed to the posses, which gave chilling notice that conventional policing methods were not going to be enough to combat this new threat. Officer Scott Gadell had pursued a reputed Shower gunman into an apartment block, but lost the ensuing shoot-out in the stairwell. He was killed by bullets from a 14-shot 9mm pistol while desperately trying to re-load his standard issue six-shot revolver.

Before the end of the year, Walter Arsenault, New York County assistant district attorney, was asked to look at a string of unsolved murders in the city where Jamaicans were either involved or suspected. The NYPD had no meaningful intelligence on the problem, and so Arsenault was given permission to set up his own homicide unit to investigate. Given its head, the team quickly identified 90 such unsolved killings. Arsenault declined to be interviewed for this book, but a later Scotland Yard report on his activities says that this unit developed the first authoritative index of Jamaican criminals in the US, eventually building to over 40,000 computerised records and photographs. "He now employs a number of retired but highly skilled police officers as field intelligence officers and pursues an aggressive strategy so far as information, developed intelligence and informants is concerned," says the report.

It was the successful nurturing of informants that opened a window onto a whole new world for Arsenault and the rest of US law enforcement. Detectives were told that far from being just a collection of local drugs dealing operations, the initial motivation of many of the gangs remained political and involved barrel-loads of money being sent down to Jamaica along with large quantities of guns. This explained why the rivalries were so intense, and also why the gangstas were viewed as heroes by their communities back home. It was all starting to make some sense.

One particularly vicious crew that was discovered around this time operated in the Bronx and simply called themselves the Homicide Posse. Their speciality was to rob Jamaican social clubs and those of other West Indian groups in the area. Their calling card was to pick out a woman from the crowd, then take her off and rape or sodomise her.

The main efforts of Arsenault's team, however, were directed against the Spanglers and its leader in New York - Toywell Phillips, otherwise known as 'Cow', the man held responsible for many of its murders. The

Toywell Phillips, alias 'Cow'

posse originated from the PNP Matthew's Lane area of central Kingston (pronounced 'Matches' Lane), right on the front line with Tivoli Gardens. Unusual amongst the US posses, they seem to have been in existence before the move to America, whereas most of the others developed their identities after the move north.

The Spanglers' modus operandi in Edgecombe Avenue was to take over a store or apartment on the street for dealing purposes and then to progress to another, either moving the occupants out through force or giving them money for the use of their property. Before long they were effectively running the whole area with an iron fist. The personnel of this posse was a combination of older members, including Cow, who had been established in New York for some years, and younger 'guns' brought up from Jamaica, including the delightfully street-named 'Strangle Face'.

As Arsenault's team had success against one branch of the team, they found that the younger members then moved into the same buildings and carried on business as usual until they too were taken out. By 1991, the whole crew had been effectively broken up, either prosecuted or dispersed and one small reign of terror was ended.

Cow, however, was to meet his end in Jamaica that year in a struggle for control of the home base of Matthew's Lane. The story, which reads like a Jacobean revenge tragedy, illustrates the close links that still remained between US operations and the situation in Kingston, but also the fragility and complexity of personal alliances and the murders associated with them.

Cow's right-hand man was Glenford Phipps, aka 'Early Bird', the Matthew's Lane Don who had been brought up to boost the Spangler's firepower in New York. As the American authorities closed in, Early Bird flew back to Jamaica - where he was promptly shot dead by men paid by Cow,

Donald Phipps alias 'Zeekes'

who wanted to take over as 'Matches' Lane Don-man. When Cow went to collect his inheritance, he was in turn killed by a gunman paid by Early Bird's brother, Donald Phipps aka 'Zeekes', in a revenge attack. Zeekes then became the Matthew's Lane don.

But the shooting did not stop there. Zeekes had not only paid for Cow's assassination, he had also provided the gun to the hitman, known as 'Manson'.

Afterwards Manson refused to give the gun back and Zeekes sent other gunmen to kill him and retrieve the weapon. He was shot but only wounded. As he lay in a hospital bed trying to recover, the gunmen returned to finish the job. Again Manson was shot and again he escaped. Trying to follow that kind of story line, it is perhaps unsurprising that the American law enforcement agencies took some time to fully appreciate the problem they were facing.

Glenford Phipps, alias 'Earlybird"

THE FIRST major blow by the ATF against the posses came in late October 1987, in a series of co-ordinated raids known collectively as Operation Rum Punch. The scale and breadth of the operation, which involved targets in 13 states, showed just how far the posses had come and how wide their influence was then spread. It was the first that most Americans had ever heard of them.

Stephen Higgins, ATF director, told a press conference that 124 posse members had been arrested in the sweep and described them as probably the country's most violent organised crime gang. He implicated the posses in more than 600 drug-related murders and in kidnapping, narcotics trafficking, gun trafficking, robberies, assaults and money laundering. Arrests were made in New York, Miami, Philadelphia, Boston, Cleveland, Dallas, Denver, Kansas City, Houston, Baltimore, Chicago, Atlanta, Detroit, Los Angeles and Washington DC.

"They're shooters," said another ATF agent at the time. "They'll shoot cops, they'll shoot each other and they'll shoot bystanders. They scare the hell out of us."

New, exotic posse names also emerged. As well as the Shower and the Spanglers, there was now the 'Dog Posse', the 'Tel Aviv Posse', the 'Dunkirk Boys', the 'Waterhouse Posse' and the 'Banton Posse'.

One of the big surprises was the extent of posse activity in Texas, already mentioned, where heavily armed local and federal officers in Dallas arrested 45 people believed to be linked to the posses there and to dozens of gang murders since 1984. Of that total, 29 suspects were Jamaican nationals. Charlie Storey, of the city police's intelligence division, described the situation as follows: "It's new: it's moved fast into Dallas and it's multiplied fast."

BY 1991, after the experience of 'taking down' some of the posses' big players and trying hard for the rest, the ATF's view of things had crystallised into an even harder picture. A confidential report from that year, simply

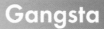

entitled 'Jamaican Organised Crime', opened with this pronouncement: "Jamaican posses are one of the most insidious, ethnic-based crime groups in operation today. They pose a major threat in virtually every major city in the United States. Their activities span borders, traversing international shores. They have grown faster than any other organised drug trafficking network."

This expansion in search of new and lucrative markets was by then known to have taken posse merchandise to virtually all the eastern and western states, as well as large sections of the mid-West. Many other states were suspected of harbouring posse activity. There were even reports of gangstas in Anchorage, Alaska. In all, the report estimated that there were 40 different posses then in operation, with an approximate total of 20,000 members. A depressingly similar story was turning up almost everywhere.

"The configuration of the groups, the methods of operation, and the identities of members may alter, but what is constant is their greed, a need to reap the monetary benefits of drug trafficking, and the pervasive violence that accompanies their trade," said the report.

In both of these areas of consistency, the given figures are startling. The posses were estimated to be making one billion dollars a year from drugs trafficking; and they were held responsible for more than 3,500 murders within the US since 1985. Given that nobody enters the drugs market except to make large amounts of money, it is the readiness to indulge in extreme levels of violence in pursuit of such money that is the posse's real trade-mark. It is how they captured their drugs markets, it is how they hung onto them and it was how they punished anyone who stepped out of line or threatened their position.

"Extreme violence continues to accompany the phenomenon of Jamaican crime," said the ATF report. "Retribution, retaliation, protection, rip-offs, machismo and saving face are all words and phrases repeatedly used to describe motives for Jamaican-related murder." Most killings were over drugs but others could just be to enhance a violent reputation. "Often, it may seem to investigators that there is no apparent motive," the report continues, "shoot-outs that occur during social gatherings are often mysti-fying. These incidents usually involve saving face or retaliation for a minor incident."

What is being referred to here is the practice of pulling a gun in response to any real or imagined sleight or show of disrespect - known as 'dissin'. Common provocations reported elsewhere involve dissin' a gunman's 'woman' or even, in one oft-quoted case, the fact that someone stepped on a Don-man's foot in a night club. But not even these factors seemed to explain everything the ATF was coming across. Another example quoted in the report was of a gunman who produced an Uzi machine pistol at a party in Boston and sprayed the crowd with bullets, leaving three dead and a dozen injured. Again, repeats the report: "On the surface, these types of incident seem completely without motive or purpose. They are reported annually and in various parts of the country."

Planned, cold-blooded murders involving multiple victims are also documented in the report. In May 1990 a gang burst into an apartment in Dallas and herded five black American youths into the bathroom. They were ordered to strip and stand in the bath, and then were raked with fire from two Uzi's. Two died and the rest were seriously injured. Suspects were identified as members of a Brooklyn-based posse.

A year later, in Brooklyn itself, a family of five was murdered by Jamaican dealers, apparently over a drugs feud. The dispassionate details given have more impact than any emotive description: "The victims, who were also Jamaican, included a man and a woman, both about 28 years old. They were found shot in the head. The woman, who was pregnant, was also shot in the stomach. Two boys, 2 and 12 years old, were found shot in the head, as was a young woman of about 17."

The report also noted a new trend in the increasing use of explosives and arson by the posses. As an extension of shooting, this was seen to be primarily used for purposes of retaliation and protection with firebombs in particular becoming something of a 'signature'. Examples quoted include the fire-bombing of a crack house in Washington, which led to three deaths, and an arson fire in south Dallas causing another five deaths where locked security bars prevented those inside from escaping. Booby traps inside fortified drug houses were also used 'to deter any intruders'. Operation Rum Punch in 1987 had led to the first discovery of hand grenades forming part of the posse arsenal; "a grenade was used in a recent bombing of a lounge frequented by rival Jamaican posses in the Chicago area", the report said.

Torture was seen as another 'signature' in Jamaican-related murder. Setting the victim on fire, shooting them in the face, forcing them to play Russian roulette, throat slashing and dismemberment had all been reported by ATF field officers.

As the influence of the posses spread, so the killing increased dramatically in cities outside New York and Miami. In Boston, the Jamaican-related homicide rate leapt from 17 in 1989 to 33 in 1990. In the single month of January 1991, there were a record 15 murders, 12 of which were related to wars amongst groups of Jamaicans, Colombians, North Vietnamese, Chinese and Dominicans. In Hartford, Connecticut, 1989 saw 42 drive-by shootings resulting in 19 deaths as a Jamaican posse fought for control of the drugs market with two local black American gangs.

Other smaller cities, as far afield as Tucson, Arizona and Orlando,

Florida, were by this time seeing their first Jamaican-related killings, leading to fears of dramatic escalation as the posses sought to increase their activity. It all makes for depressing reading.

THE MAN who shot someone dead for stepping on his foot was Delroy 'Uzi' Edwards, a young Don who operated out of Crown Heights, Brooklyn with a posse that had a bigger reputation than most for ruthless violence - the Renkers. The two names say a lot about the brutal and dirty business of dealing crack. Edwards acquired his street name from the killing machine of his preference, the Israeli-made Uzi sub-machine pistol, with enough rapid fire in a single clip to cut a man in half. 'Renk' is ghetto-speak for stench or stink, particularly that of stale urine against a wall.

True to classic posse form, Edwards had been a hired gun in the JLP area of Southside in central Kingston, the same patch from which the victims of the Green Bay massacre had been plucked in the struggle for political dominance. Having carved 'nuff notches' during the 1980 election campaign, he joined the exodus to New York where he helped run his father's ganja business from behind the counter of the family grocery store in Brooklyn. Part of his fearsome reputation was based on a rumour that he had killed his own father a couple of years later in order to gain control of the oper-

Delroy 'Uzi' Edwards

ation.

Come the crack explosion, he was in the forefront, shipping in cronies from his former Southside 'corner' on false passports to build his crew and showing some of his family's entrepreneurial flair by offering special deals for the weekend to undercut the local opposition. At the height of their influence Renkers were said to be coining in up to $50,000 a day from sales in New York, Washington DC, Baltimore and Philadelphia. They were also attributed with six murders and 17 woundings, mostly from shootings including drive-bys, and indulged a taste for gruesome torture in pursuit of internal discipline and an even bigger 'rep'.

One recipient of this tactic was a local black, recruited to the Renkers' ranks, but accused of stealing money and crack from the crew. In December 1986 he was taken to a derelict basement, handcuffed to some overhead pipes and beaten with baseball bats. When the boy threatened to pass out under the punishment, one of the posse poured boiling water over him to bring him round. He died as he hung there, and his frozen body was found in a skip three months later on the turf of a rival gang.

The Renkers were finally taken out by a joint task force of police and federal agents, and 'Uzi' Edwards was brought to trial in the summer of 1989. Among his many other 'distinctions', he was the first posse leader to be prosecuted under the Racketeer Influenced and Corrupt Organisations Act (RICO), designed specifically to deal with organised crime, and the prosecutors accused him of being one of the first dealers to introduce crack into New York. Behind bars, and unable to exercise his strict regime of discipline any more, Edwards saw the rest of the crew plead guilty and testify against him. Still only 28, he was sentenced to 501 years in jail, without parole, and fined $1m for good measure.

Not all the Renkers were immediately captured. In a chilling reminder that this kind of behaviour was not just some strange, foreign aberration, one of Edwards' enforcers turned up in Britain a year later.

Victor Francis was arrested with his brother, Leroy, following a police raid in Acton, west London. They had been selling crack from a council flat on a White City estate, keeping their drugs stored in scaffolding poles outside. As in New York, local youths had been recruited to help run the operation while the brothers posed as a reggae act called 'Lemon and Lime'.

Their sophisticated deception ran to a host of false documents, including accounts for the supposed business and false receipts and bookings from local record shops and promoters. Both were sentenced to seven years in prison at Knightsbridge Crown Court.

JUST HOW sophisticated and organised the posses and Yardies are, or ever became, is still a point of debate in law enforcement circles. Put crudely, the British view leans heavily towards the 'disorganised crime' or 'organised chaos' point of view, whereas the Americans see something far more co-ordinated.

The 1991 ATF report, for instance, outlines a three-tier structure for the posses, consisting of an upper echelon, a middle echelon, and the workers. The leaders of the upper tier co-ordinate the supply of drugs to the 'outlet cities' and maintain overall control of the organisation, typically living in

Above, Victor Alexander Francis and to the left his brother, Leroy Francis – they posed as a reggae act 'Lemon and Lime'

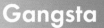

'source cities' such as New York or Miami and only going out of town in case of serious problems arising elsewhere. In turn, the daily operations of the 'outlet cities' will be controlled by those in the middle echelon, or 'overseers', normally from the same area of Jamaica as the supplier and so trusted.

Their job would include the recruitment of locals and bringing in others to perform the role of 'workers'. These would carry out tasks such as: "retail sales, protection, look-outs, couriers for drugs and money, weapons purchases, and rental of apartments and vehicles."

When the posses first started emigrating to the US , they typically formed small, closely-knit groups mainly recruited from the same areas of Kingston - hence the names relating to ghetto 'corners'. This, and the threats of intimidation, meant they were hard to penetrate with undercover agents or informants, says the report. As the scope of their operations grew, they increasingly moved into recruiting 'outsiders' both to supply drugs and as workers. These were mostly drawn from the indigenous black population but white females had been used as couriers and for buying guns, and Jamaican Chinese and Indians had also been recruited. One result of this was to further 'insulate' posse leaders from detection as these outsiders would not know who was ultimately in charge.

Some non-law enforcement analysts have dramatised this situation by putting the factors of violence and supposed organisation together to paint a picture of a highly disciplined network of criminality. This managed to spread its influence for years, without law enforcement agencies noticing, because its troops were held in line by local loyalties or fear of vicious reprisals. There was, in other words, a cell structure similar to the Mafia or any other established crime group, which was at the same time ingenious and highly dangerous.

Having watched the Jamaican criminal scene closely for more than five years, this, in my view, simply does not stand up. On the contrary, the main danger from the posses or Yardies comes precisely because of their lack of organisation and the instability which this brings with it.

What faced the authorities was a collection of loosely-associated groups all chasing the same thing: quick, huge profits from the drugs trade. This inevitably brought conflict, both with each other and with existing dealers. Add to this the pre-eminence of the gun as a means to power in the Jamaican ghettos and you have the blueprint for the quite horrendous levels of violence. Taken from the other direction, if there was anything resembling a co-ordinated network, such violence would not be necessary.

Certainly it is not desirable for the smooth operation of business as any mobster will tell you. It was the huge number of murders that brought down the full weight of the American law enforcement on the posses and has led to many of them being broken up. In Britain too, violence was the thing that finally convinced the authorities that there was a serious problem. It is not ironic, as has been suggested, that the gun was both the power behind the posses' success and the seed of their downfall. These are just two sides of the same coin.

The simplest way of understanding the issue is to say that Jamaican criminals are no more or less than extreme entrepreneurs. Being 'badder' than anyone else was the way in which they gained a foothold in the highly competitive drugs market and sought to maintain and expand that position. Rapid expansion of their influence over most of the US was, then, just the operation of free market economics. Competition was less in the undeveloped markets of the mid-West and other small towns, and the local law enforcement was less aware of the gangs' potential, therefore the move into these areas was a natural one to make.

Adaptability to local market conditions is another argument in favour of this analysis. ATF figures show a broad range of drugs sold across the country and a great variability between what is sold where. In Buffalo, New York, for instance, the activity is entirely in powder cocaine; whereas in Washington DC it is almost all crack and in Trenton, New Jersey, it remains predominantly ganja. Elsewhere, Jamaicans have been known to deal in heroin, PCP and amphetamines. What remains constant, however, is the violence - the particular marketing tool of the posses. "To argue that one kind of dealing is more dangerous than another is to miss the point," said one Trenton detective. "It wouldn't matter if they were dealing in hair-spray, the violence would be the same. It's the culture they come from."

Perhaps the most persuasive argument against the high organisation model is simply the number of Jamaican bad bwoys that get caught, as evidenced by the extraordinary deportation figures already quoted. No classic criminal organisation could possibly sustain such losses and remain in action. The only way that the posses do remain a threat in the US is because there is an almost infinite supply of willing labour from Jamaica, young men with nothing to lose and everything to gain from chancing their arms (in more ways than one), and because there is no central organisation to be broken. Where one team is taken out, another one quickly moves in to fill the gap in the market - a whole new set of players with a whole new set of connections, meaning that law enforcement agencies must start all over again.

Where great successes have been registered, they have largely been due to the availability of willing informants. This, finally, shows that the notion of strict code of discipline within the posses is misguided. Once arrested for a particular crime, gangstas have frequently been 'flipped' to offer information in return for the promise of a reduced sentence. The

Renkers experience is an extreme case in point. "Once you catch them they will give up everybody," said one agent. "They don't seem to have any sense of loyalty at all." Gross punishments meted out to those who do break ranks, then, are not signs of stringent control, but symptoms of panic about the security of any particular operation.

Vivian Blake, leader of the Shower posse in the US

THE NEAREST thing to a 'Mr Big' that the American posse scene ever produced was probably Vivian Blake, the man said to have masterminded the Shower's business out of Miami and New York.

He first linked up with Jim Brown in Florida around 1979, and stayed in America to establish the posse's operation there with Richard 'Storyteller' Morrison while Brown returned to Tivoli. As the guns bust of 1984 showed, the contacts between the Shower's activities in the US and Jamaica remained closely tied together for years and were at least in part politically motivated. It was around this time that the name of 'Shower' started to be widely used - reputedly because of its members' fondness for showering their opposition with bullets.

Initially Blake's job was to facilitate the importation of ganja into Florida, and then organise its distribution locally and to New York. Money and guns would then go back down the line to Tivoli, hidden in cardboard barrels of food and clothing. Alternatively, the guns were broken down and their parts smuggled in the backs of TV sets or refrigerators.

Blake is also said to have been one of the first to start dealing cocaine in New York, as early as 1980, having established contacts with Colombian dealers in Miami. When this took over as the high-profit staple of Shower business, an increasing flood of couriers were heading north on internal flights, body-packed with the lucrative white powder.

By the time of the nation-wide sweeps of 1987, US federal agencies estimated that the Shower had built a network of over 5,000 operatives in a dozen cities around the country. It had also led to further expansion into Canada, by setting up a big operation in Toronto. Blake and Morrison were major targets of the Operation Rum Punch but both escaped the net and went back to Jamaica.

Those who have met Blake describe him as urbane, charming and a flashy dresser. Certainly, he is not your average 'Yard' boy, having been a student at Jamaica College - the most prestigious boy's school in the country. Highly intelligent, he originally went to America to take up a college scholarship. His qualifications for ruthlessness, however, are not in question. When his name appeared prominently on an ATF indictment in 1988, along with 33 other Shower members, he was charged with nine murders as well as firearms and drugs trafficking. By 1992 the ATF reward offered for his capture stood at $20,000, but there were no takers. He was eventually arrested in Jamaica in 1994, when he described himself as a 'businessman' but he has so far successfully fought extradition.

Richard Morrison, known as 'Storyteller'

Morrison was not so lucky. He was arrested with Jim Brown in 1990, and the two embarked on a lengthy appeals process which went right to the Privy Council in London. Following a mistake at the Jamaican appeal court, however, he was sent back to Miami in 1992. A legal battle then ensued between the US and Jamaican governments as the Jamaicans sought his return but, having finally got their man, the American authorities were not about to give him up again. Storyteller was tried and convicted on cocaine trafficking charges and received a jail sentence of 25 years. He is still waiting to see if he will face additional charges, including murder. Jim Brown, as we have seen, was due for extradition but never made it.

WE ARE sitting in a car in a parking lot across the road from an isolated, derelict building in Brooklyn. Boarded up and abandoned, it does not look much different from many others in a general scene of urban decay, but it has a special place in the history of Jamaican gangs in America. This was once the base of the Jungle Posse which unwittingly provided police and federal agencies with an important key to gang operations.

"There were seven people shot on that sidewalk, right there," says ATF special agent Joe Green, who is giving me a daylight tour of the area. "As you can see, the building is surrounded by empty lots and they used to post lookouts on the roof who could see people coming from any direction."

This three-storey, isolated building is near the corner of Osborne and Legion Street, in an area of Brooklyn known as East New York. There is a shop front, with two doors next to each other, one leading to the upstairs apartments. The crew who sold drugs out of there pronounced the address as 'Leg-iron Street', no doubt having worn such things in the past or expecting to in the future.

"Ganja was sold out of the store, crack was sold in the other doorway, and anybody wanting heroin was sent straight upstairs," says Green, who carried out surveillance from the same parking lot we are sitting in before

the gang was raided and finally broken up in 1989. Green is another big man, with a big laugh and usually a big cigar to match. "The store used to work as a Laundromat, and if the look-outs spotted anyone coming along on a drive-by they would just pull the metal shutters down."

This was the centre of the Jungle operation which also had tentacles spreading to Kansas City, Missouri and Miami. It was set up by Ralvin Duffus, aka 'Wally Dread', who came from the Concrete Jungle ghetto and who was known to have high-level contacts in the PNP. The way that agents found out about this posse was again through guns.

In September 1986, ATF agents in Miami arrested a Jamaican who was found to have given false information while buying 12 weapons there the previous spring in three different transactions. The man was convicted but the whereabouts of the guns remained a mystery.

Then in November, the Olympic Gardens police station in Kingston was attacked by gang members from the PNP Waterhouse area using American para-military weapons. Three people were killed, a number of others wounded and the police station was set on fire. The Jamaican police asked the ATF to trace the guns recovered after the shoot-out and it was found that some of them went back to the Miami buy earlier that year.

Further research had by this time traced others back to a group in Kansas City and a major 'task force' operation was mounted there involving the ATF, local police, the Drugs Enforcement Agency (DEA) and immigration officers from the INS. A series of raids in November and December netted another three of the guns and arrested several members of what emerged to be the Waterhouse Posse. Criminal records of those arrested showed they had previous convictions in both Miami and New York for drugs and firearms offences and many were found to have false drivers' licences from the same area of Brooklyn - 'Little Kingston'. Further information came from a number who 'flipped', revealing a loose hierarchy to the group, its political affiliations and the fact that the Waterhouse was largely subordinate to the Jungle Posse.

As 1987 went on, other related guns started to turn up in murders in New York until the total number of firearms thought to be involved in this same gun deal grew to more than 50. Bodies of murder victims with similar Brooklyn drivers' licences were also being discovered as far away as Dallas. Agents realised that they had found a new group to rival the Shower Posse and all fingers pointed to 'Wally Dread' as the guiding hand behind it.

Ralvin Duffus, otherwise known as 'Wally Dread'

While Green largely subscribes to the 'organised chaos' model of gang activity, he says that Dread's was a fairly sophisticated operation. He would look after his workers well, putting up bail money for them when they were arrested and continuing the ghetto tradition of giving money to families or babymothers of those who were killed. He even had a private health benefits programme for his 'employees'.

Hewlit West alias, 'Crack of Dawn'

Among these were some notorious names. Hewlitt West, aka 'Crack of Dawn' was one, who got his street name from the time he liked to carry out his shootings. The original 'Jackal', who we later spent so much time looking for in London, was another. Willie 'Haggart', whose name comes from the patois for 'hog-heart' and who has also enjoyed periods of brisk business in Britain. He was eventually arrested on a gun charge, was deported and then turned up again in Brooklyn three weeks later.

By 1988 the group were under heavy surveillance in a joint operation by the ATF and the NYPD's Brooklyn South homicide unit. But pressure from other dealers in the area, like 'Uzi' Edwards, led to a period of in-fighting which saw the group gradually fall apart. Wally Dread himself was killed by a .22 calibre pistol when he moved off his patch. He had been on his way to collect his daughter from school and stopped off to buy a pack of cigarettes. On his way back to the car, two rivals shot him in the head.

"Every two or three weeks someone would turn up dead in front of Osbourne Street," remembers Green. One day, while watching the building, he and a homicide detective called John De Carlo literally plucked one of the gang members from the same corner. "This guy, Keith Silvera, had been part of the power struggle within the gang and had gone off to run other drug houses. We had a warrant for his arrest in connection with a man who turned up dead on the fire escape outside one of these places, and suddenly there he was," remembers Green, grinning through a characteristic fog of cigar smoke. "We didn't want to risk losing him so I just drove the car out onto the sidewalk, De Carlo rolled out while we were still moving and grabbed him.

Keith Silvera, known as 'Peter Skeng'. 'Skeng' means gun

He never knew what happened."

Shortly afterwards the place was closed down in a big joint raid. "There were people running all over, I've never seen so many people run," says Green. "Inside, people were crowded into the stairs so we couldn't get past. It was chaos."

Before this, however, it was the troubles of the Jungle posse which had indirectly opened a window onto an even more violent and sinister Brooklyn crew - 'The Gullymen'. Things had deteriorated to such an extent that the Jungle crew were only selling ganja. Undercover ATF agents trying to buy cocaine from them were told none was available but, helpfully, they were redirected from Osbourne Street to another source of supply. The new supplier was based in a large local record shop and, while the agents were waiting around to buy half a kilo from there, an informant suggested they also try yet another nearby address. "It's the hottest spot in Brooklyn," he told agents. That address was 1367 Stirling Place on the corner of Schenectady Avenue in Crown Heights and it was to become known both as a notorious killing zone and the scene of a significant blow against the posses in New York.

The whole building, called Irene Court, was owned by Eric Vassell, known as 'Chinaman' because of his slightly oriental looks, who was a former hit-man from the PNP area of McGregor Gully in East Kingston. Seeing the way that the political wind was then blowing, he had got out of Jamaica the year before the 1980 election and had been running a lucrative drugs and guns business in Brooklyn ever since. His reign began with the traditional turf war against those already in the business in that area, in this case a Panamanian gang. Police later said that the Jamaicans had "literally shot them off the block. "By the time that the Gullymen were broken up, they were estimated to be making $1m every 10 days.

There were two reasons why Vassell and his crew had gone undetected for so long. Firstly, Vassell had specialised in dealing heroin, then virtually unknown among the posses, and the concentration of law enforcement effort against crack had passed his operation by. The other reason was that those who did know of his existence were a group of corrupt cops from the nearby 77th Precinct who were later prosecuted for selling him drugs, skimmed off from raids against other dealers.

After the accidental discovery of Irene Court by the ATF and Brooklyn South homicide, however, detailed surveillance of the place was set up using a video van, and computer checks were run on those seen coming and going. One night the officers on duty got lucky when a man was seen standing on the corner with a gun sticking out of his waist band. He was arrested, and with a gun in hand the now familiar pattern of tracing could begin. Astonishingly, it was discovered that this gun was part of the same series of 1986 purchases made in Miami.

As more gun arrests followed with similar results, it was found that the man running this gun-buying operation was none other than Eric's brother - Clement Vassall. One member of the group was arrested while trying to board a plane in Florida with guns, and he had three driving licences with different identities on them. When these were checked out, the picture just got bigger and bigger, and it was then that the ATF realised that up to 50 guns had been bought by the group, most of them shipped north to New York.

When others started to turn up in Dallas, the full extent of Vassell's activity started to take shape. While dealing mainly heroin in New York, crack was the chosen commodity for trade in Texas. The cocaine was bought and 'cooked' in Brooklyn, and then driven down to Dallas at a rate of about three-to-four kilos a week. Hiding it in consignments of children's disposable diapers was one favoured method of transportation. After sale, some of the money was used to buy more guns in Texas, notorious for relaxed firearms regulations, and driven back to New York, and the rest of the cash was sent back in wire transfers. One series of such transactions that was monitored showed that $320,000 had been returned to Vassell in this way over a six month period. Further evidence against gang members was built by automatically photographing those who went to pick up the money from Western Union offices.

Vassell had been helped in building his posse by a contact in the New York passport office. He had provided false US passports for extra troops to be brought up from McGregor Gully, and at one time had also been supplying Delroy 'Uzi' Edwards in the same way. A typical arrival would be met at JFK airport off a flight from Kingston and driven to a safe house. There his passport would be taken from him and then sent back down to Jamaica to have its picture changed. It would then be used to 'bring up' someone else.

Not only passports were going back down to the Gully. Vassell fulfilled the role of beneficent Don by sending down guns and drugs as well as barrel-loads of food, clothes and electrical goods. Every Easter, he would pay for an annual 'treat' for the folks back home, complete with a beauty contest of girls - each sponsored by a different bad bwoy.

Since April 1990, the Gullymen had been subject to a huge joint investigation, known as an Organised Crime Drug Enforcement Task Force (OCDETF). The approach had been pioneered in Kansas but this was the

biggest of its kind. Starting with the New York ATF and Brooklyn South homicide, it eventually drew in the FBI, the Internal Revenue Service (IRS), the INS, the Department of State, the Brooklyn District Attorney's office and Dallas's own OCDETF task force. After an eight-month investigation, some 44 members of the Gullymen posse had been identified and indicted on crimes ranging from drugs and firearms trafficking to robberies, rapes, assaults and approximately 22 murders.

The killing, as ever, was cold and clinical with bodies making a regular appearance on the Schenectady corner. In one case a man was shot in the building's lobby after which the murderer handed his gun to another gang member so that he could have a go. A number of murders took place upstairs, after which there was one crew to remove the body, another to cut up the carpet and wash down the walls to get rid of the blood, and another to come in and fill the bullet holes. One member of a rival JLP-orientated gang was shot with one bullet to the head as he walked by on the opposite side of the street.

One of the early arrests from the street was of a Gullyman called Anthony Williams, known as 'Modeler' for his young good looks. While awaiting trial in prison he received word from Vassell that if he were to give evidence against him or the gang, then his family in Jamaica would be killed. Williams hung himself in his cell.

On December 6, 1990, the law enforcement team went into action, executing a total of 22 search warrants in New York, Dallas, Philadelphia and Washington DC. Agents arrested 24 gang members but a further 20, including Vassell, escaped the net. He was finally arrested in Jamaica in September 1994, and at time of writing he was fighting extradition to the US, but had lost his first round of appeal. Both he and Vivian Blake remain in Jamaican prisons.

The biggest raid, of course, was on Irene Court which featured a huge turn-out federal agents and police SWAT teams. Inside, as well as large amounts of drugs, they found one empty apartment in which there was a cupboard containing seven loaded handguns, available for use at all times. They also found large amounts of paper work which further incriminated the gang.

Joe Green, who was on that raid, remembers that some of this evidence bordered on the bizarre. Part of the front for the Gullymen was a football and domino club located in the basement of the building. This had been properly incorporated at City Hall where the organisers had been told they had to follow certain rules, including keeping minutes of all their meetings. Incredibly, they did, and these were found.

"It was amazing stuff, like: 'Mr Brown said that on a drugs buy there should be one car in front and another behind to act as look-outs and support'," says Green. "Stuff like you couldn't swear in meetings, but that trophies should be bought because someone had done a good job on a shooting. They wrote all this down - incredible."

This almost touching naiveté, taken together with the brutality of daily gang life, gives a new twist to the understanding of posse culture. It also provides further cautionary evidence against ascribing too much 'evil genius' status to gang leaders.

"No one could accuse these guys of being rocket scientists," says Green, chuckling again. "You just couldn't make this stuff up."

DESPITE such spectacular law enforcement successes, the problem did not go away in America. The posses were back in the headlines in August 1992, following a night of murder and mayhem in suburban Miami.

About 100 people were enjoying a Saturday night out at the Taste of the Islands restaurant and club when some kind of row erupted between two groups of men and the shots began to fly. It happened so quickly that youngsters on the dance floor did not have time to react before they started to go down under the hail of gunfire. Among them was Hilda LaToy Reynolds who was celebrating her 17th birthday. She was killed outright.

"We were dancing to Caribbean music and the shots started. I was dancing with LaToy," said one of her friends afterwards. "One shot just led to another and people started falling. The last time I saw her, she was lying on the floor."

A 16 year-old youth described the ensuing panic. "There was no argument, no warning. They just started shooting and people started running. People jammed up the door yelling, 'Get out!'. Everyone was running out."

In all four people were killed and 17 wounded. Two of those shot were identified as posse members, but official police reaction was cautious when it came to attributing the blame to a gang-related dispute. Some, however, were in no doubt as to who was responsible.

"It's a classic, textbook example of the way posses settle disputes," said Captain Al Lamberti of the Broward County Sheriff's office, and an expert on Jamaican gangs. "The Mafia does it cleanly. The posses make big messes. They don't give a damn about anybody." A classic, textbook response to the posses, if ever there was one.

Lamberti also rehearsed the origin of the 'posse' name - derived, as mentioned, from the gangstas love of American Wild West shows. They liked the way the cowboys ride in "shooting up the place," he said.

For the law-abiding Jamaican community, the cost of the incident on their collective reputation was equally obvious. "I might go to certain places and tell them I'm not a Jamaican," said one local nurse. "You feel embarrassed."

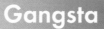

THE FOLLOWING year, immigration officials launched a daring operation in the same area which was to prove that links between illegal Jamaican immigrants and cocaine were as strong as ever. Undercover agents literally set up shop behind a store-front, offering genuine US immigration papers in return for half a pound of cocaine or $5,000 in cash.

By the time that the 'sting' operation was completed, in September 1995, gangstas from as far away as New York and Los Angeles had been lured by the bait. The deal was that in return for their investment, punters received temporary resident cards with the promise that they would be notified when the full 'green cards' arrived. When officials were ready, word was put out and those who turned up to collect the green cards were arrested. Co-ordinated raids around the country netted other suspects.

Operation Island Green, as it was known, was another startling success. In all 119 people were indicted following the raids - including 61 on cocaine charges and a further seven for smuggling. Agents had seized $60,000 in cash and 110 pounds of cocaine, and in addition uncovered seven posses and 25 drug smuggling groups. Of the first six people arrested, four were armed.

Some, however, escaped the net. Officials said that five of those issued with temporary cards were murdered before they could be arrested.

ELSEWHERE, the American posse picture continues to develop. Where most drugs were usually flown direct into Miami or New York, posse couriers are now increasingly using the border with Mexico to bring in 'body-packed' cocaine. As a result, there is now a resurgence of gangsta activity in Texas and a move into Arizona.

New problems for the authorities are posed by the fact that the scene now features increasing numbers of American-born gangstas, whose roots may be in Jamaica but who are legal US citizens and so not subject to immigration controls such as those used so effectively in Island Green.

"We have had people here since the 1970's, so we are now seeing kids who are third or fourth generation bad boys. Their mothers and fathers were posse members, even their grandmothers were posse members," said one law enforcement official. "They have been bred for this. They're like posse thoroughbreds."

Chapter Eight

OPERATION DALEHOUSE

W E ARE standing on a narrow concrete walkway outside a 1930's council flat on a grim south London council estate. It is February. It is bitterly cold. It is just before 7am, and it is getting crowded. There are eight casually dressed police officers, all with bullet-proof vests on under their bomber jackets. There are the civilian door openers, or 'ghost busters' as they like to be known, setting up their hydraulic ram. And then there's me. This is my first fully-fledged 'spin'.

The early morning yawns have disappeared as have the banter and schoolboy giggles that accompanied our drive down to the estate after the 5.30am briefing. Now there is silence, apart from the odd whispered order, as we wait for the party to assemble and for the door men to get their equipment into position. The two officers chosen to go in first are particularly subdued if 'pumped up'. One drags furiously on a cigarette and his hand is visibly shaking. Probably the cold. If it is something else, then he can be easily forgiven. He is about to go looking for a gun and he hasn't got one.

When it happens, it happens very quickly. We cram up to the door in something like order, the crouched men on the ram nod to show they are ready, and the inspector in charge shouts "GO!". There is a loud bang as the ram is released and shards of door frame go flying. This is not in the plan. The idea is that the frame is forced apart by two hydraulic arms and the door, locks disengaged, is knocked inwards by the blow from the ram itself. The weak frame means it only half works, and the two leading men have to finish the job with their boots. One mutters, "Fuck! Fuck!" as he kicks at the door. The other screams, "POLICE! POLICE! POLICE! POLICE!" in rapid fire mode as he lunges through the opening.

In the following surge I find myself about fourth into the flat, in time to see the three officers in front, still screaming maniacally, charge through another door and jump on a startled black man, naked in his bed. The idea of this dramatic entrance is to stun all inside with the sudden impact of noise, so that they freeze solid. It works. A second or so later, however, the noise of terrified, crying children is added to the cacophony, and then an extremely angry woman emerges from a back room, baby on hip, to add her own vocal contribution. It is scary stuff and I feel a bit giggly again. Rising hysteria, or something.

It soon passes. There is no gun there. The man, a Jamaican, has been fingered by an informant who had said he was holding one. Maybe he was, maybe he wasn't, but it is not there now. A search of about an hour, in which the flat is systematically dismantled and then (mostly) put back together

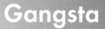

again, establishes that. Rather like raids with the Jamaican police, once it becomes obvious that there is no more excitement to be had everyone becomes very relaxed. Where more than one unit is involved, they can even become something of a social occasion where gossip is swapped with former colleagues as the tedious business of searching is carried out. Now, even one of the previously terrified children is toddling around grinning.

The only substantial thing that the officers do turn up are two tightly rolled 'spliffs' of marijuana. "Are you aware that this is a controlled drug, sir," asks one straight-faced policeman.

"Wha'?" says our man, who has regained his trousers and some of his cool "It's jus' a bit a' weed."

"I am afraid it is against the law. I am arresting you for possession... anything you wish to say,"... etc. This is not as stupid or vindictive as it may at first seem. An arrest, after all, is an arrest and allows a suspect to be taken to the police station for interview, fingerprints and pictures. All grist to the intelligence mill.

Otherwise we depart empty-handed, leaving one officer behind to wait for the council workmen who have been summoned to mend the door. Then it is back to the local 'nick' for breakfast. No one today has fallen foul of 'breakfast rules', whereby anyone turning up late for an early morning briefing has to buy for everybody else, so we all pay for our own.

THESE are scenes that were played out, with variations, many times over the next few weeks. Sometimes it was the large uniformed gentlemen of the Territorial Support Group (TSG) and their sledgehammers (or 'keys' as they call them - they'll open anything) that effected our entrance. Sometimes there was an immigration officer present. Sometimes a 'sniffer' dog to root out drugs. On one occasion a dog found a large plastic bag of cannabis resin stashed behind the cooker. On another we got the gangsta we were looking for who was subsequently deported. But the general, well-practised routine was the same in each case, as was the initial impact it caused. It was, literally, all in a day's work for Operation Dalehouse.

Set up in August 1991, Dalehouse was the logical successor to Roy Ramm's Yardie Squad which had been disbanded almost two years before. In the interim, the problems predicted by Ramm and others were making themselves felt. As the Crack Squad was beavering away at Scotland Yard trying to plot the spread of the new drug, or indeed find it in any large quantities, the special nature of its trafficking in Britain was becoming increasingly obvious. Again as predicted, this showed itself in a rocketing of statistics for drugs related crime - almost entirely attributable to the use of firearms by crack dealers and their associates, mostly Jamaican.

Dalehouse, however, did not begin life as a bold new policy initiative, or even as a brave policy reversal to redress the mistakes made in previous years. Rather it was an ad hoc squad that evolved from the investigation of a particularly vicious robbery and which carried out its work for 17 months under almost constant threat of being shut down.

Brass hats at Scotland Yard (headquarters of London's Metropolitan Police - the Met) were still wary of being seen to target a particular community with a central unit, and so Dalehouse was a purely 'area' squad, run locally by one of the Met's eight policing areas which divided up the city until reorganisation in 1994. In this case it was Area 4, the large swathe of the city south of the river which covers the boroughs of Southwark, Lambeth and all the way out to Croydon in the south. A measure of the precariousness of the operation, to be a trifle cynical, was that a journalist (myself) was allowed to spend almost a month with unfettered access to it and all its workings. A little high profile publicity does no harm in the game of internal police politics. The other thing I could offer was the fact that I had actually been to Jamaica, unlike almost every officer on the squad. This was where I worked with John Brennan and Steve Barker, who were on attachment to Dalehouse at the time. This was where my own investigation, into whether the Yardies were a real threat in Britain or just a myth, began in earnest.

DALEHOUSE was based in the unpromising surroundings of a brick monstrosity on a busy corner in Thornton Heath, south London. More municipal refuse depot or Territorial Army barracks than high-tech nerve centre, the building was shared with the area dog section and the aforementioned TSG. Inside, however, a total of 36 officers worked with the HOMES (Home Office Major Enquiry System) computer system in one of the most successful operations mounted by a British police force against Yardie-connected violence.

In command was Detective Superintendent John Jones, a highly experienced detective who then had a 100 per cent clear-up rate for murder inquiries. He got the job almost by accident, having been the duty officer for the local AMIP (Area Major Investigation Pool) team on the weekend in April 1991 when the robbery took place which started it all.

What he and his original team discovered when investigating that robbery was a list of new violent crimes which were not only unsolved but were completely unknown about to the police. As links were made and the net widened, a whole new criminal cast emerged, based around Brixton, which was causing mayhem to the law-abiding majority in the surrounding community. More officers were drafted in to help, and Operation Dalehouse stuttered into life. A quietly spoken, avuncular character, Jones, now retired, was unusual in his willingness to speak out about what he was

doing in an attempt to win the confidence of the local, predominantly black, community. His press statements often raised eyebrows amongst colleagues, as did his willingness to co-operate with other agencies such as customs and immigration. The operation had a number of setbacks, principally with cases falling down in court, but Dalehouse was attributed with vastly reducing the incidence of gun crime in the area during its time in existence.

"Our main objective is to deal with crack-related violence in south London, particularly in Lambeth," he told me at our first meeting. "The reasons for that are: firstly, we have found that this kind of violence is escalating and, secondly, that when we look at an individual occurrence of violence we are getting very little help from victims or witnesses. In fact, there are no witnesses." The most worrying aspect of the whole situation, he said, was that shootings were routinely happening up to four times a week on the streets of London, and no one outside the immediate area had even heard about it.

Right on cue, then, Stutman's prediction was coming true. In 1991, Britain was experiencing the beginnings of a serious crack problem. It was not the same problem that the outspoken American had envisaged with whole areas devastated by the drug itself. For a society unused and unprepared for the widespread use of guns by criminals, however, it was a crisis in its own right. In the years since then it has altered, perhaps permanently, the nature of British society.

For Jones, even then, there was little doubt about the source of the problem. "There is a fairly wide-based criminal fraternity of black British people, most of whom were born here or who have been here for years, just as there is for other ethnic groups with their own criminal groupings," he said. One of the most common offences among this indigenous group had been dealing in soft drugs, particularly cannabis. But then he added: "The Yardies coming and the invention of crack cocaine has brought in criminals of a very different ilk from abroad."

They had come both from Jamaica and from the USA to set up new bases and extend their operations, using 'illicit migration' and the historical links with Britain to find support and a new market for their product. In response, the home-based gangs had brought in more of these characters to settle their own territorial disputes and had increasingly taken up the use of the gun to defend themselves. "That's where the whole criminal culture comes from," said Jones.

How this new collaboration was beginning to work was shown in the first set of cases investigated by Dalehouse, involving a group of black criminals who became known as The Syndicate. The gang, consisting of one Jamaican and four British youths, set out to become 'The Kings of Brixton'

Operation Dalehouse

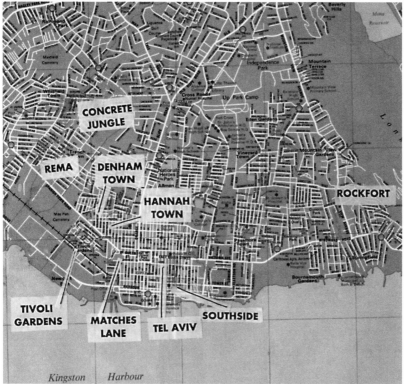

CONCRETE
JUNGLE

REMA DENHAM
TOWN

HANNAH
TOWN

ROCKFORT

TIVOLI
GARDENS

MATCHES
LANE

TEL AVIV

SOUTHSIDE

Kingston *Harbour*

with a brief but vicious reign of terror that ran between March and June 1991. It first came to light with the armed robbery of Fisher's jewellery shop in Brixton, when the owner was gratuitously blasted with a sawn-off shotgun despite having already given the gang all that they had come for. Charles Fisher, the owner, miraculously survived.

Another three, earlier robberies on jewellers then emerged. Two weeks before the Fisher shooting, the gang had held up a gambling den and then 300 young people at a disco, robbing them of all their jewellery at gun point. No one reported it to the police. Other crimes associated with the group included aggravated burglary, abduction and grievous bodily harm. In June, a fund-raising event at a local community centre also received the Syndicate treatment, when the gang pulled out their guns and fired them into the ceiling before relieving both the centre and the 400 people present of all their cash and valuables.

The point of all these crimes was not an overwhelming desire to own a lot of fashionable jewellery or even to live off the proceeds. In a move precisely mirroring the bank robberies and pay roll rip-offs of 1970's Kingston, the strategy was to accumulate cash quickly in order to finance

drugs runs from Jamaica and the USA using a string of female couriers. Raids on Syndicate members recovered cocaine with a street value of about £90,000, all of which was destined to have been turned into crack.

For Jones, the community centre case was particularly astonishing. "A local restaurant rang the police, saying they had heard the shots. But when the police arrived there were 400 people coming out of the centre and all said no shots were fired." The following week he heard about the incident from an informant and got a warrant to search the place. The police eventually found what they were looking for, but only after getting round an elaborate ploy to cover it all up. "They had papered the ceiling," said Jones. "We just peeled away the new paper and pulled out the bullets."

Suspicion of the police on the part of the black community was not news. Perceptions that the force is racist and out to harass anyone without a white face are commonplace to this day, fuelled by horrendous tales of treatment suffered in custody and heavy-handed operations on the street. The view gained extra currency in London after the excesses of the SPG (Special Patrol Group) which helped to spark the Brixton riots in 1981. The shooting and crippling of Cherry Groce in 1985 by armed officers looking for her son, was another cause célèbre which led to more rioting in the area. The 1994 death of Joy Gardner, who suffocated after having her mouth taped up by police seeking to deport her to Jamaica as an illegal immigrant, is yet another.

Even seasoned officers like Jones, however, saw something different in this kind of active non-co-operation. The extra element, they believed, was quite simply fear. The law of the ghetto, with its dreadful reprisals against police informants, was one well-learned and still commanding respect - even thousands of miles away among people who might never have been there. Don't mess with bad bwoys with guns, is the message. Look the other way. Pretend it never happened. Lie, if necessary, to protect yourself and your family from the gunman. While they were in operation, it was a law that the Syndicate's members sought to enforce. One man who did inform on them had his house fire-bombed and gutted, and his family had to be rescued. After this bungled attempt, he was finally shot through his own car window.

Faced with such problems, Dalehouse was forced to use a combination of intense surveillance and computer analysis to gain its own information, independent of any witnesses or victims. "The only way we could deal with it was to actually catch people in possession of a firearm," said Jones. In practice this meant large numbers of 'spins', both looking for guns and to accumulate intelligence from interviewing suspects and analysing sheaves of their documents, or 'corries'. Names and numbers in address books were particularly fruitful, as were numbers on itemised mobile phone bills. Fed into the computer and cross-checked with all dedicated Yardie databases in the Met, a detailed pattern of connections were built up, aliases and street names were unscrambled and addresses targeted. It was a laborious and often tedious process but, given the initial lack of co-operation from the local community, Jones and his colleagues saw little choice. Once they had demonstrated that they were serious about doing something, even this silence was slowly punctured and people became more willing to contribute snippets of information to the mix.

ONCE a likely suspect or address was identified, hours of patient 'sit-ups' would attempt to land vital incriminating evidence. Often this was done by the area surveillance team, plain-clothed experts specially trained to see without being seen and to follow without being spotted. One operation involved two of these officers spending night after night on the roof of a building, watching the entrance to a night-club opposite where one of the doormen was known to carry a gun. As there was only one way up to their observation post (or OP), the stairway had to be guarded by two armed officers. An armed response vehicle was parked nearby in case of real trouble, as were the nondescript cars of other surveillance officers.

I joined this operation one night for the second part of the proceedings, where the suspect is 'followed off' when he leaves the club. The first couple of hours are spent in what was becoming a familiar pattern of boredom, backache and bad jokes. Hunched in the back of a small saloon, waiting for something to happen, there is nothing to do but smoke and gossip. Important strategic decisions have to be periodically taken about whether it is safe for someone to risk running off for five minutes and "get the teas in". Someone else at any given time is trying to catch up on some sleep. The occasional radio check is made. For the rest, there are lots of gags along the lines of, "Who farted?", and endless 'wind-ups' where the rest gang-up momentarily on a victim – trying to kid them into believing something outrageous or that they are for some reason "in the shit" with their superiors. If the poor, exhausted soul takes the bait then there is general laughter and rejoicing. Another five minutes gone. In the next car, the armed police keep themselves to themselves with the self-conscious air of an élite. Nobody tries to wind them up.

Again, when we do finally move, we move quickly. The radio informs us that our man is on his way and the surveillance team goes into action. We are back-up in case there is an arrest so we keep out of the way, shadowing the chase a couple of streets behind, leaving the real business to the professionals and tracking them from the constant babble of radio traffic. They sound very good. One car tails the suspect for a while before overtaking him or turning off and leaving him to the second car. A third car is up ahead,

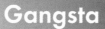

anticipating where he is going so that they too can join in. After its short stint in pursuit, the first car will work its way around the back streets to pop out ahead again and do a bit more. It is a kind of rolling relay race on a constantly changing track, tearing up and down the dark, wet roads of south London. We scramble along behind as best we can with the two in the front arguing over the map like an elderly married couple, somehow managing to keep in touch. This is fun. Once we think we've lost them, after an inspired decision by our navigator apparently sends us the wrong way and everything goes quiet. "Where the fuck are they?" is one of the more polite phrases uttered during an anxious few minutes. Then the radio crackles again, they are heading back our way and all is forgiven.

After a couple of hours of this, the unsuspecting suspect has been successfully tracked to a take-away, on a short visit to a friend's house and then home. No sign of a gun, no result. It is about 3am, back into work at nine. A policeman's lot is not a happy one... as the song says.

RESULTS, however, did come for Operation Dalehouse. Its officers made over 270 arrests and charged 25 suspects with murder and attempted murder before it was finally disbanded in December 1992. About 30 illegal guns were removed from the street and £1m worth of crack was seized. If Dalehouse's conviction rate was disappointing, it was because of the continuing problem of witness intimidation led to the late collapse of a number of important cases. Working closely with the immigration service, many more known criminals were deported back to Jamaica as illegal immigrants when there was insufficient evidence to bring charges.

Perhaps the greatest success of the operation was in the co-ordinated use of intelligence from a number of different agencies and force areas to discover links between Yardie-related violent crimes which at first sight might have been taken as isolated or sporadic. It did not establish a classic, Mafia-style level of organisation; indeed it confirmed the earlier "disorganised-organised crime" analysis. But it did demonstrate how, at any given time, a relatively small number of criminals, either from Jamaica or with Jamaican connections, were using previously unheard-of levels of violence in pursuit of huge profits from the growing crack trade. It was a pioneering approach that still informs the current police response to the problem.

One of the men responsible for making sense out of all this information at Dalehouse was a bright-eyed, shiny-headed Scot called Reg Ferris. A humble police constable, Reg was nevertheless an acknowledged master of the intelligence databases who spent days and weeks at his computer screen finding obscure connections and recording them on complicated flow-charts. Copies of these charts festooned the notice boards in the

Thornton Heath incident room, and one afternoon he attempted to explain just one of them to me.

Ten crimes were arranged in a circle, with friendly headlines like MURDER, ATTEMPTED MURDER, KIDNAPPING and ASSAULT-HAND GUN DRAWN. The incidents happened in a number of different London areas but all had 4 Area connections and as such were part of the Dalehouse remit. So the victims of a shooting at a night club in Hackney, north London, in December 1990 were found to be rival gang members from Brixton. The gun involved was the same as that used in the attempted murder of a prominent Brixton drugs dealer two months later (carried out by a Jamaican hit man brought in from Birmingham for the purpose) and the same weapon later turned up in the Syndicate's arsenal. Promoters from the night-club, meanwhile, were suspects in the kidnapping of a drugs courier from Toronto and the Brixton dealer had become a suspect in an assault case against another dealer over a heroin shipment from West Africa. Yes, it is confusing but there was more.

A Jamaican enforcer, employed by a different Brixton dealer, was implicated in an attempted murder at another night-club, in shots fired at police investigating an open-air crack market on a Brixton council estate and in the murder of a US Embassy employee, herself a suspect in a visa fraud operation to facilitate the free passage of Yardies between Britain and America. Yet another dealer, thought to be behind the visa scam, was killed by a different Jamaican gunman in Hackney, and he was also responsible for a murder and attempted murder of two large-scale cocaine importers in Brixton two months later. There were still more links but that is about the simplest way of explaining it.

Reg had reached an even simpler conclusion: "The same names keep coming up," he said. "These people are organised, even if it is in a ramshackle way." The status reports tagged to the bottom of each crime box illustrated a depressing conclusion to all this work. Only one said 'Suspect Convicted'. The rest ranged from: 'Case not proceeded with', to: 'Victim refuses to co-operate with police', to: 'Suspect acquitted and deported' to a stark: 'Unsolved'. Messy stories like these do not have neat endings.

A DIFFERENT flow-chart hung on the wall of a side office at Thornton Heath from which Brennan and Barker were pursuing some connections of their own. The pair were attached to Dalehouse as resident experts - 'Blondie' was the only officer on the squad who had been to Jamaica and who had contacts with the JCF (Jamaican Constabulary Force), while 'John Wayne' had his own invaluable sources of information on the streets of Brixton. Both had excellent contacts with the tight group of 'Jamaican hunters' in

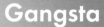

America. They operated outside the four operational teams into which the rest of Dalehouse was organised, free to pursue their own inquiries. Their most important job was to take a 'pro-active' role of running registered informants and finding new ones in order to keep the vital intelligence information flowing. Apart from chasing the Jackal, their main preoccupation when I was with them was a 'job' where they were able to pool their joint expertise. They called it 'Operation Big Apple'.

The five characters involved followed the classic pattern of a loose-knit group of Jamaican criminals, forming themselves into a temporary 'posse' for the purpose of completing a cocaine run into Britain from the US. All had considerable form on both sides of the Atlantic and links to some even more frightening gangstas. The operation to stop them, or catch them in the act, again showed the strengths and weaknesses of the British police's attempts to tackle the problem at this stage, and how the vagaries of disorganised crime could be harder to deal with than something a bit more disciplined.

IT IS ANOTHER early morning start, which this time finds us at Gatwick airport, south of London, to meet one of the two weekly direct flights from Kingston. There is news from an informant who has managed to penetrate the gang. Having set up their stall in London, complete with a cache of weapons, gang members had split up and gone back to Jamaica and the US to organise transhipment of the cocaine and assemble couriers ready for the final run. The man who had been to Kingston, to pay for the drugs in advance and see them on their way to New York, is due back in London on this morning's flight. We'll call him 'Jubba'.

This is to be a joint operation with customs at the airport, and we meet in their offices at about 7.45am, ready for the 8.30am arrival: Brennan, Barker, myself and the inevitable Brian Fotheringham from immigration. The greeting is polite if a little cool. This is the first time I have encountered police and customs officers in the same place and on this evidence they are clearly different animals. The policemen are street casual and relaxed with distinct working-class London accents. Customs are young, middle-class and intense – very collar and tie. They remind me of BBC graduate trainees, obviously bright and good at what they do, but perhaps lacking a bit of earthy savvy. My attitude is no doubt biased by Brennan who is no great lover of your run-of-the-mill Revenue man. 'Fothers' is definitely policeman 'styley'.

Things get particularly prickly when our hosts want to know who I am and, frankly, what the hell I am doing there. They do not want to let me play. It has not been authorised. A couple of calls to Customs House eventually sorts that one out (the nice lady in the press office vouches for the fact that I am not a terrorist or anything similar) and, just in time, we are all off to the 'Wendy House'.

Occasionally, when passing through the customs channel into Britain, you may be surprised to see no one there or just a couple of white-shirted officers watching you at the entrance. Do not worry, HM Customs have not abandoned their posts. They are watching and the action is going on in the Wendy House. In the case of Gatwick, this is a temporary-looking structure with blacked-out windows which sits in the corner of the customs hall. Inside are banks of TV monitors, fed from close-circuit cameras at points all around the arrivals area. An unsuspecting suspect can be watched all the way through without even knowing it. Two uniformed officers sit at the control desk, flicking images from screen to screen and operating the cameras with joy-sticks. Our collar-and-tie sits behind, directing their efforts, at the same time rattling off instructions and a running commentary into his radio for the benefit of plain-clothed men out among the queues and baggage carousels.

"Target, IC3 male. Purple shell-suit. At immigration now. Do you read? Over."

Pause. "Roger control. Target identified," comes the cool reply.

"Watch, do not intercept. Repeat, do not intercept. Over."

"Roger."

Longer pause. "Target, IC3 male. Baggage hall...," and so on, right through to the 'Nothing to Declare' channel. There, Jubba is given the customary 'tug', just in case he has decided on a little instant importation. Not altogether surprisingly, he hasn't. A purple shell-suit and a direct flight from Jamaica is not the subtlest of smuggling techniques but then you never know. At the desk, the uniformed man does a brilliant matter-of-fact search - "only a routine, sir" type of thing. Jubba - relaxed, athletic and sporting a new 'Ragga-style' haircut - is all smiles and politeness as he opens his huge bag. So far so good.

Fothers, however, is not happy. Jubba, of course, is on a false passport and so is an 'illegal'. The deal with immigration had been to let him through so that he could be 'followed off' to find out where he is staying, and so where the rest of the gang is based and where drugs are likely to end up. But at the last minute the surveillance team had been cancelled - cost again - and Fotheringham thinks the deal is no longer worth the proverbial biscuit. His immigration instincts tell him to pick the guy up and throw him out again, after a cosy chat to see if any bits of information can be picked up. The police want to let things run, so that at least his "meeters and greeters" (the people who come to pick him up) can be identified in the arrivals lounge.

It is a fine decision to take. Hasty, and animated, a discussion concludes

that to arrest Jubba at this stage and disclose what we know about his crew would undoubtedly put the informant at great risk, and jeopardise the whole operation. Customs, meanwhile, agree to try and tail the party into the car park so that at least their vehicle's registration can be logged. Brennan and I slip out of a back door to take up position in arrivals and wait.

In the event, its a bit of a wash-out. Brennan doesn't recognise any of the welcoming committee and there is no surveillance photographer to record them for posterity. He snorts in disgust at the efforts of one customs man to remain inconspicuous - repeatedly going up and down the same escalator while reading the Daily Telegraph - but, in fairness, no one seems to notice. We do not even get the registration number. Customs only have two men available at such short notice to attempt the follow, and after a quick try they give it up rather than 'spook' the suspects. All we have got out of the morning is the knowledge that Jubba is back, as planned, and so have established the reliability of the informant. It is something, but it is not a lot.

The following weeks were a mixture of progress and frustration, both for the police and the gang. New information was that, having done this thing a time or two before, the bwoys were now going for the big one. While a normal run will use a number of couriers, or 'mules', to bring in a total of one or two kilos of cocaine, this Atlantic crossing was aiming to import five kilos. That was as big a shipment as had been seen from a Jamaican operation at the time, and so from the police point of view it rose in importance. If the run could be successfully 'boxed off', and the intelligence through Barker in particular was consistently proving to be accurate, then it would be a major feather in everyone's cap. The down-side for all concerned was that it was taking a long time to organise in New York.

At the same time other things were happening. Barker also received information that a different gang were now the proud owners of a sub-machine gun. Much had been heard of such automatic weapons being around, but up until then none had been found by the police. To take one would be a big prize and would concentrate some senior minds about the development of the Yardie situation. A lot of time was taken up tracking the weapon and trying to organise raids to seize it before it could be used. But again, two had to be cancelled so as not to expose an informant and sign his death warrant.

Jubba, meanwhile, was far from idle. While waiting for the New York consignment he had found an alternative supply through a big African dealer and was busy selling small amounts of crack with the other gang members then in London. The decision was taken to clip the wings of this little operation, hopefully getting one of their guns at the same time, while still leaving the big importation to go ahead. Yet more frustration followed. An address would be identified and staked out and a 'job' organised, only to see the gang move off somewhere else. In one case, even the gun's hiding place was identified, under the sink, but the informant rang the next day to say that the gang had just been evicted by the council.

Eventually they did settle in another south London council flat and started to deal again, and a successful raid was mounted. Brennan was one of the lead officers who went in wearing riot helmets, because of a suggestion that acid might be used against them, and two of the gang members were arrested. One was found to have over £3,500 in cash in his back pocket, and 4ozs of cocaine was seized. There was no gun and no Jubba, but first blood had finally been taken.

On the down-side, it was to be Brennan's last job at Dalehouse. A dose of internal politics saw him taken off the squad days afterwards and returned to a desk job at a north London 'nick'. There, among other things, he processed paper work for traffic offences.

Events in New York also went awry, in a particularly Jamaican way. All the cocaine had been bought and assembled and the couriers organised. But days before it was due to be shipped, one of the mules made off with the whole stash. It turned out that she was the baby-mother of a rival gang member who had infiltrated the operation in order to rip it off.

A Yardie poses for the camera with a gun in one hand and a small quantity of crack in the other

It is not known what happened to the drugs after that, or indeed to her. Such a stunt is not normally associated with a long and happy life. Another of the couriers was monitored and searched on her return to Britain, to see if the gang had managed to pick up anything else to import, but she had nothing.

Their plan in ruins and all their 'investment' gone, the remains of the gang was breaking up back in London. Jubba's address had by then been traced, and it was decided to arrest him and send him home before he could disappear again and get into any more 'badness'. This raid was also a success but, due to a set of circumstances that could not have been foreseen, it degenerated at one stage into something perilously close to farce. Even one officer involved, laughing about it afterwards, just shook his head

and said: 'Keystone Cops'. I tell the story not as a criticism, but as a caution-ary tale, if one were needed, that when dealing with Yardies it is always wise to expect the unexpected.

BY NOW the cold winter mornings have turned into sharp spring and we gather in bright sunshine in yet another council estate car park. It is about 6.30am. Because events have been moving so quickly, this is a hastily arranged job, for which Barker has marshalled four detectives from Dalehouse and a small contingent of TSG support. And Fothers. Head and shoulders above the rest is a huge Glaswegian with a pock-marked face and a very large sledge hammer. Our 'keys'.

It is also an awkward operation because the target address is in a neat row of modern terraced houses, gardens back and front, making an unde-tected approach more difficult than to the door of a flat. Such stealth and a speedy entrance are essential as any warning allows drugs and other evidence to be flushed down the toilet. Jubba is also still thought to have a gun, and no one wants to give him an opportunity to find it.

So, while two officers go round to cover the back, Barker and the hammer man decide on a quick reconnaissance of the front door before the rest of us pile in. They set off down the garden path, almost tip-toeing in an attempt to be inconspicuous. With Barker at 6' 5" and his chum perhaps even bigger, this is the first amusing sight of the day. We gear ourselves up for a late charge but after some animated whispering at the door they are on their way back.

"OK, there is a glass porch with a door that opens outwards. It would make too much noise to get through that so we'll have to go through the back," pants Barker, as we huddle behind the garden fence. After a quick radio call to the others, and leaving two behind to watch the front, the rest of us set off to jog round the block, moving uneasily in our bullet-proof vests. I'm starting to get giggly again.

More problems. The back garden is barred by a six foot fence and the gate is locked. More huddled whispers decide that we are not going to mess about any longer, and it is everybody over the fence and running up the path - towards an identical porch to that on the front door. Our TSG hero, already puzzled by the preceding subtlety, is not going to be denied a second time. Without breaking step, and with a half-grunt half-curse, he swings his hammer and sets about destroying the whole structure. Plate glass and splintered wood fly everywhere, shattering the morning still. But we are through. A second glass door gets the same treatment and the team rush through the hall, launching themselves up the stairs: "POLICE! POLICE! POLICE! POLICE!".

Above, all hell breaks loose - screaming and shouting from multiple voices that I do not understand and the unmistakable thump of a heavy body hitting the floor. Momentarily alone in the hall and at a loss about what to do next, I gingerly toe open one of the downstairs doors. There is Jubba - I recognise him immediately from the airport - fully dressed, good as gold, sitting on a bed with his palms placed flat on either side. He looks at me and I look at him, suddenly aware that the vest I am wearing says 'POLICE' on the front in large friendly letters. What do we do now? What do we do now? Much as some might wish it otherwise, journalists do not have the power of arrest and so I respectfully advise him to stay where he is. "Yes, boss. No problem," he says. What a nice man.

Thankfully at that moment the cavalry arrives in the shape of exhibits man, plastic bags in hand, who has come back downstairs to start 'hoovering up'. I whisper to him that this is our man and he takes over the vigil while I go to find Barker. The reason for this last piece of subtlety is that we are not supposed to know who Jubba is. Again, in order to protect the informant who tipped off Barker about where he was living, the pretence of the raid is that it is a routine immigration event and we will 'discover' Jubba's illegal status during a normal round of questioning.

Upstairs it is still chaos. The up-side is that our immigration cover story is getting an unexpected boost. About a dozen black people are shouting animatedly in French, waving hands, passports and paperwork at a bemused Fotheringham. Children are screaming as usual, and the crowd seems to be growing by the second. We have stumbled, apparently, on a house full of recent arrivals from French Guiana who are protesting their rights to be here. Fotheringham is trying to impress on them that they are not his primary concern while he is also taking a tongue-lashing from a Jamaican woman who does turn out to be an illegal. Whoever is supposed to be renting the house from the council must be making a fortune. They do not seem to be there. "What's going on? Where's Steve?" I ask, squeezing myself past the ruck. "How the fuck should I know?" replies Fothers. Fair comment.

In one of the bedrooms, a tall black guy in his underpants is eating serious carpet. He was the thump I had heard earlier. "When we come into a room and say, 'Stay where you are and shut up', you do it. All right?" shouts the officer, pinning the youth down, into his ear. The young man is already cuffed and immobile but still gamely trying to raise his head to say something. Interpreting this as another struggle, the policeman keeps pushing him down again, oblivious to the fact that this is not the target. Some time later, when he does get a chance to speak, it transpires that the youth was trying to explain that he had recently signed up for the Met Police and that he was due to begin his course at Hendon Police College the following week. I think he is beginning to have second thoughts.

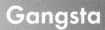

Things calm down quickly and Barker and Fotheringham get into the charade of interviewing Jubba to 'discover' his immigration status. He answers all questions quickly and politely, if untruthfully, but clearly knows that the game is up. Perhaps he is thinking that Jamaica is very pleasant at this time of year. Indeed, throughout the raid, he is the only person in the house who doesn't cause any trouble. He is a pro, you see. The one time Jubba's cool demeanour is shaken for a moment is when one officer, in the course of searching the room, snags his hand on a cupboard and snaps on a surgical glove to protect against infection. Jubba's eyes widen, and he has to be assured that an internal examination is not on the agenda.

As we are leaving - with Jubba and the Jamaican woman in tow, bags packed - the prospective police cadet returns with his lawyer, who has been raised from his bed for the purposes of lodging a complaint. "I mean, I'm shocked, man," said the youth. "Here am I about to join the force and you treat me like that. I'm wondering what I'm getting into. I'm shocked, man." Barker, ever the diplomat, apologises for any inconvenience caused, but adds that we had been in a potentially dangerous situation in which you couldn't afford to take any chances. He should have done what he was told. He'd learn about it in training. Barker also asks what, in any case, was a future officer of the Queen doing living in a house that had been illicitly rented to persons of questionable immigration status? The lawyer, short, stout and also black, is all smiles and conciliation despite the early hour. He advises his client to let the matter drop, and he does. With that little coda, the morning's excitement is over.

OPERATION Big Apple was also drawing to a close. The gang's leader was picked up in north London a few days later, and also deported. Both he and Jubba were last heard of in New York. Jubba probably never knew how much trouble he had caused.

A detail that later emerged, however, confirmed just what a cool customer he was. On their arrest, all the gang were found to be carrying false British passports, and in Jubba's case the identity was of a 16-year-old boy. He had apparently bought the birth certificate off a friend's son. After submitting his application, he had been down to the Passport Office to collect the new 'book' only to have the clerk ask him to wait a moment because of a query from further up the line. In that situation you would expect most people to do a runner. Not Jubba. He waited patiently to be told that, because of his age, he would have to get his mum to sign the application form. He took it back, got someone to sign it and later received his passport. With front like that, he could be expected back in Britain at any time.

Operation Dalehouse

DESPITE my surprise at coming face to face with Jubba during the raid, he was not the first bad bwoy I had encountered on a police exercise. That had come some weeks before, following a late night call-out from Dalehouse. For someone coming to the subject through hysterical headlines about 'evil' gangsters and 'cold-bloodied murderers', the real surprise was that Jubba's courteous demeanour was not untypical for your average Yardie. From the ghettos of Kingston to the police cells of London, most of the Jamaican criminals I have met were intelligent, articulate and appreciative of a good joke even at their own expense – in short, quite charming. Yet there was never any question that they were capable of all the things attributed to them - torturing women with electric irons and boiling water being just one delightful example. It is yet another of the many complications and apparent contradictions in the Yardie story.

Those who know the scene just take it on board and act accordingly. I saw Barker, Brennan and Fotheringham repeatedly play on this line of mutual respect and cordiality when interviewing suspects and get a lot of change back for it. In Britain, no doubt part of the reason is the contrast the bad bwoys find between this kind of treatment and what they could expect, certainly until recently, at the hands of the Jamaican constabulary. In the past they have been shown to be not above a bit of tactical torture themselves; "a few licks never did anyone any harm" being an accepted rule of thumb.

One afternoon at Brixton police station, Barker got a call from the charge room 'skipper' (sergeant) to say that a yout' had been picked up on the street for dealing spliffs and that no one could understand a word he was saying. Could Steve assist? It was small beer but still had to be attended to. Even at a modern 'nick' like Brixton, the cells are not designed to be particularly welcoming places, and when we got to him the kid was cowering in the corner of one, clearly terrified. The skipper had a point. Thick patois was all the boy had to offer and his nervous state made it even harder to decipher.

A couple of doses of the Barker treatment – Was there anything he needed? Was there anyone we should contact to tell where he was? Would he like a cup of tea? - confused the hell out of the poor fellow. Asking intelligent questions about where he was from in Jamaica also helped, and soon he relaxed and became more coherent. Barker is not a social worker, however, and in the course of his little chats managed to trap the boy into lying about his home town. A bit more pressure and he had established that that he was going under a false name. Finally, probably out of gratitude, he confessed that he shouldn't have been there at all. Sorted. Quick call to immigration, and he was booked on the next flight to Jamaica. It was a technique I was to see more of, with a much tougher nut, a few days later.

THE END of another long Dalehouse day, Brennan and Barker are packing up for the night and contemplating the joys of a quick pint in the 'office' with Fothers and friends. As we are heading for the door, however, the telephone rings. It is a call from Special Branch (the police arm of the security services) at Heathrow airport, who have just 'tugged' an unsavoury-looking Jamaican character arriving on a British passport from Los Angeles.

His bags had contained nothing incriminating but the Special Branch officer, we'll call him Clive, "just didn't like the look of him". In the absence of any more conventional intelligence, the game of chasing gangstas often relies on this kind of intuition. It had seemed to pay off when Clive checked the man's identity as given on his passport and found that he was wanted in Birmingham. He was held while the file pictures of the wanted man were sent down for confirmation only to find that they didn't match. Clive (very collar and tie) is confused.

On arrival in the cells at Heathrow, we can see why his suspicions were raised in the first place. Our man is big, very big, with a heavily scarred face. He is also extremely cool in his baggy Ragga 'threads' and has a smile to die for.

In the rest area, where we grab a cup of tea, one of the local boys is extremely excited about the whole thing. "Aren't you the guys who deal with Yardies?" he asks. "Is he a Yardie, is he? I hear they are really bad bastards who'll kill anybody as soon as look at them. Wear lots of gold chains and stuff. Isn't that right?" So much for the standard police view of the issue at the time. Barker adopts his own kind of cool and shoots the man a withering look, "Something like that," he mutters. "Jesus," says Brennan, rolling his eyes, as we go back to the cells.

The Yardie, who is going under the unlikely name of John Brown, readily agrees to an informal 'chat' and so waives the need for a properly structured, taped interview. He seems more than happy to chance his arm with these civil-tongued policemen and the boys go into action - polite, as ever, casual and funny. Brennan does most of the talking with Barker cutting in with the odd, sharp question. Nice cop, (not very) nasty cop.

For about two hours the conversation revolves around endless innocuous inquiries about where he comes from in Jamaica, what he was doing in America and where he is supposed to come from in Britain - Birmingham, as it happens. Brennan asks about the geography of that city, football teams and even the numbers of bus routes. To all questions, our suspect answers confidently, pausing occasionally to raise his eyes to the ceiling or suck his teeth in the classic Jamaican expression of disgust or boredom. In general, he adopts a poise of puzzled innocence that anyone could doubt his word. Throughout, Clive sits quietly in the corner, looking equally puzzled. It is quite a performance. Towards the end of it all, Brennan moves in for a low-key kill: "Lots of respect to you, man, nuff respect. You've done very well and on any other day you'd have walked through here. Coming through Los Angeles is a new one, I like that. Very clever. But today, you see, you're unlucky. So unlucky, man, it's hard to believe." He has the undivided attention of his audience.

"You see, in this room right now you have the two policemen in Britain who know more about Jamaica and Jamaicans than anybody else." A shift in the chair, perhaps. A cock of the head. Otherwise, no response.

"I don't know who the fuck you are but you're definitely not John Brown and you don't come from Birmingham. Why don't you just tell us who you are, we'll put you on the next plane to Kingston and we can all get some sleep. Come on, next time you try it on you're almost certain to get in… "

"Yeah man, mi John Brown. Mi from Aston, Birmingham," cuts in our man, defiantly.

"You're not John Brown and you are going back, so lets get it over with," says Brennan. He opens his wallet and tosses a Polaroid photograph across. It is a picture of Trinity, with his arm around Brennan and with the inscription "To my good friend Blondie" written across the bottom. It is an old,

favourite trick. "Do you recognise this man?" he asks.

"Yeah man, 'im Trinity. 'Im big man in Jamaica."

"How would you like me to call him now and get him to meet you off the plane tomorrow?" asks Brennan, innocently.

"Mi John Brown. Mi from Birmingham," comes the reply, less confident but holding his ground.

"Okay, okay. You're doubly unlucky because I'm from Birmingham. Aston is not on the south side of the city, it's on the north. The Outer Circle bus route is the number 11; anyone who's lived in Birmingham knows that.

Detective Sergeant John ('Blondie') Brennan with the legendary Keith 'Trinity' Gardner

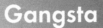

And Aston Villa don't play in orange. I know, I used to play for them myself!" It is all true. Our man laughs nervously, he is shaken.

Brennan goes in again. "On top of all that, he used to live in Birmingham and he knows Jamaica as well," he says pointing at me, who has been sitting silently in the back corner, scribbling furiously. The man swivels round and shoots me a frightened look, caught off balance at last. So am I, but it is also true, so I nod sagely.

"Roll up your sleeves," demands Brennan. The man's arms are covered with scars. He opens his shirt and his chest tells the same story - huge, angry-looking gashes. "Those are machete scars from fighting, aren't they? You're a bad boy and you're going back, I'm sorry."

"No man, dem is from when I fell off mi bike when I was about 10," he offers, recovering rather well I thought. "Dem look so bad because it's some 'ting to do wi' mi skin, yeh knaw. It no heal properly. It's a black man ting."

"And what about the scars on your face? Are those from when you fell off your bike as well?"

"Deese? No man. That was, wa' yu call it now? Dat was some 'ting I do wi' mi razor."

"You mean you cut yourself shaving?"

"Yeah man!" he says, triumphantly. The room collapses in laughter. Even Clive has completely lost it.

'Mr Brown' never does give up and tell us who he really is but, eventually, he resigns himself to a free trip home, courtesy of HM Government. Charming to the end, he agrees to have his fingerprints taken and even mends the police's Polaroid camera so that we can get a picture of him "just for the records".

"He'll be back in a couple of weeks," said Brennan, pocketing the photograph.

He was probably right. In any case, this was not a false alarm. The fingerprints were checked with the Yard the next day and revealed that our man, while not John Brown, had previously been convicted for drugs offences in Birmingham and then deported after serving his sentence. Checks in America showed that he was currently wanted in Los Angeles, also for drugs trafficking.

The latest intelligence is that he is now back there.

Chapter Nine

TUFFY

I F Rankin' Dread was the most high profile gangsta to make his impact on
Britain during the first wave of Yardie activity in the late 1980's, then
'Tuffy' can be seen as the most influential figure of the second, more
deadly, influx of the early 1990's. As with 'Dread', his legacy has as much to
do with the reaction he elicited from the British authorities as anything he
actually achieved. But he has the classic 'bad bwoy' profile from this
period, and his story provides evidence to develop a number of arguments
already touched on. Most brutally, he illustrates the much-quoted cliché
that Jamaican gunmen do not expect to live until they are 35. Tuffy was
gunned down in London in May 1993, a few months short of his 34th birthday.

Christopher Alexander Bourne, aka Mark McGibbon, aka Leroy
Matthews, aka Lloyd Barnett, aka Peter Bolan, aka Amos Benjamin, aka
'Tuffy', first came to the attention of the Met as early as February 1988
when he was arrested on suspicion of supplying cocaine. This was the
period when the Yardie problem was first being taken seriously, indeed by
coincidence this first arrest came the day after Roy Ramm's Operation Lucy
was announced. Tuffy was quickly identified as a potential player in what
was then known as Jamaican Organised Crime in north London, but the
charges against him didn't stick and he was released. Over the next five
years he was to lead the authorities a merry dance as they pursued him
through a maze of deception and false identities. Their gradual realisation
of who they were really dealing with ran in parallel with their develping
understanding of the whole problem.

Tuffy was arrested again the following September, this time for selling
cocaine on the notorious 'front line' of Sandringham Road in Hackney, east
London, and for possession of heroin and cannabis. He was also charged
with assaulting a police officer during the arrest. This time he was held in
custody, as police and immigration struggled to establish his true identity.
Officers suspected that he was the brother of a Jamaican calling himself
Andrew Washington Green, who had been arrested during the high-profile
raid on the Four Aces club in Dalston, east London - also in February 1988.
Tuffy was thought to be operating with Green and another brother to establish a cocaine importation operation.

His story, however, was that he was called Christopher Bourne and had
been in the country since the early 1970's when he had been brought here
from Jamaica by an aunt. He had a steady girlfriend and a child, he said,
and was trying to make an honest life for himself. It was a story he stuck to

for over a year in custody, despite growing evidence that he represented something far more sinister. The matter remained unresolved by the time his cases came to court, and following conviction he was deported as an illegal immigrant in late September 1989.

Two months later he was back with a brand new identity of Amos Benjamin and a Jamaican passport to match. He was stopped by a suspicious immigration officer at Heathrow after his cover story failed to check out; his forged passport was taken away and he was told to report back a few days later. Tuffy, unsurprisingly, failed to turn up, and disappeared into the growing Jamaican underworld of north London.

By the time police heard that he was on the scene again, the stakes had risen considerably. Checks through Interpol had finally borne fruit, revealing that the innocent-sounding Mr Bourne was in fact Mark McGibbon, raised in the ghettos of west Kingston and with the unmistakable credentials of a dangerous political gunman. He had twice been convicted by the Gun Court in Kingston for firearms and robbery offences, in 1975 and 1978, finally receiving two life sentences, reduced to 15 years hard labour on appeal. It later emerged that these charges related to the theft of ballot-boxes. He had been released on parole in 1985.

As the months went by, and the search for him intensified, more details of his past were added to the picture. Tuffy was born on the 24th October 1959 in the Victoria Jubilee Hospital in Kingston, Jamaica. He grew up in Tivoli Gardens where he set about building a fearsome reputation for himself as a JLP gunman and enforcer. He became a trusted lieutenant of Jim Brown, and following his release from prison in Jamaica had spent some time in Miami as a hit-man for the Shower Posse. He remained a committed Labourite, describing the former PNP government as communists, and boasted that he would return to Jamaica to fight the good fight with bombs, bullets or mortars should the need ever arise. At one time he had even been talked about as a possible successor to the Brown dynasty, and his name has been linked to 25 unsolved murders in Jamaica and America.

His family shared a similar 'illustrious' background and two of his brothers were to meet similar fates. Andrew Washington Green, real name Joseph McGibbon, was eventually sentenced to three years for drugs offences in Britain, but he fled the country after being granted a weekend's home leave. He was last heard of in Rikers Island prison, New York, serving a long stretch for murder and robbery. Another brother, street name 'Booba', was removed from Britain four times as an illegal entrant and for his suspected involvement in cocaine trafficking. He was killed in New York in 1991.

BY 1990, the renewed hunt for Tuffy had moved south of the River Thames. Following the drugs-dealing fashion of that time he had moved into crack and, together with a small posse of like-minded gangstas, was running a string of crack houses on the Myatt's Field estate in Brixton. His influence was such that at the height of his powers he and his confederates, 'Honey', 'Lippy' and 'Showy', were said to virtually control the whole estate. He was also known to have links into a notorious crack estate in north Peckham.

During this period Tuffy twice narrowly escaped the police dragnet. On both occasions he was stopped by routine patrols and charged with minor offences but he gave yet more false names and was allowed to walk away.

In January 1991, however, the police were ready to move on his operation. Officers from the crack squad, with local back-up, mounted a large raid on one of the Myatt's Field crack-houses where a 9mm handgun, over 60 'rocks' and bundles of cash were seized. Tuffy, however, got away again. He jumped out of one of the third-floor windows as the team crashed into the flat, his fall cushioned by a passer-by who suffered a broken leg. Showy was not so lucky. He also made the leap, but broke his own leg and was caught while trying to crawl away from the scene.

Tuffy was finally arrested almost two weeks later after buying an air ticket to bring in another of his brothers using two forged £50 notes. He and the people arrested during the raid were all charged with selling crack and for possession of an illegal firearm but, again showing the difficulty of making such charges stick, none of the cases ever got to court. There were nine people in the flat at the time, and it proved impossible to find enough evidence to link any of them to either the gun or the drugs for a conviction to be secured. Tuffy, however, was prosecuted on a forgery charge and, having spent another year in jail, was deported again in January.

During his time inside he had married his girlfriend in an attempt to avoid being sent back. This part of his case, however, was weakened by the fact that he had fathered another child by a baby mother on the Myatt's Field estate while operating from there.

For Showy, his leap for freedom eventually proved to be his salvation. He was allowed to stay in Britain to receive medical treatment for his shattered leg but he checked himself out of hospital and melted away.

Like so many Jamaican gangstas, Tuffy was nothing if not persistent. Having tasted the possibility of the good life in Britain, he was determined to return again.

Over the next year he made several attempts to elude immigration controls at Gatwick on direct flights from Kingston but each time was turned away. Ever inventive, on February 5, 1993, he hatched the plan of flying to Brussels and then taking the short flight to Birmingham on yet another set of false documentation. Again he was stopped at immigration while the single officer on duty there ran checks. After about an hour of sitting on a bench in the immigration hall, and while the officer was distract-

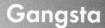

ed dealing with another incoming flight, he simply picked up his suitcase, jumped over the barrier and ran out of the airport. He caught a taxi outside and was gone.

When he surfaced again in London shortly afterwards, it was as the head of the 'Robin Hood' posse.

THE ROBIN HOOD was a fascinating and frightening development on a number of levels. Firstly, as the name suggests, it was at least in part politically motivated. The idea was to rob from the rich, in this case anybody living in the 'rich' society in Britain, in order to generate funds for the poor 'sufferers' of the ghetto. Evidence from informants indicates that Tuffy came under a lot of pressure to deliver cash and gold jewellery to feed the coffers of the Tivoli operation, itself coming under increasing pressure from more effective police activity in Jamaica and the success of American law enforcement action against its US-based drugs networks. By the time the posse met its end, it was also said to have acquired hand grenades, semi-automatic pistols and other heavy weaponry in order to pursue these goals.

On the other side, the activities of Tuffy and his 'cru' showed the relatively modest ambitions that motivates such criminals to violent action. All Tuffy was trying to achieve for himself, according to the word on the street, was to accumulate £150,000 so that he could build himself a nice house with a pool somewhere on the hills around Kingston, retire and live 'large'.

In order to satisfy these various demands, Tuffy teamed up with his old friend 'Showy', aka Howard Williams, and also with Christopher Daniels ('Pekos') and Andrew Bambury ('Bambury' or 'Mackerel'). All were originally from Tivoli Gardens, all dyed-in-the-wool JLP men. In addition they recruited Eric Marcarno, a Trinidadian, to act as their driver, and a couple of British-born criminals with Jamaican connections. Together they went on a robbery spree around Stoke Newington and Hackney, both traditionally dominated by PNP gangstas, holding up Jamaican dances to take chains and other jewellery and robbing shops and illegal gambling dens at gun point. At one dance in Dalston, some of the victims were said to be members of a local off-shoot of the Spangler posse, and there was much talk of a fully-fledged gang-war developing. It never had the time to happen.

Proving again, however, that nothing in this world is simple or easily reduced to tribal loyalties, at one stage the gang linked up with some soldiers from Tel Aviv, a big PNP area in central Kingston. This reinforces the view that, while political business might hold some sway, when in Britain the primary concern is making money - as much and as fast as possible.

SOMETHING of a 'Don-man' in his own right, the tawdry business of importing cocaine, converting it to crack and selling it on street corners was by then somewhat beneath the view of himself that Tuffy had developed. So he re-entered the drugs market by ripping off dealers and then forcing others to sell the proceeds for him. All he and the bwoys had to do was carry big guns, talk big and pick up the money. One of the more audacious operations that the Robin Hood was said to have carried out was the robbery of Harry's Café - then a known centre for crack dealing in Brixton. In the end, it was this high-risk strategy that was to prove Tuffy's downfall.

The gang first came to the attention of the police after reports of a 'hit' on a drugs dealer in Notting Hill - targeted for sleeping with the wrong woman. Detectives tracked Tuffy to a flat in Clapham, south London, but during the raid he escaped again, out of a back window. Despite a prolonged chase, he was lost. By the spring of 1993 he was back in Brixton, setting up what was to be his last act of badness.

His plan was a variation on the lucrative formula mentioned above - stealing a consignment of cocaine from other dealers and then selling it for him through an established crack house. The chosen venue was a flat in Vassall Road, Brixton. The story goes that he phoned up the dealers who ran it, they agreed to his demands of using the place for a couple of days and told him to come round and collect the keys.

At 9.15pm on May 30th, he went down with Showy and a couple of his other bwoys to complete the deal. But once inside, with the metal security door shut behind him, things went very badly wrong. His three intended Jamaican victims were ready, as it was said that they had already been ripped off by Tuffy on a previous occasion. Their leader, Raymond 'Emma' Grant, started an argument, saying to another of those present: "Tell your boy I've got a gun on me", before pulling it out. When Tuffy grabbed for the gun, the other two also produced weapons and opened fire. In a shower of at least 13 bullets Tuffy was hit four times at point-blank range, including three shots to his chest. Still, he managed to escape outside and ran off down the street with his attackers firing after him. He ran for over half a mile before collapsing, and died in hospital later that night. A local police inspector described it as being: "Like a St Valentine's Day massacre - a killing of frightening proportions".

WITHIN HOURS, and showing the close connections between events in Britain and those in Jamaica, reprisals started on the streets of west Kingston. Suspecting a political motive behind the shooting, gunmen from Tivoli attacked neighbouring PNP areas, killing one man and leaving many others wounded. The resulting 'warfare' continued for weeks, accounting for up to 20 deaths.

It culminated in another horrifying massacre at dawn on June 29 when

an old man and two young children were murdered in Hannah Town. At 6am, about a dozen men had cordoned off parts of Drummond Street before opening fire with high-powered weapons on the house where the three were sleeping. Lamar Mitchell, aged seven, received several shots in his young chest from an M-16 rifle and one of his knee caps was blown away. His five-year-old sister, Audrey, had her face torn off by bullets. Harold Hines, a 65-year-old shoemaker, was shot through the head. One witness said they had heard the young boy pleading for mercy before the killers had cold-bloodedly dispatched him. The children's mother was also shot, but survived with a deformed arm.

Pictures of the disfigured corpses, splashed over front pages in Jamaica and on national television, shocked the country. Despite being hardened by decades of violence and gun law, this slaughter of the innocents was something of a very different order. One newspaper editorial spoke of 'the swelling tide of barbarism on our island' while local young people broke the traditional code of silence to go on television and condemn the killings and the gang war. By October, the Special Anti-Crime Task Force had tracked down and shot dead two of the main suspects.

In Britain, people were also speaking out. Another unprecedented development saw more than 50 witnesses from the Brixton community come forward to give evidence over the Tuffy shooting. It led to the conviction of Raymond Grant, then 28 and with previous convictions for drugs offences. He was jailed for life at the Old Bailey in 1994 with a recommendation that he serve 20 years. He claimed he had been framed by witnesses, and supporters shouted "Racist! Racist!" when the sentence was handed down. Three other co-defendants were cleared by the jury.

Speaking outside the court, Detective Inspector Jim Webster of Brixton police station said: "People are sick to the teeth of their streets being taken over by gun running and drugs. We are delighted with the public's response in this case. It seems people are realising that without the help of the public we will not get anywhere in our fight against crime."

After Tuffy's death, the rest of the Robin Hood posse soon fell apart. Showy, his right-hand man, was arrested in Brixton, charged with illegal entry and deported. He is since said to have returned to Britain. Pekos and Marcarno were arrested after robbing a local Jamaican grocery shop. They threatened the owners with a .44 Magnum and a .22 revolver and got away with about £1,000 in cash - but not very far. The premises were under police surveillance at the time over a completely separate matter, and the pair were arrested round the corner. Each got nine years in prison for armed robbery and illegal possession of firearms.

Bambury was killed in Stoke Newington. After having robbed a group of Trinidadians and Guyanese, he foolishly returned to the scene, was stabbed in the neck and bled to death.

As for Tuffy, his body was flown back to Kingston for burial. On the wall of his tomb above his head is a large inscription of an automatic pistol surrounded by a laurel wreath. "He lived by the gun and died by the gun," said one detective involved in the case. "He even had a bullet hole in his manhood from a previous shooting."

THE POLITICAL impact of the Tuffy shooting in Britain was immediate and significant, bringing to an end official reticence on the subject of Jamaican gang crime that had prevailed since the winding down and closure of Operation Dalehouse at the end of 1992. The reason was that the problem, assumed to have been over-estimated and then to have gone away completely, was re-asserting itself on the streets of London with a vengeance.

To re-cap, Dalehouse had been established in August 1991 following a spate of Yardie-related killings in the Metropolitan Police's 4 Area, principally Brixton. Official figures show that in the 10 months between July 1990 and April 1991 there had been seven such murders. Once up and running, the operation's main problem was in getting convictions when cases it investigated were brought to court, not least due to witness intimidation. But figures also provide strong evidence that Dalehouse was a highly effective deterrent against gun crime in the area, and succeeded in dramatically reducing the murder rate. In the next ten months between April 1991 and February 1992 there were three such killings. From then until the end of the year, there were none. This, ironically, was given as one of the reasons for closing the squad - if there were no longer any crack-related murders in 4 Area, then what was the problem? Dalehouse had done its job of making the streets of Brixton safe again and could be shut down with pats on the back all round.

The fatal flaw in this logic was exposed with poetic speed. On January 1, 1993, the very day after Dalehouse finally closed for business, the killing started up again. The victim was a 20-year-old identified as Richard Higgs, who was blown away by a sawn-off shotgun on the Landsdowne Estate in Clapham, south London. He was taken to hospital and put on a life-support machine but this was switched off after his mother came to visit him from Jamaica. Detectives investigating the case believed he had been an 'enforcer', brought into the country to settle drugs disputes, and linked him to three previous crack-related murders - in Harlesden, north-west London, in Stoke Newington and in Jamaica.

The day after the Higgs murder there was another drugs-related shooting in south London.

At the beginning of February, also in Clapham, Wesley Barnett, 25, was

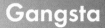

shot dead outside an off-licence in an execution-style killing. He had been blasted in the chest outside his home but then managed to run 100 yards up a residential street before being 'finished off' by three men who chased him in a car. Although a nearby estate had some reputation for drugs dealing, this was by no means a ghetto area. A further 200 yards up the road is a gentrified strip of shops, wine bars and restaurants popular with local 'yuppies'. Again, however, a drugs dispute was given as the reason.

The violent litany continued. On February 28th, four people were attacked at a flat in Vauxhall, south London. Three were shot and a fourth thrown out of a window.

By the time Tuffy was shot at the end of May, the Area-4 toll was six Yardie-related murders in five months. The situation was worse than it had ever been. Elsewhere in London the appearance of enforcers from Jamaica was also being reported. At least six punishment shootings had taken place in the previous few months on estates in Harlesden and Wembley, with victims being shot in the legs, apparently on the orders of drug dealers. In Stoke Newington, a high technology surveillance operation was set up to combat the growth of crack dealing in that area. Police in Birmingham, Bristol and Manchester were also seeing the problem of crack-related violence intensifying.

In June, Paul Condon, the Metropolitan Police Commissioner, admitted the gun battles between Yardie factions had got out of hand. In an interview with the Independent on Sunday, his first since taking over the job some five months before, he said: "It is day-to-day turf war. The level of violence is such that they do not mind shooting each other just to save selling that day." Condon also revealed that a review of anti-Yardie intelligence gathering had been ordered.

Most dramatically, he said that rises in terrorism and gun crime could lead to Britain's policemen being routinely armed. An armed service would take shape by a 'creeping process' as increasing numbers of officers would need to carry weapons. "There will be more and more specialist units and more and more officers on the streets who will have to be armed," said Condon. "I don't seek it but it could happen within 10 to 20 years. I do not believe it is inevitable, but it is probable."

Such unusual candour from the country's top policeman, apparently signalling another U-turn in policy, was no coincidence. On the subject of fresh, concerted action against Jamaican gangs Condon had already had his orders from no less than Michael Howard, the newly-appointed Home Secretary, in charge of the police. No doubt prompted by widespread press coverage of the Tuffy shooting, Howard had visited Brixton shortly afterwards and was told by officers that new initiatives were required if the resurgent problem was to be contained. He in turn demanded action from

Condon, saying that the gangs were a serious threat to law and order.

The immediate response was to dispatch Detective Chief Superintendent Roy Clark, deputy head of criminal intelligence (SO11) at Scotland Yard, to Kingston and New York for yet another assessment of the situation. Clark's report was to make explosive reading for his Yard bosses, and led to the setting up of the latest squad targeted against Jamaican criminals.

DETAILS of this highly confidential 'Executive Summary' remained unpublicised until 1997. It is easy to see why. The report contains strong criticism of the Met's policy on Yardies as it then stood and backs up the views of those working in the area which had for so long been dismissed as special pleading or crying wolf. It pin-points Jamaican criminals as the most dangerous threat facing police in the capital and overturns the orthodoxy that they presented only a localised and temporary problem.

Clark concludes with his own ringing call for action: "It has been made abundantly clear by all I have spoken to that unless there is a consistent, aggressive and long-term strategy to deal with Jamaican criminals in London there will be ever and sharply (sic) increases in murder, violence, drug related crime and crack availability."

The first point to make about the report and the squad that it subsequently spawned is that they were specifically aimed at the threat from Jamaican criminal gangs. This only needs stating because that fact has been denied by the Yard ever since. Hog-tied by the political need for racial sensitivity, the targeting of elements within this specific, black ethnic group can still not be acknowledged - despite all the evidence that such a policy is necessary.

At one confidential, background briefing I attended in 1993, a senior Yard intelligence officer tied himself in knots to avoid admitting that such targeting was taking place. This was a performance worthy of the most elusive cabinet minister being interviewed on breakfast radio. After much persistent questioning, he closed the subject with the despairing statement: "You must write what you want, but I couldn't possibly say it."

Clark's report is, thankfully, unequivocal. Entitled 'Jamaican Gangs in London', its introduction begins: "The purpose of this paper is to explore the problem and background of Jamaican criminals who are increasingly active in areas of London and some other cities within England." It continues with an eerie air of deja vu. "The document makes several strategic and tactical recommendations to combat what is clearly an increasing threat to London by violent criminals who have almost unlimited access to firearms and drugs, and an ability to carry them across borders with apparent ease." After praising the work of the informal team of police, customs

and immigration officers whose exchanges of information in the south London pub I have previously mentioned, the section concludes with this damning criticism of the direction of police policy: "There has been an almost complete breakdown of a Metropolitan Police Strategic response and of the formal intelligence gathering and development structure."

Two of the report's key recommendations involve developing greater co-operation between police in this country and the Jamaican Constabulary Force (JCF). In his background notes on the situation in Jamaica, however, Clark accurately assesses the problems with this idea, given the historic splits within the JCF along party political lines. Again, he pulls no punches: "The Police Force is regarded as thoroughly corrupt, brutal and inept by very influential people on the island," he says. "They are regarded as the biggest and most powerful posse. They are part of the problem."

It only fair to note that these comments were made before the appointment of Colonel Trevor MacMillan as police commissioner later that year, and the serious attempts at reform that he undertook. Clark also goes on to commend a number of JCF officers for their dedication and willingness to cooperate.

To illustrate the stark realities of Jamaican life he includes the weekly list of murders, published by the Sunday Gleaner, from the time that he was there. This 'frightening picture' shows that there had been 23 murders that week, 14 of them involving the use of firearms and taking place within Kingston, a city with a population of 700,000. "It is said that almost every child has witnessed at least one shooting, or seen the body of a murder victim, by the age of 10 years," says Clark.

On the political front, he describes the island's turbulent history and claims of links between senior party figures of both sides and the posse leaders. Even at the latest election, which took place in March 1993, he notes that there was evidence of ballot-rigging - with some polling areas returning 100% votes in favour of one party or the other. Anecdotal evidence from Jamaicans working at the British High Commission is also quoted. They were allowed home early to vote but reported the next day that either they had not been allowed near their polling station or that someone had already voted in their name. "Not one successfully voted," says Clark.

He adds that the police and army clampdown introduced at the time of the election, known as Operation Ardent, may have contributed to an increase in gang activity in Britain. The wider implications for the country of the parlous state of Jamaican society are equally gloomy. "There is no sign of improvement in the economy or the life of Jamaicans. The main industries: sugar, bauxite and tourism are all in decline. The latter is a direct result of violence and general lawlessness," he says. "With generations of young Jamaicans within the ghetto having no hope of success other than through the gun and involvement in crime, it is clear the Yardie problem will be with us for many years. Our strategy must therefore be long term if we are to prevent the Jamaican gangs infiltrating and taking a permanent hold in London and then spreading elsewhere."

On the nature of the Yardie criminal himself and the threat that he poses, Clark is characteristically forthright. "Whilst it may seem obvious from the record of shootings in Jamaica, the gang member is probably the most violent criminal police in London may have to face. A Yardie will not hesitate to commit acts of violence against police officers, members of the public or other Yardies," says his report. "Whilst many criminals will resort to violence as a last resort, a member of a Jamaican gang will use violence as a first step and without hesitation, indeed many people have died at their hands for no apparent reason. A casual bump into one of them has been known to result in murder."

It then re-rehearses the thirst of the Yardie for trappings of success - expensive clothes and jewellery, an expensive car to drive and the most powerful gun possible at his disposal - all to add to his status, all financed through drugs dealing or robbery. "He will not hesitate to 'rip-off' another Yardie of drugs or cash but he lives in constant fear of being so treated himself. They will lie and not hesitate to make allegations against police officers."

Clark backs this up with an example from New York where one gang member demanded that three female associates give evidence accusing a police officer of throwing another gang member from a roof. The officer was about to be indicted for murder when it was found that the women had been lying, and that they had done so through fear. "Equally, a Yardie accused of a crime will seek to intimidate witnesses as a matter of course," says the report.

The use of multiple identities is also highlighted, with its attendant market in stolen passports and other documentation. A Yardie's street name will be maintained as far as possible as the basis of reputation but even this will be changed when necessary. "The only constants are his fingerprints and he is very aware of that weakness in his plans to beat the law," says Clark. Experience in New York showed how gang members deliberately smudged fingerprints while they were being taken, or used 'chapstick' and other chemicals in order to alter their condition and fool identification experts.

Also from the USA, there is a telling story about the close connections between Jamaican criminals on both sides of the Atlantic and the speed with which they can communicate. An officer in the New York District Attorney's Office received a call from an informant to tell him about Tuffy's

murder the day after it happened, even though the man was in jail at the time. "The informant had not only heard of the murder of a fellow Jamaican over 3,000 miles away from within prison, but was also able to suggest who was responsible, the motive, and background," says Clark.

Finally, he draws a frightening lesson as to where the problem is heading in this country. "The Jamaican, American and UK experience has shown that the Jamaican Yardies become role models for young and impressionable black youths," he says. "Young British boys are being lured into crime and possible imprisonment and death by the sight and word of the rich trappings with which Yardies surround themselves."

THE IMPORTANCE of this report cannot be overestimated. It shows the extent of police knowledge at the time, and so the basis on which future policy was formulated. Clark's report is quoted here at such length not in the interests of sensationalism, but to show that there is a realisation of the scale of the problem at the highest levels in British policing - whatever may be said in public. Yardies, and the particular dangers they represent, are not figments from the imaginations of hysterical journalists in search of an easy, or racist, scoop. They are a reality that has been officially recognised as such for years.

Indeed, some of the most sensational or fascinating details in this report cannot be reproduced here for security reasons or because of a lack of supporting evidence. Nor can the impressive list of sources from whom Clark drew his conclusions. What can be said with authority, however, is that according to all official assessments over a period of almost 10 years, of which Clark's was just the latest, the threat has increased not diminished and has the potential to continue doing so 'for many years to come'.

In order to combat this threat, Clark made 35 detailed recommendations. These centred on the need to build a powerful, intelligence-led unit within SO11 which could collate and co-ordinate all the disparate records on Jamaican criminals and use this information to direct operations against the gangs. The unit should be manned by the small number of Jamaican experts who had continued to operate in the field, and the informal working relationships they had formed with customs and immigration officers should be formalised within the unit. Links with police in Jamaica should be strengthened with a free exchange of information, and formal links with law enforcement agencies in the USA and Canada who were tackling the problem there should be established. Priority should be given to the use and development of informants both in this country and Jamaica as the most effective means of gathering new intelligence.

All of these specific recommendations were implemented, and quickly. By September 1993 the new squad was already being set up, led by Clark and ultimately answerable to Commander John Grieve, then the head of SO11. Its brief was to concentrate on gathering intelligence for the Met, but also to provide a national resource for other forces with a Yardie problem. Officers from drug squads who have worked closely with the unit say that it now boasts the most comprehensive data-base on Jamaican criminals in the world. This facility was particularly boosted by gaining access to the 40,000 computerised records and photographs accumulated by the New York District Attorney's Office and to the 'gangbusters' data-base of the Federal Bureau of Alcohol, Tobacco and Firearms.

The positive response to his report must have surprised even Clark. At one point in it he anticipates the political and financial difficulties of his proposed action. "I am aware that the formation of such a group is against current policy and management practice and will probably be opposed," he says, before driving home his message again. "However it is clear that failure to deal decisively with the problem of Yardies will result in an increasing number of murders and violent offences which will, in all probability, result in even greater abstraction from Division and Area."

Two of his key recommendations, however, did not bear fruit. The first was the highly sensitive idea of imposing visa requirements on Jamaican nationals wishing to enter Britain. This was aimed at counteracting the 'active trade' in forged or altered passports by putting an extra hurdle in the way of roaming Yardies. Given that Jamaica is a Commonwealth country, whose head of state is still the Queen, this was apparently regarded as too radical by the powers that be at the Foreign Office.

The second rejected idea was that any new 'active strategy' against the Yardies should be publicised through the media. In his report, Clark stated that: "The criminals are attracted to London as they see the police as less of a threat than elsewhere, the profit available from drugs is much higher and, at present, there is less danger from opposing gangs. They also consider the sentences imposed by Courts as very lenient." His argument was that publicising a new response would deter them from seeing Britain as a "soft and easy country to base their criminal activities".

As we have seen, this was not welcomed. Indeed politically correct constraints on the new squad even extended to its name. The obvious thing to call it would have been the 'Jamaican Crime Unit', but this was watered down by the Yard to the 'Caribbean Crime Unit'. The name was changed again following apoplectic complaints from the Foreign Office, after one of its officials visited the unit's offices and saw the name on the door. Since then it has laboured under the snappy title of the National Drugs Related Violence Intelligence Unit, or NDRVIU for short.

It is true that during 1995 the operation was augmented and its brief extended to gather intelligence on other crime groups, particularly Turkish

heroin dealers and the advanced guard of the Russian Mafia. The majority of its work, however, has remained focused on Jamaican criminals. Outside officers who have made use of its database say that more than 90% of the names on it are Jamaican nationals, or British-born black criminals with strong Jamaican connections. Those who have been to its office, on the seventh floor of Scotland Yard, say that its walls are covered with pictures of the Kingston ghettos, maps of the city and the island, and photographs of Jamaican suspects. There is even, apparently, a Jamaican flag.

SIMILAR decorations also festoon the office of Drugs H (Hotel) team in Customs House, the magnificent headquarters of HM Customs and Excise by the Thames. It is from this office that customs runs its own low-profile operation against the Yardies.

One of the undoubted achievements of the NDRVIU was that it initially managed to overcome the inter-service rivalry previously described and establish formalised co-operation between police and customs officers. The H team's remit is to track and intercept all drugs trafficking from north America and the Caribbean, but again most of its work is taken up with Jamaican criminals. Experts from the team are regularly on attachment to the Yard, and intelligence material from their extensive contacts both in the USA and Jamaica flowed freely into the police computer.

As Clark noted repeatedly in his report, this relationship had already been going on informally for a number of years with members of the H team being regular visitors to that other 'office' in the south London pub. Having met some of them there, it is easy to see how the partnership flourished. These customs characters are different again from the collar-and-tie colleagues encountered at Gatwick. Like their police and immigration counterparts, they have extensive knowledge of Jamaica and Jamaicans and have to some extent gone 'native' - absorbing themselves in the culture and language of the place. After spending a lot of time there, one of them has even acquired his own street name - 'Bellyman', after his proudly-borne, rotund build. Watching him perform the 'bogle', a once-fashionable dance on the 'ragga' scene, is an experience one doesn't forget in a hurry.

Again, the precise role of these officers must remain confidential for security reasons but they have been vital in building up relations with the Jamaican police and with the American law enforcement agencies. Although the size of cocaine seizures made from Jamaican 'mules' are tiny compared to the huge hauls coming in from South America, the record for which is more than a tonne, H team's work is still regarded as extremely important. The wider threat to Britain from the culture of violence that is imported with Yardie drugs is seen to amply justify the team's continued involvement.

Chapter Ten

OFFICERS DOWN

THE imported Yardie gun culture made its most devastating impact on police and public alike on the night of October 20, 1993 when a community policeman called Patrick Dunne was shot dead on a south London street.

Dunne was a policeman from a different world, from cosy black-and-white television days on the BBC when Sergeant George Dixon would salute viewers under his blue lantern every Saturday tea-time and say, "Evenin' all", before delivering his homily for the week. Dunne, 44, had come to the police late, having worked for years as a maths teacher. He patrolled his 'patch' on a bicycle. He was trying to calm a routine domestic dispute at a house on Cato Road in Clapham when the new world caught up with him.

Hearing bursts of gunfire nearby, he had gone outside the front door of the house to investigate and was killed by a single shot to the chest from a 9mm automatic handgun at a range of 30 yards. He had just pushed two occupants from the house behind him to protect them. The fluorescent vest that he wore to stop him being knocked off his bike made him an easy target. Instead, he was knocked backwards through the doorway by the force of the blast. His last act was to grab for his radio to try and call assistance. Dunne was simply 'blown away', and with him died the last vestiges of a certain kind of national innocence.

Police officers, tragically, had been shot at, hit, and even killed by armed criminals before. But in the main they were involved in dramatic chases or planned operations to thwart armed robberies. There was something different about the murder of Patrick Dunne, to do with the casual callousness with which it was carried out against an officer who was posing no physical threat. A line had been crossed. In the words of the ghetto, it was 'cold'. As Dunne fell, the murderer fired a victory salute into the air and ran away laughing with his two accomplices.

Seconds before, they had shot down a small-time Ghanaian drugs dealer in a hail of bullets at a house across the street. William Danso, 31, was chased round his own front room as the three gunmen kept firing. He was hit by five bullets, and a further 12 were later dug out of the walls and furniture.

The official line on Dunne's murder was that he had been 'incredibly unlucky'. From more street-wise officers who had spent years watching the situation develop, there was little surprise, only a grim acknowledgement that this was a tragedy waiting to happen. Some used to say, cynically, that it would take the shooting of a, "white, middle-class pregnant mother with

a pushchair on a zebra crossing", before the public and powers-that-be woke up to what was going on. Instead it was one of their own number who had to die.

The next day, another man was killed at the hands of gunmen. In an unrelated incident, Anthony Melhado, 29, was shot on the pavement outside Shepherd's Bush Tube station in west London. He was also thought to be the victim of a drugs feud. In that 24 hours, London had recorded more shooting deaths than New York.

Once again the headline-writers caught Yardie fever, and once again Commissioner Paul Condon was in front of the TV cameras. "There are people fighting turf wars over the sale of crack," he said. "They are armed, desperate criminals, prepared to shoot indiscriminately." No one needed to ask who he was talking about.

In fact, of the three main suspects in the murders of Dunne and Danso, none of whom have never been brought to trial for these offences, only one is a Jamaican. But this did not mean that everyone had got the wrong end of the stick. Indeed, it can be argued that the prospect of British-born youths carrying out these attacks is far more frightening than if they had been done by some little-understood, exotic foreign Mafia. For it meant that the Yardie culture had taken firm root among black youth in Britain (the other two suspects are black). Put another way, it meant that the 'threat' posed by the gangstas, which for so long had been denied or dodged, was no longer a threat. It was a fact, a part of British society. The country had turned a highly dangerous corner.

The process of absorbing this culture had been going on for years. From the very first stories about the arrival of the Yardies in the mid-1980s, police had complained about the scale of the problem being confused by black British youths claiming the title for the kudos it carried. Apart from these 'wannabes', there had also been a steady recruitment of local yout' by the gangs to act as runners or street-corner salesmen. It was a development mirrored by earlier American experience. The activities of the Syndicate, investigated by Operation Dalehouse, had shown that local groups were starting to pursue 'badness' on their own account. Clark's report, written only four months before Dunne's murder, had warned that there was more to come. Now, apparently, the process was complete.

Such was the outcry over these shootings that the debate even drew in PJ Patterson, the Jamaican prime minister. Days afterwards, on a routine visit to Britain, he gave a press conference at the Jamaican High Commission in London. The event was packed and, after giving a dull account of talks about trading relations with Britain, Patterson was showered with questions about the Yardies. By then the police had already given a steer that the early suspects were either British or had lived here for many years, and Patterson retorted that Jamaica could not be held responsible for the actions of people who had little or no connection with his country. He contrasted the shining example of Linford Christie, Britain's champion sprinter, who was born in Jamaica. "I find it strange that when Linford Christie wins gold medals for Britain, no one turns round and says that he is really a Jamaican," he said, noting that when somebody did something bad then it was a different story.

THE MAN chosen to lead the Dunne investigation was, once again, Detective Superintendent John Jones, former head of Operation Dalehouse. He was one of those who had seen such a murder coming, and today he is still angered and saddened by the fact that it was allowed to happen.

As a rolling operation, rather than an established squad, Dalehouse was obliged to seek funding on a quarterly basis from the Met's Force Tasking Group, made up of senior operational commanders. Jones remembers that as time wore on, some members of the group became more and more reluctant to continue putting up the money. 'Tut-tutting' and other ostentatious signs of boredom were not uncommon when the

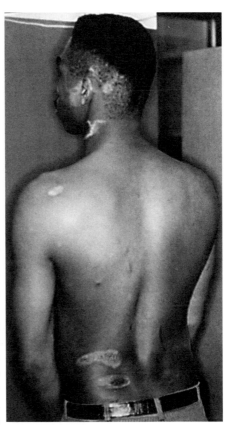

Yardie torture: This victim had red-hot spoons applied to his head and back

subject was raised. "There seemed to be an awful lot of blinkered people around that table," says Jones. "People who, because of their experience or whatever, either couldn't or didn't wish to see the writing on the wall."

In order to keep the show on the road, and backed by a hard core of supporters in the group, Jones found himself having to be ever-more 'adventurous' in the way he addressed them. Some might call it rudeness, he says.

"One thing I did say, particularly towards the end when it was getting difficult, was – 'If we don't do something about this, then these people are

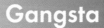

going to start killing policemen'," says Jones. "Of course they did. It happened."

While accepting that the Met had many other funding priorities at the time, he is troubled by the belief that Dunne's murder could have been prevented. "I feel it's highly likely that if Dalehouse or something similar had still been operational in October 1993 then Patrick Dunne would not have been killed. I really believe that," he says.

Jones's reasoning is that the amount of intelligence gathered by Dalehouse was prolific, focusing on the very kind of people who are thought to have carried out the murders and the very area in which they happened. Suspects had become very high profile by that time, and would almost certainly have been targeted by the operation had it still been working. "It makes me very angry, but I don't know who to be angry with," he says.

AFTER THE murders, however, finding Dunne's killers became the Met's top priority. Jones was given a squad of 50 detectives to solve the case and the area around Cato Road was immediately swamped with police activity. Many of the officers involved had the added motivation of having been colleagues of Dunne at Clapham police station. Jones was in part driven by the fact that he had been on the team which investigated the death of WPC Yvonne Fletcher, shot from a window of the Libyan embassy in 1984. On that occasion he had watched the known killers board a flight home, protected by diplomatic immunity, and was determined that this time the police killer would be brought to justice.

Initially, all seemed to be going well and three suspects were quickly identified and watched closely. On the night of November 23, they and two other men were arrested, some following a shoot-out with armed police in north London.

A surveillance team had followed this group, who were travelling in a black BMW and a Peugeot with personalised number plates, from Brixton to Highbury Hill where it was believed they were planning to 'rip-off' a crack house. On the way, it was said that they had stopped off to pick up a gun from an associate waiting in a south London pub.

By coincidence, two local officers were on plain-clothes patrol in the same Highbury street. When the suspects' cars arrived, these officers became suspicious and decided to stop and question the occupants. Shots were fired as the men jumped from the cars into neighbouring gardens and hid behind dustbins. Terrified residents dialled 999.

Armed members of the surveillance team then moved in to cover their colleagues and an armed response unit also arrived to lend support. The gunmen were persuaded to lay down their weapons, and the police did not return fire.

Six days later, three of the men appeared before magistrates in connection with the murders of Dunne and Danso. Richard Watts, then 34, was charged with both murders. Gary Nelson, 23, was charged with conspiracy to murder Danso and with an attempted murder from the previous July. Anthony Francis, 28, was charged with conspiracy to murder Danso. It seemed that the investigation had been a quick success.

After spending weeks in custody, however, all charges against these men were dropped. The Crown Prosecution Service (CPS) had decided that it had insufficient evidence to secure convictions. To date, and despite the fact that both of the murder weapons have since been found, no new charges have been brought against these three men or anybody else. The investigation still continues, although much reduced in the number of officers involved. Jones retired before being able to see the job through.

The failure to get a conviction for Dunne's murderer is something that still bothers him. It is only one of two murders that Jones has had to leave unfinished in more than 34 years as a policeman. "The frustrating thing is that I know who killed him. I know why and how and what they killed him with," he says. "But at the moment it is the decision of the lawyers that we shouldn't proceed with any litigation."

The public interest in the case should override legal niceties, he says. It would be better for people to be acquitted than for them never to be brought to trial at all, particularly given the callous nature of the crime. "This murder was celebrated by the people who committed it in the most horrendous fashion," says Jones. "It actually gave them pleasure and joy to have done it, as far as I can understand, and that is certainly unique in my experience."

Experience of horror is not something that Jones is short of. In the five years before he retired he investigated the murder of a baby only months old, the rape and stabbing to death of a young woman, numerous Yardie shootings, and the rape, attempted murder and setting on fire of another innocent young woman going about her business. Of all these cases, however, he regards the murder of Dunne as the worst of all.

"It's not that I feel any more sorry for Pat Dunne than for any of the other victims," says Jones. "It's that I feel a lot more sorry for society as a whole."

This is not just to do with who Dunne was or what he was, which by coincidence was a very special kind of policeman. It is because he was a representative of what everybody holds important for their day-to-day safety, says Jones. "He has been crushed underfoot and allowed to stay there without retribution because of the vagaries of the criminal justice system and those who interpret it."

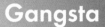

JOHN JONES'S last case for the Met began less than five months after the murder of Pat Dunne and also involved gunfire. The depressing parallels do not stop there. The new incident happened in nearby Brixton, about half a mile from where Dunne was shot, and again the targets were police officers.

The old 'front line' in Brixton was Railton Road, an unlovely stretch of urban decay following the route of a commuter railway and punctuated with struggling shops, boarded up businesses and the odd bomb-site. As it runs down to the junction with Coldharbour Lane, the name changes to Atlantic Road which gave its name to a large Victorian pub on the corner, 'The Atlantic', a once noisy centre for 'community' activity and drugs dealing. This area was also an apex of other kinds of activity during the Brixton riots. The pub is closed now and most activity of all kinds has drifted off elsewhere, but in its notorious hey-day the 'line' was host to scenes worthy of any American ghetto.

Knots of hooded and insulated youth would gather there at respectful distances from each other throughout the coldest weather, sometimes chatting and 'sparring', mostly watching. They were not waiting for a bus. They were selling crack.

The police response at one time was to move into Railton road in force, with vans coming from both directions, and simply hoovering the dealers into the back. But as time went on, a combination of the requirement to be 'sensitive' to the area, and the developing techniques of the dealers, meant they could do little else but watch and wait for someone to make a mistake. To lift a dealer in those days would be fruitless, as he would have no drugs and no appreciable amounts of cash on his person. Both were held elsewhere, to be whistled up as necessary from even younger 'runners' operating on foot or on mountain bikes. It was, literally, a stand-off.

It was into this situation that an unarmed two-man police patrol wandered at about 9.30pm on the night of March 9, 1994. Constables Jim Seymour, 31, and Simon Carroll, 23, were on Rushcroft Road, a curving street round the corner from The Atlantic. They approached two young men about to mount a powerful Suzuki motorcycle with a view to running a vehicle check. It was, said Seymour afterwards, the kind of routine incident that happens, 20 to 30 times a night in Brixton.

This time, however, things went very differently. As they were walking over to the men Seymour's attention was distracted by 'something suspicious' and he momentarily turned away. "As I turned my back, I heard shouting, a shot and PC Carroll screamed out. I remember a bang and straight away Simon screaming. As I turned round, I just saw the gun and was shot in the back. It all happened in a split second," said Seymour from his hospital bed two days later. One of the suspects had pulled a semi-automatic gun from inside his jacket and opened fire. Carroll had been shot in the thigh, shattering the bone.

"I knew Simon was quite bad from the way he screamed. I tried to get to him but the pain was so terrible I couldn't move." He heard more shouts and further shots, and feared the worse. "I thought they were going to kill us. I managed just to hit the floor, beside a vehicle for some protection. I really thought the man was going to finish us off," said Seymour. "I just started shaking with fear. Then, after a short while, I heard the motor cycle roar off up the road."

Seymour, a married man with daughters aged three and 21 months, had been incredibly lucky. The bullet which hit him had ripped through his back and exited at the front, narrowly missing his kidneys. Both men were treated at the nearby King's College Hospital, which has acquired a gruesome reputation for its expertise in dealing with gun-shot wounds.

Immediately there were renewed calls for the police to be armed. Seymour himself related how his best friend in the force, Sgt Derek Robinson, had been stabbed to death the month before while trying to stop raiders at a south London post office, and called for all operational officers to be given body armour. He also said that "without a doubt" he would have been better protected if he'd had a gun. Later, both he and Carroll said that they thought the police should be armed. Ironically, the attack came in the week that the Met had started to distribute 600 sets of new dual-purpose bullet and knife-resistant armour.

Commissioner Condon this time took firm action, announcing that in response to the shooting he would authorise 70 more armed officers for routine patrol in London. "I have always said the arming of the Met will be event-driven and this shooting takes us closer to being armed," he said. "There is only so much I can ask these officers to take." The way ahead for British policing was becoming clear.

THE MAN behind the high-tech gun used in Brixton was Leroy Smith, or 'Schemer'. He is perhaps the most frightening 'home grown' product of Yardie gun culture that Britain has yet seen. Born in the UK of Jamaican parents, Smith had spent a lot of time on the island. Once grown up he showed himself particularly eager to embrace the worst aspects of Jamaican life. At the time of the shootings he was an escaped prisoner who had been on the run from the police for almost a year.

Smith had been locked up in August 1992, pending trial for a particularly vicious burglary on a post office in Leicester. He and an accomplice had allegedly held the postmaster's family hostage at gun point, forcing the man to open the safe and hand over the money. In April that year, still before his trial, he was transferred to Brixton prison.

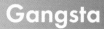

Gangsta

The transfer took place in a hired BMW car, with Smith escorted by three prison officers and handcuffed to one of them. When they reached Clapham, the driver had to ask Smith for directions to the jail as he didn't know his way around London. Smith saw his chance. He directed the car down a back street, produced a four-inch penknife and held it to the throat of one of the officers. "Get the cuffs off or I'll kill him," demanded Smith. He then forced the prison officers out of the car and drove off to freedom.

Shortly afterwards he flew to Jamaica where he began setting up a crack smuggling operation, using young British girls he recruited to go out and bring the drugs back to Britain, concealed in the hollowed-out soles of training shoes. Towards the end of the year he returned to Britain himself with a score to settle against a rival crack dealer who he believed had ripped off one of his consignments. His revenge was to fire into the window of the other dealer's 18-year-old sister, leaving a bullet in her bed. After the shooting Smith phoned the house and told the girl's brother: "You saw what came through the window? Next time it's going to be one of your lot's head."

Weeks later Smith was one of an armed gang involved in a bungled raid on a jewellers in Battersea, threatening staff with a gun. But the robbers only got away with £1,000 after the two staff courageously fought back with CS gas and baseball bats, hitting Smith on the head.

On the night that he shot Seymour and Carroll, Smith had been in the Atlantic pub discussing yet another drugs deal. When he came out and was approached by the policemen, he couldn't afford to be searched because he had his gun on him. So he pulled it out and shot them. Before leaving the scene he had fired a 'victory salute' in the air, just like the murderer of Pat Dunne.

Three days later he fled to New York, and quickly got back into the business of smuggling crack, again using girls specially flown in for the job. He was arrested by a heavily armed American police SWAT team on 26 April in the town of Bridgeport, Connecticut for firearms offences, and also for the attempted murder of a 21-year-old woman. In July he voluntarily returned to Britain in the hands of Met detectives, having found life in a US correctional centre too hard. Smith, then aged 25, stood trial in December 1995 charged on 14 different counts.

The key prosecution witness was Natalie Oluwa, who had to be housed under police protection while the case was prepared and who still lives at a secret location in fear of her life. Her evidence was devastating, and shed further light on Smith's warped character. She told of how she had first sheltered him on his escape from prison, how he had confided in her over his various acts of badness, including the shooting of the two police officers, and how she had briefly been inside his drugs operation. She was also the woman he had tried to kill in America.

Asked during the trial why she was giving evidence, she said: "Because he threatened my life and I'm scared that if he does, you know, get out he is going to kill me. I know he is going to kill me because I led to his downfall."

She described how Smith would play with his gun and its ammunition when she first met him in London, and how he would sleep with the weapon. It was a high-tech Sig Sauer, 9mm with a laser sight, a variation on the Yardies favourite weapon, known as the 'Desert Eagle'. During arguments with his girlfriend he would point it at her, illuminating a target spot on her head with the red dot from the sight.

He boasted to Natalie about what he'd done to the policemen who he described as 'pigs' and 'buzzards' and told her: "I'll never get caught. Anyone gets in my way and I just pop them."

She went to visit him shortly after the police shootings at his new base in Brooklyn, where Smith persuaded her to do a drugs run from Jamaica to New York. While in Kingston, however, she got cold feet and returned empty-handed. Smith, who met her at the airport, was furious. Once they were in his van he pistol-whipped her about the head and threatened to kill her.

By then Smith had moved again, this time to a four-bedroomed house in Bridgeport, Connecticut, where he kept his latest group of female couriers. He told Natalie that to make up for her earlier failure she would have

Images such as this of a dead Yardie have prompted calls for increased police action

to take a package of crack to Britain, but again she refused, and again she was beaten. Things came to a head when Smith returned one day to find the package he had prepared for her had been broken into. She denied she had done it but Smith told her she would now definitely be shot.

The next day he woke her and told her to get up and get dressed: "Today you die," he said. Natalie was taken in Smith's car, with another girl as a witness, to a deserted street. "This is to show you what will happen to you if you try to rip me off," he told the other girl. When he coolly asked if Natalie had any ID on her, she knew he was serious. She refused to get out of the car, pleading for her life so Smith fired three shots out of the window. She just ran. Smith fired shots after her but she managed to get away. After sheltering for hours in a nearby store, Natalie went to the local hospital and called the police.

The SWAT team closed in on the house, and arrested Smith when he returned there. In his car they found an Ingram Mk II machine pistol and a Glock .45 handgun. In the house they discovered another machine gun that Smith was planning to break down and import into Britain.

At the end of his five-week trial, Smith was found guilty of all but one offence. The judge said: "Throughout the trial you have shown no sign of remorse or hope for the future," and sentenced him to a total of 25 years in prison. As he was being taken to the cells, a smug-faced Smith cocked a finger as though it was a pistol and 'fired' it at the police officers who had tracked him down.

Chapter Eleven

THE WHEEL COMES OFF

THE driving drum-and-bass rhythm was suddenly silenced in the early hours of Sunday morning as five armed men stepped up to take the floor at the 'blues' party in a disused warehouse in Nottingham. Shots were fired in the air to further command attention but this was no gun salute to the house DJ, common enough at such events. It was the beginning of an audacious robbery.

"We are S.A.D," shouted one of the bandits. "Seek and Destroy". Within minutes, as the terrified crowd of about 150 were covered by hand guns and a sawn-off shotgun, women and girls had been separated from the men and the methodical theft of all their valuables had started. Everything was taken in the haul - wallets, cards, cash, jewellery and mobile phones. Even gold rings were unceremoniously yanked from people's fingers. Complaints and curses were exchanged, but no serious resistance was put up among the women. It was only when it came to the men's turn that someone was brave, or foolish, enough to stand on his rights. He was immediately, almost casually, shot in the leg. As he writhed on the floor, screaming in agony, his assailant taunted him. "Bleed, pussy, bleed," said the gangsta.

That single shot was fired on May 31, 1993, but it is still reverberating around Scotland Yard. It set in train a series of events that were to seriously embarrass the Metropolitan police and which have resulted in yet another major set-back in the fight against Yardie crime.

In the course of two subsequent trials about the robbery it was revealed that the gunman who fired the shot was none other than a top Scotland Yard informant, on the police payroll at the time of the shooting. The trials also heard allegations of obstruction by the Met to Nottinghamshire police's investigation into the incident and that Met officers had misled the court. Most damaging, it was alleged that police and immigration officers had conspired to bring other known gunmen into the country as part of their strategy for infiltrating Yardie gangs.

In turn, and quite understandably, these allegations have led to serious questions being asked about the whole policy of using informants to carry out what is known as 'pro-active' policing of Jamaican criminals. The net result, amidst a flurry of recriminations and apologies, has been the hamstringing of one of the most effective tools ever used against the gangstas.

THE MAN with his finger on the trigger that night was Eaton Green, otherwise known as 'Leon'. The details of his past, like so many in this story, read like a depressing photo-fit for a Yardie gangster. Green was born in

1967, the year of Jamaica's first violent election, and brought up in the staunch PNP area of Tel Aviv in central Kingston. His twelfth birthday came a month before the murderous 1980 election campaign, during which he had a gun thrust into his hand for the first time and took on the traditional local role of a young political hit-man. In the years that followed, during the period described by Michael earlier in the book when the 'yout' came out of prison to take over the 'runnin's', Green grew up to be a prominent member of the powerful Tel Aviv Crew. He was arrested on a number of occasions for crimes of violence and in all spent the best part of five years in jail.

He was on the run from further firearms charges in Jamaica when he came to Britain in February 1991. He had again been arrested, this time for shooting with intent to kill, and was awaiting trial in Kingston when his nerve went. Out on bail at the time, but fearing that he was about to be re-arrested and the bail removed, he took the British Airways flight to Gatwick and, like so many before him, was quickly absorbed into London's Jamaican crime scene. Within months of his arrival, however, he had started working for the police, quickly establishing himself as a 'Category A' informant who fed his handlers with some of the highest quality intelligence on Yardies in this country that detectives had ever seen. He became, quite simply, the best single asset the police had access to.

The man who discovered this 'star' was Steve Barker, the 6' 5" policeman I was to work with a year later, who was then a lowly uniformed constable on attachment to the crime squad based at Brixton police station. Predominantly, this unit involved young officers working in plain clothes but still carrying out routine beat patrols with the idea of observing street dealers and criminals at work and arresting them. They were also encouraged to pick up any gossip they could and, if possible, 'turn' petty offenders into informants.

Eaton Green, captured on a Hertz car rental security camera in 1993

In May 1991 Barker arrested Green for a minor traffic offence which, whatever police might say to the contrary, is still used as a standard method of stopping people who look 'tasty' (potentially interesting),

enabling the officers to check them out. This was the approach taken by Police Constables Seymour and Carroll with such terrible results when they were shot down. In Barker's case the tactic paid off when Green was found to be carrying an offensive weapon and was taken back to Brixton 'nick'.

The process of recruiting informants is not subtle. Basically, the more that the police have on someone the more leverage they have over them, making it more likely they can be persuaded to co-operate. At its simplest, someone might just be broke or in debt and desperate for some extra source of income. At the other end of the scale, they may be very keen for a court action not to proceed. In this case Barker had the perfect lever, whether he knew so or not. Court action on an offensive weapon charge would lead to awkward questions about immigration status and possible checks being run with the Jamaican police. As a wanted man there, who was travelling on his own passport, Green would almost certainly have been deported right back into the arms of the authorities he had just run away from. He started to help British police with their inquiries.

I heard a lot about this 'super informant' during the time I was working with Operation Dalehouse, without ever knowing his identity, and some of the 'jobs' I participated in were based on information he had given. Not all bore spectacular fruit, but I saw or was told of enough to be convinced this was no ordinary 'snout'. There were many more examples. Documents provided to the court during his trials showed that Green had given police 168 intelligence reports on Yardie-related activity during his time under their wing - including murders, arms and drugs deals - which led to a number of successful prosecutions. On top of that must be added the number of crimes that were prevented by the arrest and deportation of Jamaican criminals who were illegally in the country, before they had a chance to commit any further 'badness'. His information was also regularly checked with New York in order to keep track of trans-Atlantic movements by the gangstas. In return Green was paid handsomely - up to £1,000 a job.

Certainly, his contribution did no harm to Steve Barker's career. From pounding the Brixton beat Barker suddenly found himself at the centre of the Met's fight against Yardie crime. He was teamed up with John Brennan on Dalehouse and then was an obvious candidate for the new unit at SO11 (Scotland Yard's criminal intelligence squad) when that was set up in the summer of 1993. He received invitations to conferences in America and found himself giving lectures to other police forces in Britain on the Yardie threat and how to combat it. Not bad for someone who was still only a police constable, although later he began training to be a detective.

It is equally certain, however, that Barker's superior officers were more than happy to let this relationship flourish, often with minimal supervision. As long as Green kept putting up the good 'jobs' which brought in attrac-

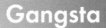

tive 'results', they were satisfied to let Barker get on with it. With the events in Nottingham, however, this mutually beneficial situation went horribly wrong. In police jargon, 'the wheel came off' - in a major way.

AT THE CENTRE of the controversy was the arrival on March 28, 1993, of another notorious gunman on the Gatwick flight from Jamaica - Rohan Thomas, better known as 'Colonel Bumpy'. An old friend of Green's and a known killer, he was also a member of the Tel Aviv Crew who had previously served 14 years for shooting a Jamaican police officer. He was eventually sentenced to another 14 years for his part in the Nottingham raid after being convicted of conspiracy to rob, two charges of possessing a firearm with intent to endanger life and possession of a gun without a firearms certificate. Another man, Cecil Thomas (no relation) who entered the country at the same time was acquitted but deported after the trial.

The problem was that both men had been encouraged to come to Britain by Green while he was an informant, and that police had been fully aware of their impending arrival and had warned both immigration and customs at Gatwick. Green had even paid for their tickets, although Scotland Yard has denied giving him the money for this purpose.

Why these men were allowed in at all, or at least not picked up before they could do any damage, goes to the heart of the issue. Tying themselves in knots again, senior Met officers have since admitted that letting them into the country had endangered public safety, that police had lost touch with the group before the Nottingham attack, and that both facts were a source of 'profound regret'. It was hoped, they said, that Green would gain 'street credibility' by helping the men to come here and so could gain further information for the police on a series of unsolved Yardie crimes, including 13 murders. What has been consistently denied is that rules were broken to facilitate the men's entry or that the full nature of Colonel Bumpy's gangsta background was known at the time.

The man taking most of the flak after the trials was Commander John Grieve, then the head of SO11 and Barker's ultimate boss. "We were involved in an international intelligence operation," he said after the second trial. "We took a view that it is better to know where some of these people are if you have no grounds to bar them from your country at the time."

Defence lawyers, on the other hand, saw it differently. They alleged a 'conspiracy' between Green, Barker and the immigration service. "There is a war going on in Jamaica between different Yardie gangs," said one during the trial. "The authorities seem to be letting some of these warriors into Britain and that war is spilling onto the streets of this country."

WHILE THE full picture remains confused, if Scotland Yard had got its way none of the information that has emerged would have become public knowledge at all. Once it became unavoidable that Green would have to be named as an informant in the first trial, which opened at Leicester Crown Court in September 1994, Grieve and other senior officers at the Yard did everything in their power to have the whole prosecution dropped.

Green, no doubt trying to improve his own position, had been involved in betraying all the other defendants in the case. When the lawyers for these men demanded to be told if their clients had been named by an informant, the trial judge decided to reveal his identity.

The row that then ensued between the Met on one side, and Nottinghamshire police, the prosecution and the trial judge on the other dragged through most of October. Eventually no less than the Attorney General and the Director of Public Prosecutions were brought in to adjudicate. They upheld the judge's decision to identify Green and to release his informer file to the defence lawyers. By the time the whole matter was resolved, however, the jury had been away from the evidence for almost a month and it was decided that they could not be expected to pick up where they had left off. A re-trial was ordered, with bad blood having been spilt on all sides. When that finally ended, in September 1995, Green was given a reduced sentence of six years for his part in the robbery.

So what was going on? Was the Met simply trying to protect an informant, as is standard practice, or was it trying to hide its own involvement in a highly irregular relationship with Green which culminated in him bringing Colonel Bumpy in under their noses?

The fact that evidence has since emerged that Green was involved in quite a few other bits of badness while on Scotland Yard's books - including running protection rackets, selling crack and regularly carrying a gun - does not help its case. If officers knew about any of these matters, and did nothing, they would be in violation of strict Home Office guidelines on informants. Nor did it look good that when Green's informer file was finally released whole sections had been shredded. Steve Barker's version of events has still to be heard. When called to give evidence in Green's second trial, Barker was on holiday in America.

In the days before this book was published, the Green case was again the focus of intense media interest. In newspapers and on television fresh allegations were made to add to the controversy.

One was the Green, just two weeks before he was arrested, was sent to Holland by Scotland Yard on an intelligence gathering mission. While there, he was said to have used an Uzi sub-machine gun to rob drug dealers. Another was that, after his conviction, SO11 moved him to a safe-house to try and 'milk' him of more information on the Yardie scene. While there, he confessed to 11 murders, including one carried out on the instructions of a senior Jamaican politician. No attempt was made, it was reported, to investigate these crimes.

IN JULY 1996, Scotland Yard's policy on fighting Yardie crime sustained another serious public blow when Delroy Denton, or 'Epsi', was sentenced to life imprisonment for murder. Marcia Lawes, his 24-year-old victim, had been raped and then stabbed 17 times in the neck and once in the heart. She had two young children. After the trial it was revealed that Denton was also a registered police informant at the time of his frenzied attack.

Michael, real name Delroy Denton, the sex-crazed killer who was a police informer

This was a tragic disaster. The Green case had shown a bending of the rules, at least, which had led to the public being endangered. Now a young woman was dead, brutally murdered by a man known to have a violent past who was probably only in the country because of his work with the police. Described in court as a "sex-fuelled psychopath", Denton had pursued her to satisfy an infatuation born of only two meetings, and Marcia died because she refused to respond to his advances. Incredulous relatives asked how such a man could have been on the police payroll. How did such a thing happen?

The immediate answer is a story with a familiar ring to it. Denton had been caught up in a police raid at the Atlantic pub in Brixton in 1993 and arrested for carrying a knife and a small amount of drugs. After initially giving a false name he had confessed to immigration officials his true identity and violent history in Kingston - which included shootings, robberies and an eight year jail sentence. He also admitted he had entered the country illegally on his brother's passport. Immigration in turn referred him to SO11 as a potential informant, and Denton was signed up. He remained in the country by claiming political asylum on the grounds that if he returned to Jamaica he would be killed by rival political gangs.

But after a period of 18 months, during which he provided regular information, things began to go wrong. In December 1994 Denton was charged with the rape of a 15-year-old girl. He was then de-registered as an informant, according to procedure, but re-registered after charges were dropped for lack of evidence.

When Marcia Lawes was raped and murdered in April 1995, Denton was charged on the basis of DNA evidence, and again de-registered. While admitting to having sex with the woman, he claimed to have slept with her on the night before she was killed. With a lack of conclusive proof, these charges were also initially dropped. Fresh evidence, however, led to him being charged again in December that year, and this time the case went to court.

Most of this story emerged at the time of Denton's trial in 1996. It was a case I followed closely, out of personal as well as a journalistic interest. For it also emerged then that Delroy Denton was none other than the man I knew as 'Michael' and whom I had interviewed at such length for this book.

It was a chilling discovery. This was the man I had sat in a pub with and talked with for hours. This was the man who told me about the course he was taking, learning to be a bricklayer, and who had proudly shown me his diagrams of different brick patterns. Our conversations took place months before Marcia Lawes' murder. But clearly when 'Michael' also showed me how he would kill someone, he was not just working from memory.

Fresh allegations have also been made about Denton's case. The most serious is that he was allowed to stay in Britain after his application for asylum had been rejected by the Home Office. This was also months before the murder took place. He is also said to have boasted to friends about other murders he had committed, and rehearsed strange sexual fantasies to them.

THERE IS also another, fuller answer to the anguished question from Marcia's family as to how she could have been murdered by a police informant. While in no way seeking to diminish the depth of their tragedy, or disguise the fact that things went dreadfully wrong with Denton, it comes down to a simple, hard fact. In order to combat the bad men the police need bad men on their side - and in some respects, the badder the better.

This book opened with a description of the 'strange, alien world' of the ghetto. A white face on the street, from my own experience, is immediately a source of suspicion if not actually seen as a target for robbery. Even when I was taking photographs of general street scenes in Handsworth, perfectly blameless black people would turn their faces away from the camera. Whatever I was doing could be of no benefit to them, and could possibly cause them serious problems, was the obvious logic. They didn't want to get involved.

Often, faced with this wall, police can only find out who is who or what is occurring in the gangsta underworld through paid informants.

Equally, within these communities there are high levels of secrecy surrounding the bad men and bwoys, enforced through fear and the constant threat of extreme violence that is the Yardie hallmark. To get close to them, an informant has to be 'in', and there is no way that an angel will get anywhere near. As one police officer colourfully explained: "You don't get many Sunday school teachers who are informants." People who do talk to the police, for whatever reason, literally risk their lives every time they open their mouths.

There is, then, a constant, highly dangerous, balancing act to be performed by those trying to combat Yardie gun culture. It is a very dirty world, and dirty tricks is the only coinage of value. To borrow Carl Stone's metaphor, policing that world is 'Playing with fire'. In the cases of both Green and Denton, the authorities got their fingers badly burnt.

FOR INDIVIDUAL officers to be blamed for this is to miss the point, for they are damned if they do and damned if they don't. "What you need to put in your book, man, is why doesn't the Government do something about these fucking gunmen who are running around our communities?" was a view I heard frequently expressed during my research in Britain. There is a real desire for the menace of the gun to be curbed in the ghetto where life is hard enough anyway. Policemen tell of how they have been cheered and applauded by neighbours when some particularly dangerous man has been arrested on a raid. It may sound naive, but surely the way ahead is to be more open about what is happening in these areas and about what is being done to fight it. This is the way to mobilise the groundswell of revulsion against the gunman but, instead, the reverse has happened.

One reason is that when Police Commissioner Condon tried to dip his toe in this water, by addressing the subject of muggings, it was bitten off. In July 1995 he announced the Met was about to launch a concerted effort against street crime in the black areas of London by writing to assorted 'community leaders' and asking them to attend meetings with him so that he could explain the policy and head off a back-lash before it took place. His justification for the move, he said, was that research had established that 80% of muggings in London were carried out by black youths. There was an immediate knee-jerk reaction of derision, and accusations of racial stereo-typing. Condon's position collapsed when it emerged that the research on which he was basing his 80% figure was only carried out in three predominantly black areas. Someone, again, had blundered and the hopes of a more open approach were still-born.

I was helping with research for a proposed BBC film on gun culture around this time and saw the change occur at first-hand. Initial discussions with senior officers at the Yard, including John Grieve, had been cagey, but hopeful. Cameras would never be allowed near SO11 because of fears over security but perhaps it would be possible to film street operations that utilised the intelligence which the gun-crime unit provided. Following the Condon fiasco, the Yard shutters came slamming down and the film was scrapped. Could this have been another case of 'poli-tricks' at work?

It was not the first Yard initiative to be attacked as racist. In December 1993 the 323 passengers on a Christmas charter flight from Kingston where detained at Gatwick airport for screening by police and immigration officials. Eventually 27 were deported. The government was accused of targetting Jamaicans, but this was denied by a Home Office minister. Sources say that this was in fact an SO11 operation - planned in advance - and that in giving his answer, the minister had been misinformed.

RETURNING to lessons that should have been learned from the Green and Denton cases, the most obvious one was that the very atmosphere of secrecy and denial - about how the police were actually trying to deal with the Yardie threat – had caused mistakes to be made. Part of the problem was that official blind-eyes had been turned to what was being done at grass roots level. These things should have been rectified but instead less imaginative action was taken.

Brian Fotheringham, 'Fothers' of the immigration service with his compendious knowledge of the scene, helped to 'run' Denton and did give evidence at the Eaton Green trial. Shortly afterwards he was moved away from dealing with Jamaicans and his close links with SO11 were cut. He now checks passports on the Eurostar Channel Tunnel train service.

Steve Barker still works closely with the intelligence unit, but senior police sources say that its activities have increasingly diversified away from Yardie-related crime. Crucially, its emphasis on using intelligence from informants provided by 'field officers' has been scaled down, and relations with Customs have cooled. In 1996, Detective Sergeant Tom Bayes, another officer with expert knowledge of Jamaicans who had helped set up the unit, asked to be transferred to normal CID duties. Apparently disillusioned by what was going on, he thought he could do more good back on the street.

Elsewhere, another source of expertise was lost. John Brennan, then a newly-promoted inspector at the South East Regional Crime Squad and who had addressed the 1994 Association of Chief Police Officers on the subject of Yardies, was 'required to retire' from the force after being convicted of a drink-driving charge. His appeal to the Home Secretary is still pending.

John Grieve also made a move, to head the Anti-Terrorist Branch. It is not known whether this was related to the Green/Denton controversy. At the time, in the middle of the Irish peace process, it was considered a fairly low-profile appointment. That all changed, however when, on the day he

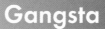

took up his new post, the huge Canary Wharf bomb exploded in east London.

WHATEVER the official position, the aim of this book has been to show that concerted action against the threat from Yardie gun culture is needed, and needed immediately. I have dealt primarily with the situations in Birmingham and London to provide an understandable focus, but that does not mean similar situations do not exist elsewhere in Britain. To say it again, things are bad and they are getting worse. Bristol, Nottingham and Leicester have all seen dramatic increases in gun crime over the past few years which have coincided with an influx of Yardie criminals.

The well-documented situation in Manchester, or 'Gun-chester' as it is sometimes known, is more complicated but obviously related, as is the case with Liverpool. A recent survey of police forces revealed that crack-cocaine was starting to show up in such unlikely places as Cheltenham and Worcester, both regarded as low-crime areas. A number of forces, seeing what is coming, have quietly set up their own specialist operations to try and cope. But success between them still largely depends on informal co-operation and personal contacts.

One such recent collaboration has unearthed a level of organisation within a Jamaican drug-smuggling operation that has never been seen before. It is said to import cocaine into London, distribute it out to Birmingham and then on to Bristol, Nottingham and as far north as Leeds and Huddersfield. Increasingly, new importation routes through Europe, particularly Amsterdam and the Belgian ports are being opened. Police and customs officers have already seized £10.5 million pounds worth of cocaine which they believe came from this single outfit. And this is while none of those thought to be ring leaders, who include a former Jamaican police officer, have even been arrested.

While speaking of the North of England, a Yardie suspect in a different inquiry has even been arrested recently in Holmfirth - a small, sleepy and picturesque Pennine town which was used as a location for long-running British TV comedy series, 'Last of the Summer Wine'.

And in London the shooting goes on, involving ever younger victims. In the summer of 1995 a 17-year-old youth was shot in Notting Hill, in the west of the city. It is widely believed that he was not the intended target, but the single bullet smashed his spine and left him in a wheelchair for the rest of his life. In the first week of 1997, a 16-year-old boy was shot dead in a club in Hackney, east London. He had been attending the 17th birthday party of two local college girls.

AT THE SOURCE of the problem, back in the ghettos of Kingston, the violence is once again reaching epidemic proportions. With an election due later in 1997, the situation is not expected to improve in the near future and another spate of gunmen escaping to Britain and America can be confidently predicted. National crime figures up to October 1996 show 707 murders compared to 597 for the same period of the previous year; for shootings the count is 1,357 compared to 995. Of the murders, more than 70% were committed in 'sensitive' areas of Kingston.

In response, the Jamaican Government has reversed the policy of Colonel Trevor MacMillan and started again to deploy 'front-line' crime fighters to control these areas, some with highly dubious human rights records. One such police officer is Superintendent GC Grant, who was head of the notorious 'Eradication Squad' during the early 1980's. MacMillan, who left the post of Police Commissioner in September 1996, is said to have resigned over the policy change.

While I believe the police in Britain could and should be doing more to fight the rising tide of gun culture, it would be wrong to close without also acknowledging the fact that, at best, they can only contain the situation. Wider forces are at work over which they have no control.

At its simplest, as long as the atmosphere of desperation exists among youths in the black communities - where they see the only way ahead, or even the only way to buy a fashionable pair of training shoes, as being through drugs and guns - then the problem will persist. This is a matter for a Government that is serious about being "Tough on crime. Tough on the causes of crime." Unless this broader agenda is addressed, then the allure of the Yardie will continue to weave its evil spell.

THE FILM 'The Harder They Come', starring reggae singer Jimmy Cliff, was made in 1973. It tells the story of Ivan, the 'country-boy' with stars in his eyes, who goes to Kingston to make his fortune but who dies like a Western gun-slinger after a short career of serious badness. While more than 20 years old, the film is still the most raw, eloquent portrayal of the gangsta's world view. The refrain from Cliff's title song, which could be the Yardie anthem, appears at the front of this book.

The film also contains an exchange between Ivan and his long-suffering girlfriend who accuses him of being a 'dreamer'. He rounds on her. "Me dreamer? Who's a bigger dreamer than you, always talking about milk and honey in the sky?" he says, fire in his voice and anger in his eyes. "Well no milk and honey no in the sky - no not for me and not for you. It's right down here, and I want mine now. TONIGHT!"

That, ultimately, is what we are all up against.

Index

Index

Index

Index

Index

Index

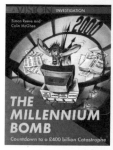

THE MILLENNIUM BOMB - *Countdown to a £400 billion Catastrophe*
by Simon Reeve and Colin McGhee
This is the first book to investigate the so-called Year 2000 problem, whereby computers across the globe will go haywire at midnight on December 31, 1999. A bizarre glitch means that most machines cannot cope with the date change. The authors reveal how anything electronic could fail including aircraft, defence systems and satellites, and they warn we are heading towards a real millennium disaster. £8.99.
ISBN: 1-901250-00-8

INSTRUMENTS OF TERROR - *Mass Destruction Has Never Been So Easy...*
by Dr Frank Barnaby
Using inside information and backed by the opinions of senior intelligence officials, a leading expert on defence and security investigates the impact of technological advances on the weapons available to terrorists. Dr Barnaby warns that terrorism has become an unstoppable threat and he says the world now faces a huge challenge from terrorists with no moral restrictions on mass killing. The book explains in graphic detail why the world is only a few years away from a renegade group obtaining and detonating a weapon of mass destruction such as a nuclear bomb. £8.99.
ISBN: 1-901250-01-6

POWER AND CORRUPTION - *The Rotten Core of Government and Big Business*
by Steven Moore
A revealing investigation into government bribery and commercial sleaze by an experienced police detective who has investigated the subject around the world. This book examines the implications for democracy of the widespread practice of using pay-offs and other financial inducements to help clinch deals and influence government policy. It surveys the impact on the world's poorer countries where corruption hinders aid and investment. It asks whether police forces have the capacity to root out the worst excesses, and warns that governments lack the will to stop the rot. £8.99.
ISBN: 1-901250-03-2

BIOWAR - *The Secret Plans for Test-tube Weapons*
by Wendy Barnaby
New research reveals frightening evidence of how the military around the world are using genetic engineering and other biological and chemical techniques to create horrifying new weapons. Written by a leading science journalist, the book shows how scientists in a small number of countries are secretly developing these devices which are capable of wiping out tens of thousands of people. £8.99.
ISBN: 1-901250-04-0

ALL VISION BOOKS ARE AVAILABLE FROM YOUR LOCAL BOOKSHOP OR THROUGH MAIL ORDER.
Please send a cheque (made payable to Satin Publications Ltd) and add 99 pence postage and packing in the UK per book (£1.49 in Europe, £1.99 outside Europe) to:
Vision Paperbacks
Book Service By Post
3 Neal Street
London WC2H 9PU

Please allow 28 days for delivery. Prices and availability subject to change without notice.